JUST SILENCES

D1714243

JUST SILENCES

THE LIMITS AND POSSIBILITIES OF MODERN LAW

Marianne Constable

PRINCETON UNIVERSITY PRESS   PRINCETON AND OXFORD

Published by Princeton University Press, 41 William Street,
Princeton, New Jersey 08540
In the United Kingdom: Princeton University Press,
3 Market Place, Woodstock, Oxfordshire OX20 1SY

Second printing, and first paperback printing, 2008
Paperback ISBN: 978-0-691-13377-5

*The Library of Congress has cataloged the cloth edition of this book
as follows*

Constable, Marianne.
Just silences : the limits and possibilities of modern law /
Marianne Constable.
p.   cm.
Includes bibliographical references and index.
ISBN-13: 978-0-691-12278-6
ISBN-10: 0-691-12278-4 (cl : acid-free paper)
1. Silence (Law). 2. Justice. 3. Sociological jurisprudence. I. Title.
K579.I6C66 2006
340'.11—dc22   2005043018

British Cataloging-in-Publication Data is available

This book has been composed in Sabon

Printed on acid-free paper. ∞

press.princeton.edu

Printed in the United States of America

10   9   8   7   6   5   4   3   2

Whereof one cannot speak, thereof one must be silent.
  —Ludwig Wittgenstein, *Tractatus logico-philosophicus*

We are always speaking, even when we do not utter a single
word aloud, but merely listen or read, and even when we are
not particularly listening or speaking but are attending to some
work or taking a rest.
  —Martin Heidegger, "Language," in *Poetry, Language, Thought*

Contents

Acknowledgments _____

THE AUTHOR ACKNOWLEDGES the circularity of her task: to show the impossibility of capturing relations of law and justice in the terms currently available to us. She warns of the infelicities that follow. The book begins by asking some interesting questions about silence, then proceeds to talk around them by writing about language, speech, words, expression, voice—anything but silence. As an engagement with law, the discussion fares no better; rather than addressing "real" law, the book grapples rather ungraciously with legal texts, legal scholarship, legal theory, legal opinions—and what they are not. As to justice, the book ultimately offers little satisfaction to those who seek principles or definitions of the justice that it claims corresponds, through law, with being human.

I thank the following readers for their patience with the manuscript; their insights inform every page: Elizabeth Mertz, Linda Meyer, Philippe Nonet, Lucy Salyer, Austin Sarat, and Jonathan Simon. For helpful comments on early formulations of the work or on particular chapters, I thank David Bates, Roger Berkowitz, Betty Lou Bradshaw, John Brigham, Frederick Dolan, Jill Frank, Bryant Garth, Christine Harrington, Leanne Hinton, Robert Kagan, Richard Leo, David Nelken, John Nelson, Peter Rush, Richard Perry, Kim Scheppele, and Susan Sterett. A decade's worth of magnificent research assistants—Jennifer Culbert, David Kazanjian, Sara Kendall, Aaron Nathan, Ellen Rigsby, James Salazar, Shalini Satkunanandan, Elizabeth Wadell—and indefatigable undergraduate research apprentices—Matt Sekits, Arden Hoffman, John Park, Terry McGuire, Jason Smick, David Djavaherian, Gerome Miklau, Lisa Pau, Rayneil de Guzman, Faisal Azam, Megan Metters, Carson Medley, Michelle Lau, Supreeta Sampath, Jason Smick, Dan Silver, Susan Louie, Jackie Cyriac, Seth Gold, Amy Vecchione, Jay Swallow, Julie Chandler, Olga Kotlyarevskaya, Milena Edwards, Leslieann Cachola, Celene Sheppard, and especially Miah Rosenberg—made the work possible.

Colleagues too numerous to name offered comments, which I have incorporated or which I have tried to respond to, in presentations at the American Bar Foundation, Amherst College, Cambridge University (Unofficial Knowledge Project), John Hopkins University, New York University, Notre Dame University, the Oñati Institute, Princeton University, University of Iowa (Project on the Rhetoric of Inquiry), University of Pennsylvania, and the University of South Carolina, as well as at meetings of the American Political Science Association; Association for the Study of Law, Culture and the Humanities; Law and Society Association (and

Summer Legal Institute); International Philosophy of Law; and Law and Semiotics. The following institutions provided research support for which I am very grateful: American Bar Foundation; Davis Center for Historical Studies (Princeton University); National Endowment for the Humanities; Shambaugh Fund; Townsend Center for the Humanities (University of California at Berkeley); and University of California at Berkeley Academic Senate Committee on Research.

Portions of this book have appeared, often in quite different form, as: "Genealogy and Jurisprudence: Nietzsche, Nihilism and the Social Scientification of Law," *Law and Social Inquiry* 19 (1994), 551–590; "Reflections on Law as a Profession of Words," eds. Bryant Garth and Austin Sarat, *Justice and Power in Sociolegal Research* (Evanston: Northwestern University Press, 1998), 19–35; "Laying Aside the Law: The Silences of Presumptive Positivism," ed. Linda Meyer, *Essays in Honor of Frederick Schauer* (Oxford: Hart Publishing Company, 1999), 61–78; "The Silence of the Law: Justice in Robert Cover's 'Field of Pain and Death,'" ed. Austin Sarat, *Law, Violence and the Possibilities of Justice* (Princeton: Princeton University Press, 2001), 85–100; "The Rhetoric of Community: Civil Society and the Legal Order," eds. Bryant Garth, Robert Kagan, and Austin Sarat, *Looking Back at Law's Century: Time, Memory, Change* (Ithaca: Cornell University Press, 2001), 213–231; and "On Not Leaving Law to the Lawyers," ed. Austin Sarat, *Legal Scholarship and the Liberal Arts* (Ithaca: Cornell University Press, 2004), 69–83.

Finally, I would like to acknowledge the students of Rhetoric 165, the librarians of the University of California at Berkeley, and Chuck Myers and the staff of Princeton University Press, for inspiration and assistance of various sorts. My greatest intellectual debt continues to be to Philippe Nonet. I thank Laureen Asato and Cathy Kudlick for listening to me and Randall Alifano and Felipe Gutterriez for helping me to hear.

JUST SILENCES

Prologue

Signs of Silence

> We had to conceive of silence in order to open
> our ears.
> —John Cage

A LIBRARIAN SHUSHING a library visitor, putting an index finger to the lips or pointing to a sign that says "silence," is a familiar image. If signs that actually say "silence" are increasingly difficult to find in libraries, and if librarians—and library designers and architects—increasingly protest that libraries no longer need nor ought to be the silent spaces of the past, then signs that say "PLEASE Turn Off Your Cell Phones" nevertheless are still somewhat in evidence, in the New York Public Library, for instance. And in popular culture too—from Harold Hill, who—in high school renditions of *The Music Man*—continues to sing that "the civilized world accepts as unforgivable sin any talking out loud with any librarian,"[1] to Ziggy, the comic strip character who in the 1990s sits at a library table beneath a sign that says "SHUT UP (FORMERLY *SILENCE*)"—the figure of silence in the library endures.[2]

One can acknowledge the figure of silence in the library and its persistence, even as one may wonder what a silent library would be, whether libraries ever are silent, and what the various silences—if any—in a library could be. One can ponder the figure of silence in the library, that is, without the actual presence of a shushing librarian or a sign that says silence and without experience of an absolutely silent library. Our familiarity with the figure of silence may help us to think about modern libraries even though they may not be silent. So too our attachment to justice may help us to think about modern law even when we can't find a word or sign that says "justice" or a definitively just law.

[1] Meredith Willson, *The Music Man* (New York: Frank Music Corp. and MW Music, 1986), 98–99.
[2] *Ziggy*, Tom Wilson, August 17, 1984, Universal Press Syndicate. Comics were identified through the Steven M. Bergson Collection of Comics Librariana, Toronto. The web site was originally found at http://www.geocities.com/Athens/Acropolis/2161/combks/combks.html. It was accessed again (July 31, 2003) at http://www.ibiblio.org/librariesfaq/comstrp/comstrp.htm.

Ziggy

Think of a sign in a library that says "silence." The sign needs to be read; it contains the word *silence*. The library of course contains a lot of other words—masses of words, in masses of books, stored and displayed in other forms and formats, too. But there seems something special about this word, the word *silence* that shows up by itself—among other words—on its sign that needs to be read. There's something special about reading a sign—perhaps *any* sign—in a library. The sign seems to draw attention to itself—not just as being readable—but as saying something that is to be paid attention to in a way different from all else that is readable in a library.

Have you by now imagined—or recalled—the sign to be discussed? Imagine entering the library. There seems something particular to the silence of a library: it is a silence that does not belong to gas stations or hospitals or record stores, for instance, although it could be confused with other silences: Dennis the Menace distinguishes the quiet of the city bus he is in from the noisiness of a school bus and thinks he must be in a library bus.[3] Broom Hilda discovers that what she takes to be the quietest library is actually—and perhaps tellingly in these difficult times for libraries—the funeral home next door.[4]

What is the silence of the library? What does the word *silence* on a *library* sign mean? How is what this sign says different from "No food or drink in the library" or "silence—massages are being given next door" (which hangs on the inside of an upstairs dressing room in the Berkeley Sauna)? One answer is that "silence" in the library means "Be quiet" or something like that. It could mean "shut up" (Ziggy); "stop chattering," as a librarian suggests Margaret is doing when Margaret prissily reminds the this-time silent Dennis the Menace about all his previous library misbehavior;[5] "don't make noise," as dinosaurs wildly come to life when Calvin reads about them in the library;[6] "*Quiet!*" as a librarian yells at Priscilla.[7] In these instances the *silence* on a library sign is a more or less polite or impolite command or instruction or request—an imperative—that, like "No food and drink in the library" or signs elsewhere that say "silence," tells someone what to do.

One might also observe—after reading *Dennis the Menace* and *Calvin and Hobbes* and other comic strips very carefully—that silence in the library seems to be a statement of a rule whose infraction will be followed by a paradoxically loud "SHHHH!," by a scolding perhaps, or even by being *kicked out.* If one takes this being kicked out seriously, "silence" seems not only to be an imperative but also to name conditions proper to being *in* a library—conditions proper to the use of a library as a place full of words to be read, including the special word on a sign, "silence."

Let us see where we are, then:

- We have thought of a sign that says "silence."
- We have "silence" as the imperative "Be quiet."
- We have "silence" as naming conditions proper to being in the library.[8]
- We have the library as a place for reading—quietly.

And we also have, as mentioned above,

- the disappearance of actual signs in libraries that say "silence."

---

[3] *Dennis the Menace*, Hank Ketcham, September 2, 1990, King Features. See note 2.

[4] *Broom Hilda*, Russell Myers, April 13, year unknown, TMS. See note 2.

[5] *Dennis the Menace*, Hank Ketcham, April 5, 1988, King Features. See note 2.

[6] *Calvin and Hobbes,* Bill Waterson, December 9, 1987, Universal Press Syndicate. See note 2.

[7] *Priscilla's Pop*, Al Vermeer, February 15, year unknown. See note 2.

[8] There are, of course, conditions other than silence that are proper and indeed necessary to the library as a place for reading, but these issues—of selection and classification and preservation of reading materials—will not be discussed here.

Thinking about silence in the library has in part reminded us of the familiarity of signs saying "silence" in a library. We all seem able to imagine or recall such a sign: it seems that there did *use* to be such signs. But it also seems as if signs that say "silence" are difficult to find, perhaps impossible to find in libraries.[9] What does that ostensible absence tell us?

Does it mean—as an anthropologist might claim—that we do not need signs as such to pass along the everyday practices or tradition of library silence? Does it mean—as a historian might propose—that silence *used* to be the rule, that silence is *no longer* the rule, that insofar as *silence* named (in the past) the conditions for proper use of a library, those conditions have changed and we should try to figure out why—or at least try to figure out what has happened to the signs? Or does it mean—as a skeptic might observe—that we could be mistaken in thinking that silence *ever* used to be the rule, that silence actually might *never* have been the rule, that "silence" never *named* the conditions for proper use of a library and *in fact*—as scientists can probably show—libraries are never completely silent anyway?

Perhaps. To all three questions. Pursuing an investigation along any of the lines suggested certainly could provide us with more information and with more accurate information than we now have about library practices or about the absence of signs and of silences in libraries. But that is not where this discussion goes. It sticks instead to the trope that has stuck, of silence in the library.

Even absent an actual sign that says silence in an actual library today and even in the absence of actually silent libraries, silence in the library tells us something. It says that a library—which nowadays still does exist in a manner of speaking,[10] even as it is in danger of disappearing[11]—is a place where an encounter with silence occurs in the midst of words and where an encounter with words occurs in silence. A library is reasonably silent—"reasonably" so, because there are after all different silences. Calling a library "noisy" itself draws attention to library silence as an issue. The silence of the reasonably silent library allows the encounter with speech that is known as reading.

---

[9] This is an empirical claim: the author, research assistants, and a reference librarian searched the University of California, Berkeley, library and its reference materials during winter and spring 2002. In one reference work only we found images of a sphinx and a clam representing silence.

[10] An early version of this material actually was presented in the Robert Frost Memorial Library at Amherst College. A vast literature refers to existent libraries, of the past, present, and future. Web sites and catalogs document library holdings and material to which library users have access.

[11] See Marianne Constable, "The University Library at the Turn of the Century," *Chronicle of the University of California* 4 (fall 2000), 138–56; Leon Litwack, "Has the Library

Although the sign with the word "silence" on it and the condition of silence in a library are clearly two different things—the sign and the condition—either or both of them may not exist. And the word *silence* itself, like the library, is something other than either the sign or the condition! To pursue empirical connections between signs and conditions that may not exist at this point seems premature. Instead, consider the word that is the configuration of relations between the sign "silence" that is to be read, the imperative "silence," the named condition of silence, and the library and its enabling of the encounter with silence and speech that is reading. Roughly speaking, *silence* on the sign names the condition of a library that enables reading and, indeed, *silence* would name the condition of a library that enables reading even when that library doesn't have a sign that says "silence." Conversely, the condition of a library that enables reading—a reasonably silent library, a library conducive to reading, that is—is what silence as the imperative (be silent) calls for—even when it is not present on a sign. (Indeed it may be easier to read in a library that does not distract its occupants with signs . . .)

But it is the absence of explicit signs that say "silence" in libraries—an ostensible silence about silence—that draws us now. Something may be unsaid because it is taken for granted. It may be unsaid because it is left out. And it may be left out because it is forgotten, or by mistake, or in error, or deliberately.[12] How is one to tell the difference? When does silence about silence in a library speak of such familiarity with silence that no sign is needed? When does silence about silence in a library signify a neglect of library silence? A library completely neglectful of silence ceases to be a library as we have known it, a quiet place for reading and thought. But does neglect of library silence point to the demise of libraries, or does it herald the emergence of as-yet-unthought-of kinds of libraries?

Let us recall how the discussion of the figure of silence in the library has gone so far. We imagined a word on a sign. We did not need to imagine the figure as word-sign; we could have imagined it as gesture or image or something else—as a librarian shushing a patron for instance—but we did not. In our thought experiment, we entered a place that surrounded us with words and books. The library we entered was silent enough that readers encountered words properly. So too in many actual libraries. Yet we recognized that one finds few actual signs that say silence or tell one

Lost its Soul?" *California Monthly*, February 1998, 15–18; and Geoffrey Nunberg, ed., *The Future of the Book* (Berkeley and Los Angeles: University of California Press, 1996).

[12] See J. L. Austin, "A Plea for Excuses," *Philosophical Papers*, 3rd ed. (Oxford: Oxford University Press, 1979), 175–204.

exactly what kind of silence is needed or what kinds of sounds (other than cell phones) are out of bounds. In this way, the silence of the library as to silence raised questions about what is happening to the library as we know it.

So too the silences of law as to justice raise questions about law as we know it.

"Silences of law?" some will exclaim. "There might not actually be any such things." "That could mean a lot of different things." And so forth.

But you followed me into the silent library although it might not actually be silent and its silences could mean a lot of different things, so try to follow me here. Justice is a little like the figure of silence in the library. It is not identical with the figure—nor with silence—and one must not push the analogy too far. But just as the figure of silence reminds us that a library is a quiet place for reading even when one cannot find—for whatever reason—a sign or word that actually says "silence" or an actually silent library, so too an attachment to justice can recall law to us even when we cannot find a word or sign that says "justice" or a definitively just law. Suppose that

- We think of texts that speak of justice, instead of imagining signs that say "silence."
- We have "law" telling its addressees what to do, rather than an imperative to be quiet.
- Where "silence" named conditions proper to acting and reading in the library, "justice" names conditions proper to doing or judging according to law.
- And, like the library, law is a place of encounters between persons and things in silence and speech: less of reading and thinking, perhaps, than of judging and acting.

Finally, as when we sought actual signs that said silence, when we begin to read modern texts of law and texts about modern law closely,

- We also find few clear signs of justice.

Texts of contemporary law do not say what justice is. Like the philosophy of law, they do not settle what it is just to do. Social science generally abstains from judgments of justice. Legal anthropology seldom claims that its depictions of the everyday practices of law are those of justice. Legal history traces changes in law by following lost signs and fragments of justice. Skeptics observe that in the absence of determinate signs or rules of justice, there may be no such thing as justice. They propose realist approaches to law: leaving justice out or grasping both law and justice in terms of social power or as ideology (in which language becomes an instrument of social power).

The trope of silence in the library in the face of the nonappearance of signs that say silence opened us to questions quite different from those of the anthropologist, the historian, the social scientist. So, too, an attachment to justice, in the face of the silences of law with respect to justice, opens us to different approaches to law than those often taken.

Granted, silence alone says nothing. There are many different kinds of silence: silences of familiarity, of struggle, of oblivion, for instance. Silence, even in context, fails to inform us correctly as to the facts. But the absence of clear signs of justice in law may tell us something. An absence of signs of justice could say that justice is so taken for granted that it goes without saying; we are seeking the wrong signs if we do not find it. The absence of clear signs of justice could mean that justice—like silence in a "noisy library"—is nevertheless still an issue. Or the absence of signs of justice might mean that justice—like silence in a library, should the very figure of silence become unfamiliar or forgotten—is no longer an issue.

Presenting issues of law and justice this way, in a questioning that continually begins with and returns to modern silences, seems strange. It suggests that law and justice—and speaking and writing about them—are not what they used to be. (It does not imply that all modern law is unjust nor that modern law cannot change.) It warns of a danger that one day, should justice stop being said, we could become oblivious to it. For words speak. They come out of silence to disclose their world. When they stop being said, they may recede into the familiar silence of an unsaid—or into oblivion. Were modern law to stop speaking of justice, would this silence herald the demise of law? Or might it point to the emergence of new and unthought-of kinds of law? And what sort of law would this be?

Silences in libraries established quiet places in which readers encountered the worlds words reveal. Even though new technologies and conceptions of public spaces challenge the traditional library and its practices, the still familiar figure of silence in the library opens us to surprising possibilities, old and new, in the world. The figure of silence, for instance, still allows us to chuckle over the toy "action figure" of a shushing librarian or to appreciate a cartoon of a librarian who scolds a patron wearing a neon yellow T-shirt and pink, purple, and orange spandex for dressing "too loudly."[13] Justice long named the way persons encountered their world through law. The practices of law are changing, such that modern law often seems silent as to justice. One wonders whether a figure of justice still keeps us open to unpredictable possibilities in the saying of modern law.

[13] *Swan Factory*, Cuyler Black, July 6, 1996, Creators Syndicate. See note 2.

Chapter 1 _____

The Rhetoric of Modern Law

> Failing to remain silent about things one cannot
> speak of is what philosophers (and many others)
> do for a living.
> —Michael Wood, *Children of Silence*

ONE OFTEN HEARS that an absence of voice is an absence of power and
an absence of justice and, conversely, that voice means empowerment and
justice. In this context, one might well expect "silences of law" to mark
the place of the oppressed, of victims, of the powerless and the voiceless
at law. That is surely one aspect of law's silence, but the silences of law
are many. They gesture not only toward the justice to be found in laying
claim to voice and to the power to be had in speech, but also toward the
possibilities of justice that lie in silence.

This work inquires into modern law, its speech and silences, and its relation to what is arguably the traditional concern of jurisprudence—justice.
It draws on texts of and about contemporary U.S. law, attending to their
language and silences, to open a new perspective on current positivist understandings of law that deny the necessity of a connection between law
and justice or (what amounts to the same thing) consider that connection
to be socially contingent. The work explores the loquaciousness—the discursive power—that sociolegal studies, political theory, and legal scholarship alike often posit—whether as attribution or aspiration—of modern
law and of its speaking subject. The work argues that the justice of modern
law lies precisely in positive law's ostensible silences—which is not to say,
despite the current predominant identification of silence with lack, that
justice is absent. Neither is it to say that positive law is just. Rather, the
conditions of justice, like those of Kantian equity—"a silent goddess who
cannot be heard"—cannot be stipulated or definitively pronounced.[1]

This chapter presents in broad strokes the issues and arguments of the
book. It shows what is at stake in modern law: a potentially new silence

---

[1] Immanuel Kant, *Metaphysical Elements of Justice*, 2nd ed., trans. John Ladd (Indianapolis: Hackett, 1999), 35; originally published as *Metaphysische Anfangsgründe der
Rechtslehre* (Hamburg, Felix Meiner Verlag, 1986), 43: "eine stumme Gottheit, die nicht
gehört werden kann."

as to justice. The first section of the chapter begins with modern law and the issue of its relation with justice. The second section shows how rhetoric approaches such an issue. The third section introduces the sociolegal positivism that today raises the question of modern law and justice most tellingly. And the fourth section shows how that question resounds with what Friedrich Nietzsche, the master rhetorician with ears behind his ears, long ago heard as the question of nihilism. In brief, *Just Silences* concerns modern law. It considers what is particular to law as modern and hence within a tradition. This chapter identifies the tradition of modern law as that of Western jurisprudence. The history and rhetoric of jurisprudence shows that one very striking feature of modern law—its social and sociological character—has not always been so. Nietzsche offers one nonsociological account of the "social" that we moderns, as he puts it, find so compelling; Heidegger another. Both turn our attention to issues of the metaphysics of law and knowledge that contemporary sciences, including sociology, largely ignore.

Law Today

Most texts of and about law today take law to be a social phenomenon. All manner of scholars take even religious law and customary law to be products of the societies of their times. Even scholars interested in what they would call the "normative" aspect of law situate law in an empirical social world. That "society" is real, that "reality" is social and empirical, holds such sway that one wonders what else law could possibly be.

Conceptions of law as an instrument of social power—as positive law— often accompany the attribution of law to the empirically knowable social or societal realm. Sociology is clearly not the same as legal positivism; there are many differences and debates within sociology; and scholars and authors may not themselves believe or intend what their texts seem to presume. The chapters that follow take sociology to refer in a broad sense to the disciplines that grasp law as an emphatically social or societal phenomenon. Likewise, there are a number of views of legal positivism and of debates within it; this book does not deal with all of its intricacies, although some of its complexity will emerge in the course of discussion. Roughly speaking, philosophers compare legal positivism to theories of natural law, which holds that an unjust law is not a law. Legal positivism maintains that the existence of law is one thing; its justice another. Positive law is human-made law. This book shows how, despite their variations and differences, sociology and legal positivism are often implicated in one another in particular ways. This implicatedness of legal positivism and sociology pervades not only legal positivism and sociological scholarship but also modern law.

The book situates what it thus calls sociolegal positivism as but one moment—admittedly the current moment—in the history of Western jurisprudence. Rather than rejecting sociolegal positivism, the social character of law or positive law as such, the book accepts as starting point the existence and social character of the positive law of the United States. It indeed draws attention to the positivist and social character of law in both avowedly positivist and ostensibly nonpositivist modern legal texts. These texts range from U.S. legislative documents and judicial opinions to law reviews and newspaper articles, sociolegal studies, and philosophical works.

The work argues—with Nietzsche, as shall be explained below—that current attachment to positive law and to the empirical and social reality of law, reveals a way (but not the only way) of conceiving of law and justice. It reveals not only a modern "conception" of law, but modern law. The work claims further that law has not always been positivist, empirical, or, broadly speaking, sociological. Nor need law always be so. Contemporary sociolegal positivism, like every other way of thinking about law, has its own particular extension and limits—and, at those limits, its own particular openings to what Heidegger and Foucault have called the unthought.

One can identify a cluster of characteristics around which legal positivism and sociology converge. First, as mentioned above, sociolegal positivism relegates connections between law and justice, if any, to empirically contingent social realities. Second, as the following chapters will show, sociolegal positivism presumes that positive law is humanly articulable power in at least one of two senses: as the declarations of officials or in scholars' descriptions—conceptual or empirical—of the order and dynamics of human social systems. Even when positive law is not the command of a distinct human sovereign or the official unification of a system of rules, it appears as a humanly made creation of society—whether as norms or practices or network of institutions—that is describable in sociological terms. Third, sociolegal positivism postulates the completeness of positive law as law. Legal positivism holds that there exists no law outside of that recognized by human positive law and that anything recognized as law is positive law. Sociology, whether attributing the determination of law to particular human actors or to social structures or everyday norms, views law as exclusively social. Sociological positivism, then, as shall be discussed in the section "Sociolegal Positivism," in effect maintains that any so-called law that precedes a given legal positivist system was itself socially powerful in the manner of positive law or was not really law at all. Sociolegal positivism thus tends toward peculiarly exhaustive and ahistorical accounts of powerful and controlling law that functions as instrument or strategy within a field of social power. The sociological and positivist commitment of our age—to the human determination of guidelines concerning what exists—threatens to discount as law anything that is not positivist and sociological—including past law.

Describing aspects of sociolegal positivism in the manner of the preceding paragraph can help identify the extensiveness and limits of modern sociolegal positive law, but it fails to show law's nonpositivist possibilities. For language, too, as the following chapters will show, is itself often grasped nowadays as an empirical, positivist, sociological phenomenon, as an expression of power or as a tool to be marshaled in the service of power. To not only identify the extent and limits of an articulate, powerful, existent modern law, but also to recognize its possibilities, one must listen to the silences of modern law and of its language.

Turning to silences suggests possibilities of relations between law and justice that are not articulated or articulable in the terms of legal positivism and that do not exist as the empirical realities of strategic social power. This turn to silence runs against much contemporary work that talks of both law and language as the powerful resources of society in a technical age.[2] The turn to silence highlights contemporary talk about law and language precisely to ask how law and language might be *otherwise* than in usual talk. It does so, again, not to discard or dismiss positive law, which is indeed modern law, but to explore openings and possibilities of law and justice that sociolegal positivism, in its commitment to the social and empirical character of law and language, does not recognize. The silences in the texts of law today are far from empty. They speak not only of limits, but also of possibilities, of justice in the contemporary law associated with actual empirical and social reality.

Far from securing a definitive truth about law, this work seeks to open—and keep open—questions about law and about law and justice. Unlike legal positivism, the work does not attempt a descriptive theory—whether empirical or conceptual—of law or legal systems; unlike sociology, it does not set out to describe as such the particular legal system that is admittedly its ground. But if the questions this work raises are not those of legal positivism and sociology, neither are they those of natural law. The work claims neither to represent existent relations between law and justice nor to prescribe what those relations should be. The concern rather

---

[2] See Martin Heidegger, "The Question concerning Technology," and "The Age of the World Picture," in *The Question concerning Technology and Other Essays*, trans. William Lovitt (New York: Harper Torchbooks, 1977), for background that informs the formulation here and the chapters that follow. See also Martin Heidegger, *Langue de tradition et langue technique* (Brussels: Editions Lebeer Hossmann, 1990), 40 (trans. from *Überlieferte Sprache und technische Sprache*). I am very much indebted to Philippe Nonet for my understanding of these and other works by Martin Heidegger.

is with the possibilities of modern law. The work is not a predictive enterprise, though. Rather than predicting what law will be, it recalls to modern law possibilities that already will have been.

In other words, within the context known loosely as that of "Western
thought," this work explores the law of a necessarily particular time and
place: the United States of the late-twentieth and early-twenty-first centuries. The work reads conventional texts of sociolegal studies, of law, and
of legal theory that are taken in this time and place to say something
about language and silence, power and voice. For many in this time and
place, the most obvious silences in contemporary law and politics are
those of the powerless. But one also finds many silences of power—of
contempt, of entitlement, of authority, of resistance. This work deliberately shifts focus from the familiar silences—and the familiar discourses—
of power and powerlessness to the sometimes neglected silences of justice.

The silences of justice that accompany contemporary law vary. Like the
familiar hush of a library in which words allow things to come to presence
in reading, silences of justice in the law may allow things to be heard. But
just as libraries may differ and silences vary, so too does law and do its
silences, as the chapters that follow show. Each chapter refers to both limits
and possibilities of modern law. In each chapter, the language of modern
law shows the extent and limits of modern law and its language; in the
interstices and at the limits of language, silences point to law's possibilities.

Chapter 2 first shows how sociolegal studies generally treat both law
and language as matters of power, while remaining silent as to justice.
The chapter then shows how appeals to voice, while also often articulated
in terms of power, may call to justice even when justice is not mentioned
by name.

Chapter 3 points to aspects of language and religion not captured in
legislation designed to protect Native American culture. The chapter highlights the notably discursive and articulate, social scientific, rulelike formulations of law in U.S. legal and political forums, while suggesting that
there are possibilities of language and law that U.S. law and social science
do not hear.

Chapter 4 looks at speech, law, and politics in the U.S. Supreme Court
flag-burning opinions and in discussions about them. The chapter shows
the pervasiveness in law today of conceptions of speech that grasp language as the resource of a technical age. But the chapter also shows how
words of law simultaneously claim and respond to calls for justice.

Chapter 5 focuses on Frederick Schauer's presumptive positivism as an
example of work that takes law to be a social system of rules.[3] That justice
drops out of Schauer's work on rules suggests both the limitations and

[3] Frederick Schauer, *Playing by the Rules: A Philosophical Examination of Rule-Based
Decision-Making in Law and in Life* (Oxford: Clarendon Press, 1991).

possibilities of rule-based approaches to law. The silence about justice in social systems of rules reminds us that in modern law, possibilities of justice lie not in statements of rules themselves, but behind the rules, in the silences where statements of rules run out and responsive action and judgment paradoxically begin anew.

Chapter 6 contrasts the silence about justice in Robert Cover's "Violence and the Word" with some of the more oblivious textual silences that have come before. Cover's silence gestures toward a need for justice—or at least toward its shocking absence in increasingly pervasive conceptions of law as violence or social control.[4] If modern law, for Cover, plays on a "field of pain and death" in which no common "normative" world is possible, Cover also implicitly appeals to a relating of persons and world that is prior to the betrayal represented by the field of pain and death, in which human beings need a common world. Out of this relating issues law. Law is the correspondence of what Cover calls a "normative order" to the human need for it. Such correspondence opens the possibilities of both the just and unjust in our world, including the possibility of what Cover here judges to be the violence and lack that characterizes modern law.

Finally, chapter 7 turns to one of the most well-known silences of law, the American right to remain silent. The formulation of this right in *Miranda v. Arizona* helps show how silences of modern law point to issues that go beyond knowledge of the social.[5] The opportunity for silence offered to an accused by the *Miranda* warning reveals an engagement with a possibility of just speech that is not simply an instrument or tool of social power. Contrary as it may be to accounts that emphasize the discontinuity of formal law and legal institutions from ordinary life, *Miranda* (and the law of evidence) recognizes, with J. L. Austin, that the justice of a trial depends on a hearing in which the judge (or jury) who speaks the verdict can presume that conventions of proper speech have been met.[6]

In what follows then, *Just Silences* attends to legal texts for what they say and don't say about justice. Sticking largely to texts of and about positive law, *Just Silences* listens to what is not positivist in law, to what is not clearly articulated and articulable at law, and to what is just. Its claims about justice are not normative or prescriptive. It refuses to relegate the justice of law to empirically contingent social realities. It reveals a multiplicity of legal silences and of possible implications for justice at precisely the limits of positive law, where the language of power and the power of language run out.

---

[4] Robert Cover, "Violence and the Word," in *Narrative, Violence, and the Law: The Essays of Robert Cover*, ed. Martha Minow, Michael Ryan, and Austin Sarat (Ann Arbor: University of Michigan Press, 1993), 203–38.

[5] *Miranda v. Arizona*, 384 U.S. 436, 86 S.Ct. 1602 (1966).

[6] J. L. Austin, *How to Do Things with Words*, ed. J. O. Urmson and Marina Sbisa, 2nd ed. (Cambridge: Harvard University Press, 1962).

It suggests that words call through voice to justice, even when "justice" is unsaid. Law is the chain of claims and responses calling to justice. Law binds us to our world. It issues from silence as the declarations that correspond with, and correspond to, the human need or necessity out of which voices appeal to justice. From law—the complex correspondence and binding of persons to a world that emerges with the calling, however silently, of words to justice—arise the possibilities of the just and the unjust in our world.

That judgments of justice and injustice today issue from law constitutes a reversal of an earlier tradition (see "The Problem of Nietzsche" below) in which law issued from justice.[7] Positive law rejects any prior necessity or binding of justice. It is a human and *social* creation. Its necessity lies in the social force or pressure that produces—through compulsion or persuasion—the obedience of subjects. It appeals to technological concepts of social reality—such as legitimacy, welfare, efficiency—to design a correspondence between social needs and social policy. From social study and opinion issue evaluations of the design and fit of law to society and society to law. Claims of, and responses to, positive law are made in terms of the values—equality, liberty, fairness, toleration, self-rule—of society.

That society stands in the former place of justice, issuing law and talking so noisily of its own values and norms, makes one wonder what has happened to justice. Is justice a modality of society? *Simply* a modality of society? Can justice be expressed in *exclusively* social terms? Is a justice that exceeds the limits of the social so nonsensical that it cannot be said? Is it so ingrained that it need not be said? Might it become (or have become) impossible?

This work explores the ways in which both "yes" and "no" can seem obvious answers to all of these questions. It seeks, as Sheldon Messinger used to say of the best of sociology, to make the strange familiar and the familiar strange. The method throughout is a—perhaps idiosyncratic—rhetorical one. As we shall see, it differs from other approaches to law, although it has commonalities with several of them. It seeks to approach the particularity of questions of law and justice in our time, keeping open to them as questions.

Rhetoric

Rhetoricians think about language and what it does and doesn't do. They think about what is revealed in the use of particular language in particular texts. They expand and contract notions of text: word, figure of speech,

[7] Friedrich Nietzsche, *On the Genealogy of Morals*, in *Basic Writings of Nietzsche*, trans. Walter Kaufmann (New York: Modern Library, 1968).

image, phrase, claim, paragraph, argument, article, book, library, event
... They play with genre: oral epic poetry, script, performance, film—
even comic strip! Rhetoricians do not commit themselves to causal accounts of change (as backward-looking historians seeking reasons for the
appearance or disappearance of signs or phenomena may do) because
rhetoricians know that causal accounts are empirically suspect. Like good
social scientists, rhetoricians would rather stick to correlations than
causes for making connections. Unlike social scientists, though, they do
not limit themselves to *empirical* correspondence: they experiment in
thought. At the same time, they shudder at precisely the thought of articulating ideals, of identifying or postulating what ought to be, of staking
out a position pro or contra silence, for instance, the way law professors
might. And rhetoricians certainly do not have the philosophers' respect
for logic and logical argument.

An example from a logic textbook helps clarify the difference between
logic and rhetoric. Citing an 1826 logic textbook, a contemporary textbook provides the following passage as an illustration of a fallacious argument and, in particular, of the fallacy of begging the question, or *petitio
principii*:

> To allow every man unbounded freedom of speech must always be, on the
> whole, advantageous to the state; for it is highly conducive to the interests of
> the community that each individual should enjoy a liberty, perfectly unlimited,
> of expressing his sentiments.[8]

Petitio principii refers to what is sometimes called circular reasoning, in
which, the textbook explains, a conclusion ("to allow every man unbounded freedom of speech must always be, on the whole, advantageous
to the state") is "buried within" one of the premises ("it is highly conducive to the interests of the community that each individual should enjoy
a liberty, perfectly unlimited, of expressing his sentiments"). To a logician,
when a premise assumes the truth of what the argument seeks to prove,
the argument is fallacious—logically problematic. To a rhetorician, by
contrast, the assertion of such a relation may be a source of wonder: How
can one claim be "buried within" another? What is the import of burial?
Isn't what is buried contained and hidden? Why isn't an argument whose
premise contains its conclusion, however hidden, true-in-itself? Truth-in-
itself is not the same as tautology. Tautology refers to the truth of a proposition. Begging the question or circularity refers to the status of an
argument. Why isn't circularity truth-in-itself? Might truth-in-itself be a
logical fallacy? How can logic answer the last question, insofar as the

question involves adjudication of logic's own relation to truth? Might logic be contained within truth? Might truth be hidden in logic?

More to the point perhaps, a rhetorician might ask what sort of world—of language and politics, for instance—the logic textbook comes out of when it presupposes that what is "advantageous to the state" ("always" and "on the whole," to be sure) is buried within what is "highly conducive to the interests of the community"? Or further, presumes that "unbounded freedom" is contained in "liberty, perfectly unlimited," just as "speech" is hidden in "expressing . . . sentiments," and "every man" within "each individual"? What sort of world—and of law—does the citation of this passage as an example of *petitio principii* reveal? Is it the same world as that of the text from which the passage was drawn? If, as the logic text implies, obligation to individual enjoyment of liberty entails allowing freedom (and who or what allows it?), is it a Kantian realm in which ought implies can? Is it a Millian world in which states maximize individual interests? What sort of world do these logicians—and their copy-editor—inhabit?

Interestingly, the 1820s textbook that the 1990s textbook cites as its source uses the passage to show how the English language—with its Norman and Saxon roots—is especially prone to circular arguments. The English language, writes Whately,

> is perhaps the more suitable for the Fallacy of *petitio principii* [than the Fallacy *ignoratio elenchi* or of irrelevant conclusion], from its being formed from two distinct languages, and thus abounding in synonymous expressions, which have no resemblance in sound, and no connection in etymology; so that a Sophist may bring forward a proposition expressed in words of Saxon origin, and give as a reason [for] it the very same proposition stated in words of Norman origin; e.g. [passage cited above follows].[9]

The world of the 1820s textbook, then, is a world in which a logician takes note of language very differently than does "a Sophist." The English-speaking Sophist (to whom the example is attributed) seeks to persuade listeners who are ignorant of the roots of their language of the infinite desirability of speech (its "unbounded freedom"), while the logician warns that phrases in even "distinct" languages can state "the very same proposition."

The contemporary rhetorician's attention to language differs from that paid by either logician or sophist. The rhetorician questions the logician's eternal faith that ideas represented by words can be grasped irrespective of their utterance in particular times and places and languages. To the rhetorician, words do not necessarily represent propositions and neither

---

[9] Richard Whately, *Elements of Logic*, 9th ed. (New York: Sheldon and Co., 1873), 223.

words, ideas, nor propositions can be analyzed independently of their use. But this does not imply that the value of words, for the rhetorician, lies only in their ability to persuade or in sophistry. One need not accept the common caricature of the rhetorician as reducing the import of language to its use as persuasive communication or to the transmission of messages from willing senders to passive—or even active—receivers.[10]

So how *do* rhetoricians attend to language? They read. They listen. They read very carefully. They read texts for what they say; and they read texts for what they don't say. They read the words of a text; they listen for its silences. They wonder, for instance, about phrases like "law is too important to leave to the lawyers," a phrase with a lovely alliterative lilt. But does the phrase mean that *law* is too important to leave to the lawyers, but that it is all right to leave some less important nonlaw to lawyers (and what might that be?)? Does it mean that law is too *important* to leave to the lawyers, rather than too interesting or enriching or complicated (and how is it important)? Does it mean that law is too important to *leave* to the lawyers, as opposed to delegating it to them or letting them borrow it once in a while? Finally, does it mean that law is too important to leave to the *lawyers*, as opposed to those with whom it might otherwise safely be left—law professors, or judges, or legislators, or liberal artists or scholars, for instance?

Rhetoricians don't just read the lines, then. They read between the lines; they read around the lines. They read parentheticals. (They read so carefully that they even read signs that are not there, as the prologue showed!) They love words and silences—and libraries, but they don't usually *say* anything about that. More often they *say* outrageous things about the scholarship of more serious disciplines—like anthropology, history, sociology, law, philosophy—while claiming that these caricatures are based on their own careful readings.

Take the philosophy of law for now. The most familiar way for jurists and jurisprudes to address the question of law philosophically today is to distinguish between positive law as "the law that is, in contrast to the law that ought to be," as Peter Berkowitz puts it. "This simple, preliminary formulation," he continues, "leaves open the question of the consequence of a conflict between the positive law that is and the law that ought to be, between the law of the city and the divine law, between human justice

---

[10] The following do not fit this caricature: James Boyd White, *Justice as Translation* (Chicago: University of Chicago Press, 1994), and *Heracles' Bow* (Madison: University of Wisconsin Press, 1985); Peter Goodrich, *Oedipus Lex: Psychoanalysis, History, Law* (Berkeley and Los Angeles: University of California Press, 1995), and *Law in the Courts of Love: Literature and Other Minor Jurisprudences* (New York: Routledge, 1996); Linda Ross Meyer, "Between Reason and Power: Experiencing Legal Truth," *University of Cincinnati Law Review* 67:3 (1999): 727.

and what is right by nature or dictated by reason."[11] The subject matter of the philosophy of law thus devolves into an argument between positivists and natural lawyers as to the meaning of law, which leaves open the question of what to do in any particular instance.[12] Natural lawyers maintain that a higher moral law is the measure of the lawfulness or justice of man-made laws.[13] Positivists provide factual, nonmoral criteria, such as procedural regularity or the command of a sovereign, as the test of a law's validity and hence existence and maintain that there is no necessary connection between law and justice.[14]

A rhetorician, after a careful reading of texts of and about law, might suggest that there are many more interesting ways of talking about law and justice than as a dichotomous conflict between natural law and legal positivism, between ought and is, divine and human. To the rhetorician, jurisprudence appears less a debate as to the meaning of "law" than an inquiry into complicated relations between law and justice around particular questions of action or of what to do—precisely the questions that philosophy does not answer.

Law, the rhetorician notes, seeks to answer the very questions of what to do that concern philosophers but that philosophy (like rhetoric) does not generally answer. Indeed, law tells those whom it addresses (and responds to) what to do. It does so whatever one's theory or conception of law. And it does so in various ways, compatible with many theories yet

[11] Peter Berkowitz, "On the Laws Governing Free Spirits and Philosophers of the Future: A Response to Nonet's 'What is Positive Law?'" *Yale Law Journal* 100 (1990): 703.

[12] For an excellent textbook introduction to the philosophy of law, see Frederick Schauer and Walter Sinnott-Armstrong, introduction to *Philosophy of Law: Classic and Contemporary Readings with Commentary* (Fort Worth: Harcourt Brace College Publishers, 1996), 1–7. Schauer and Sinnott-Armstrong are correct that the answer to the broad question "What is law?" can be a moral issue (as when positivist Hart and natural law defender Fuller argue about how the concept of law should be understood) or an ontological one (Soper), whether provided in conceptual (Coleman) or quasi-descriptive (Dworkin) terms. Each and all of these approaches leave open the question of what to do in any particular case—except, of course, in the matter of the particular case of how to answer the broad question "What is law?"

[13] See Thomas Aquinas, *The Political Ideas of St. Thomas Aquinas: Representative Selections*, trans. Dino Bigongiari (New York: Hafner Press, 1953, 1981); Augustine, *On Free Choice of the Will*, trans. Thomas Williams (Indianapolis: Hackett, 1993), and *City of God*, trans. Henry Bettenson (New York: Penguin, 1984); John Finnis, *Natural Law and Natural Rights* (Oxford: Clarendon Press, 1981).

[14] See John Austin, *The Province of Jurisprudence Determined* (London: Weidenfeld and Nicholson, 1954); H.L.A. Hart, *The Concept of Law* (Oxford: Clarendon Press, 1961); Hans Kelsen, *Pure Theory of Law* (Berkeley and Los Angeles: University of California Press, 1967); Joseph Raz, *The Concept of a Legal System* (Oxford: Clarendon Press, 1970). Note that sometimes legal positivists distinguish the two points, that legal philosophy is concerned with describing (the existence or nature of) law and that there is no necessary connection between law and morality.

irreducible to any single one. Whether law is God-made or man-made, text or behavior or something else or both, law *tells*—gestures (to), indicates, shows, reveals, states, describes, threatens, or commands—its addressee or subject what must be done. It may do so with and without words, with and without rules, as shall be seen.

Parsing out the rhetoric of particular laws raise major constellations of issues having to do with *how* law tells the one *whom* it tells *what* to do. In any particular legal event or text, the rhetorician notes, one can identify, like variations on a theme,

- an addressee or subject, the "one" or "ones" whom law addresses (citizens, residents, persons, corporations, human beings, officials, would-be spouses, Christians, moral actors, utilitarian maximizers) when it tells *someone* what to do;
- a doing, the *what to do* law calls for (the establishment of funding for language programs, the return of particular artifacts, respect for the flag, the introduction of testimony in particular ways, for instance, which may constitute a deed, a conscientious choice, social behavior, rule-following, willing, conforming, calculating);
- a telling (of what to do) in a manner (with or without words) through which, law presumes, addressees discern what must be done (via example, by cognizing statements of rules, by threats and coercion, through revelation, through moral knowledge, through legal reasoning, through deliberation or strategy).

The imperative of law may manifest itself variously as custom, tradition, practice, obligation, command, declaration, rule, sign, calculation, judgment, or something else. That a particular manifestation of an imperative—a "declaration," for instance—can sometimes be described also as an obligation or as a command or as both suggests that the claim that law tells those whom it addresses what to do is less an empirical or a conceptual answer to the question, "What is law?" than a rhetorical one, in which "must" may hold varying statuses.[15]

Furthermore, "telling" implies that one speaks (with or without words) to another in context; it implies action. It suggests that, irrespective of whether one adopts a stance that law does its telling well or badly, the strong distinctions between action and speech or between language and behavior that some scholarship adopts toward law are conceptual distinctions. This does not mean that they are "only" conceptual distinctions—or to be discarded. That the distinctions between speech and action, be-

[15] Rhetorical, in the sense of Goodrich, Meyer, White, above. On empirical and conceptual, see Jules Coleman, "Rules and Social Facts," *Harvard Journal of Law and Public Policy* 14 (1991): 703.

tween language and behavior, are conceptual distinctions means that they are *also* rhetorical distinctions—and to be explored for what they presume and what their use enables one to learn, or precludes one from learning, about law.

Rhetoric recognizes that legal language is inseparable from legal behavior. Having recognized such inseparability, rhetoric provides a language in which to speak of the ways in which law and studies of the legal system nevertheless sometimes insist on separating language from behavior. In some social scientific scholarship, for instance, scholars rely on a strong distinction between language and behavior to identify and articulate a disjunction between what law claims of itself and what it actually does. They argue also for the primacy of the standards of social sciences, which look to law in action, over the values of a legal profession that takes law as language or as "anything but behavior."[16] Law itself struggles with its version of the language-behavior distinction, as in attempts to clarify the difference between protected "speech" and unprotected "conduct" under the First Amendment, for instance, which is discussed further in chapter 3 on the flag-burning cases.

Rhetoric also notes that the various tellings and doings of law have different possible relations to justice. Jurisprudence articulates regularities in these relations. In jurisprudence, law corresponds not only to particular understandings of addressees, the collectivities to which they belong, their action and knowledge, but also to justice. The "citizens" of the polis, the "fellow Christians" of the heavenly city, the "moral persons" of a kingdom-of-ends, the "rational agents" of socioeconomic theory and the bearers of everyday life of modern society, that is, correspond to particular conceptions of law and justice. Shifting configurations of words used in jurisprudence for the identity, action, and knowledge of law's addressee—in works from those of Socrates and Plato, through Augustine and Aquinas, Kant, and the utilitarians, to the contemporary legal, political, and social theory of Rawls,[17] Unger,[18] Habermas,[19] and others—reveal changing understandings—conceptions and practices—of law and of justice. Law (as "The Problem of Nietzsche" will discuss further) may be a way of life (Socrates), natural law (the Christians), moral law (Kant), positive law (the utilitarians), or social policy (Rawls). Justice may be eternal. Or the association of law with justice may be qualified: natural

---

[16] "Anything but behavior" in Lawrence F. Friedman, "The Law and Society Movement," *Stanford Law Review* 35 (1986): 763.

[17] John Rawls, *A Theory of Justice* (Cambridge: Harvard University Press, 1971).

[18] Roberto M. Unger, *The Critical Legal Studies Movement* (Cambridge: Harvard University Press, 1983).

[19] Jürgen Habermas, *Between Facts and Norms: Contributions to a Discourse Theory of Law and Democracy*, trans. William Rehg (Cambridge: MIT Press, 1996).

law constitutes imperfect participation in a divine (law of) justice. For some, justice is that which temporal law needs or secular law lacks; for others, it may be that to which human law aspires or fails to aspire. According to some, law is doomed to try and to fail to achieve justice; according to others, justice itself is illusion, ideology, or even outright lie. Some even formulate law's association with justice (the psychoanalytic rhetorician notes) in a denial that there is any necessary connection between the two!

What is named for the rhetorician by all of these words is again not simply concepts. *Citizen* indeed carries with it a conception of law that tells the members of a polis to practice the virtues of the laws of the city. But citizenship is not only a concept; citizens do embody the virtues and law of the collectivities to which—and in the ways in which—citizens belong. Today's citizen, however contested current conceptions of citizenship, is a member of a nation-state whose law is positive law. *Citizen* today tells us about our world, not just about relations between terms in a text. It does so whether or not empirically verifiable or officially recognized citizens are present and despite factual and conceptual disputes over their identification. It does so despite conflicts of laws and contestations over the status of particular states and of state law.

The language not just of philosophy, but of law, reveals worlds. Law today, for instance, often considers the citizen to be a "stakeholder" in enterprises of government.[20] Government, conversely, may also become a stakeholder in the community and in its members. The second of the Department of Health and Human Services' six goals for "Healthy People 2010," for instance, is to "[p]romote ... personal responsibility for health lifestyles and behavior."[21] In 1997, President Clinton established an Advisory Commission on Consumer Protection and Quality in the Health Care Industry. The problems that health maintenance organizations (HMOs) were meant to address—problems with the medical profession— had given way to problems with the very "health care providers" that had replaced doctors, nurses, and medical assistants. Clinton asked thirty-four "citizen-experts" to draft a "bill of rights" protecting Americans, in the words of one commentator, "from the corporations insuring their health." Former patients became "health care consumers," in Clinton's terms, and were asked to take responsibility for declaring their rights.[22]

At issue here is both a word and a subject, the *patient*. According to the *New York Times*:

[20] United States Bureau of Census, *Census ABC's: Applications in Business and Community* (Washington, D.C.: Georgetown University Press, 1990).

[21] Consortium of Social Science Associations, *Washington Update* 17 (1998): 21.

[22] Robert Hunt Sprinkle, "Corporatism in Question: A Note on Managed Care," *Report from the Institute for Philosophy and Public Policy* 17 (1997): 13.

The chief executive of the King's Fund, an influential British health charity and research organization, says it is high time to abolish the word "patient."
. . . But if "patient" has to go, what word should replace it?
. . . Rabbi Neuberger [of the King's Fund] considered but rejected "client," which she thought made health care delivery sound like a purely financial transaction. . . .
"Consumer" also struck her as wrong, conjuring an image of the "constant ingestion of pills and potions." She finally settled for "user," a word that "despite its lack of elegance," conveys action rather than passive acceptance, confidence rather than bewilderment, power rather than dependency. "It could even suggest an equalization of status between health professional and service user that is nearer the climate in which modern health services should be provided," she declared.[23]

If Clinton differs from the British in his terminology of consumers and users, the technique he used—citizen-experts—is nevertheless one of widespread currency. Communities of service users band together to press for what they need, about which they are considered best and local experts.

Clinton called on citizen-experts to articulate not needs but "rights," a locution commonly associated with liberalism's so-called autonomous individuals rather than with their socially encumbered brethren. But Clinton's citizen-expert is not quite the individual of classical liberalism. Rather, the citizen-expert is a *user* of *services*, the complement to the *service provider* (as "consumer" is to "producer"). While the British "user" conveys "action," "confidence," "power," rather than passivity, "bewilderment," "dependency," the word *user* reminds us of the absence of perfect freedom, as Peter Lyman puts it (in the context of digital library and computer technology), since "all of these choices are given by the technical structures designed by the programmer" and presented by the server.[24]

In the context of social policies and expertise about human services, the "user" is the offspring of rational choice and marketing theory. S/he embodies the joint hopes born from the shortcomings of both "rational actor" and "consumer." While the "rational actor" assumed by policymakers is too abstract and ethereal, too ungrounded in the things of the world, to serve as a model citizen, the market "consumer" is too indiscriminating and materially oriented to be taken seriously as an expert. The "service user" is heir to both. The "user" combines the techniques of cost-benefit analysis and concern for economic efficiency with utilitarian

[23] Abigail Zuger, "Essay: Patient Suffers from Connotations," *New York Times,* August 31, 1999.
[24] Peter Lyman, "What is a Digital Library? Technology, Property, and the Public Interest," *Daedalus* 125 (1996): 7.

calculations as to satisfactions—in new civic form. The user manipulates the things of this world, yet distinguishes between needs and desires. The user draws on experience of these needs to contribute to representations of the public or publics (in user surveys, for instance). But more importantly, as citizen-expert, the user engages with others within given social structures. Indeed, as an entity already situated in relations and dependencies with others, the service user—like all members of contemporary society—engages in a particular politics of association.

That politics goes to the very matter of modern law. In the last twenty-five years or so in the United States, non-strictly-state institutions and organizations—including private and for-profit ones—have come to exercise and manage functions and tasks that, earlier in the century, had themselves come to be associated with the federal state or the states (examples: insurance companies, health maintenance organizations and managed-care providers, charter school programs, credit-checking outfits, private security companies, private prisons, partnerships between volunteer organizations and local governments, and so forth). The adoption—by state agencies, quasi-public organizations, and private parties alike—of the techniques of management, accounting, and evaluation that characterize market enterprises has meant that expertise no longer belongs either to specialists or to social researchers, planners, and efficiency experts, who were held accountable to professional norms and external goals. Expertise now belongs concurrently to the citizen—a citizen trained to community responsibility and appealed to, as responsible community member and local expert, to participate in government that increasingly administers what may loosely be termed the activities of everyday life—working, eating and drinking, learning, resting and recreating, traveling, reading, watching television, driving, and so forth.[25]

As we have learned from Michel Foucault (a rhetorician second only to Friedrich Nietzsche), particular social projects—the leper colony, the plague city, the Panopticon—carry with them their own "political dreams."[26] In the 1990s, the empowered community emerges as the political dream of the projects of administrative agencies. This dream of the empowered community coincides with the privatization of formerly pub-

[25] The public entities alone concerned with these activities make up an alphabet soup. They include for working: OSHA, SSA; eating: FDA; drinking: ATF, local liquor laws, Surgeon General; learning: local school boards to DOE; resting and recreating: the Consumer Protection Agency, bicycle helmet laws, National Park Service, the EPA; traveling: INS, Customs, FAA; television and radio, FTC; driving: NHA, Highway Patrol, DMV, seat belt laws. Quasi-public and private organizations are of course also involved in promoting and structuring these activities.

[26] Michel Foucault, *Discipline and Punish: The Birth of the Prison*, trans. Alan Sheridan (New York: Vintage, 1977), 198.

lic functions. Particular ideological political concerns for security and democracy, identified by Foucault in his work on governmentality and described further in the works of others, together with the growing significance to governance of nontherapeutic social sciences, contribute to the appeal of empowerment as political dream, political tool, and political project.[27]

As the expertise of the therapeutic professions (the human sciences to which Foucault points—public health, psychology, social welfare, city planning, and so forth) gives way to that of experts in fields of financial planning, management, administration, and public accounting, the latter experts rely increasingly for their "substance" on local knowledge, the input of the democratic citizen or local community member. The accounting and auditing fields hold out a common vocabulary for crossing between public and private, state and market, concerns. They offer tools for organizing and evaluating data in otherwise ostensibly incompatible registers by allowing the translation of data into the transparency and visibility of the ledger book or the account sheet.[28]

The experience of Health and Human Services (HHS) highlights the sorts of changes in administration that occurred from the 1970s through the 1990s. HHS shifted in the 1970s from an older professional model of evaluation and review to a new quality control (QC) model. The social work professional gave way on the front line to the clerk and at higher administrative levels to the technocratic manager with a background in business administration, argues William Simon in his analysis of the new

---

[27] Michel Foucault, "Governmentality," *Ideology and Consciousness* 6 (1979): 5; Gordon Burchell, Colin Gordon, and Peter Miller, eds., *The Foucault Effect: Studies in Governmentality* (Chicago: University of Chicago Press, 1991); Barbara Cruikshank, *The Will to Empower: Democratic Citizens and Other Subjects* (Ithaca, NY: Cornell University Press, 1999); Thomas L. Dumm, *A Politics of the Ordinary* (New York: New York University Press, 1999); Pat O'Malley, "Neo-Liberal Police: 'Partnership Policing' and the 'Empowered Community,' " paper presented at Law and Society Association Summer Legal Institute, Rutgers, New Jersey, 1999; Nikolas Rose, *Powers of Freedom: Reframing Political Thought* (Cambridge: Cambridge University Press, 1999); Jonathan Simon, "On Their Own: Delinquency without Society," *Kansas Law Review* 47 (1999): 1, and "Megan's Law: Crime and Democracy in Late Modern America," *Law and Social Inquiry* 25 (2000): 1111; Mariana Valverde, Ron Levi, Clifford Shearing, Mary Condon, and Pat O'Malley, *Democracy in Governance: A Socio-Legal Framework. A Report for the Law Commission of Canada on Law and Governance Relationships* (Ottawa: Law Commission, 1999).

[28] Michael Power, *The Audit Society: Rituals of Verification* (Oxford: Oxford University Press, 1990). The extension at least of accounting, beyond the firm and even beyond tax and government accounting into other spaces of public concern, was not unintentional: a concerted effort was made by the American Institute of Certified Public Accountants to deal with public relations and to increase the public service of its members. John L. Carey, *The Rise of the Accounting Profession to Responsibility and Authority: 1937–1969* (New York: American Institute of Certified Public Accountants, 1970).

regime. Social workers and caseworkers were replaced with "eligibility technicians" or "income maintenance workers" (1215).[29] In conjunction with the rise of the welfare rights movement, QC, with its attention to "error," as Simon shows, reinforced trends toward formalization of eligibility norms, intensified organizational hierarchy, and increased documentation requirements and shifting of costs toward recipients (1210–12). Congress likewise turned away from counseling, toward economic approaches such as financial incentives and work requirements, for fostering recipient self-support.

The 1990s saw welfare transformed once again, this time to a decentralized block grant system that aims not only to make recipients economically self-supporting but also to engage them in "community." The Personal Responsibility and Work Opportunity Reconciliation Act of 1996 replaced AFDC, Aid to Families with Dependent Children, with TANF, Temporary Assistance to Needy Families block grants to the states. The act imposes time limits on welfare benefits and requires recipients to go to work, as well as increasing the role of the states in determining and providing benefits. The act aims at not only "work opportunity," but also "personal responsibility." It stresses the importance of having some sort of "community work experience" and states that "responsible fatherhood and motherhood" are key to marriage as the "foundation of a successful society" in which the interests of children come first. The most recent state welfare program innovations include cooperative programs for child care and transportation for workfare beneficiaries, many of which are worked out via state and local partnerships.

Despite its goal of financial independence, this latest system of aid to the poor cannot be reduced to an "economic" approach to self-support. Neither does it mark a return to an older therapeutic model nor to a rights-based system. Its emphasis on goals of personal responsibility and civic competence resembles the goals of many other community-oriented programs—Neighborhood Watch campaigns, community arbitration boards, emergency and disaster preparedness programs, community health centers, city or regional planning for public facilities. These programs, too, rely on elaborate information that those who are to be served provide through extensive documentation. They often cite empowerment as a secondary goal. And they require "partnering" between "community" and agency for the integration of good citizen-worker-residents into a civic life that will be fostered by healthy or safe social and civic environments.

[29] William H. Simon, "Legality, Bureaucracy, and Class in the Welfare System," *Yale Law Journal* 92 (1983): 1215.

The epitome of such partnering is encountered in the "emerging field" of "community justice."[30] Community justice may include "a wide array of programs, and 'community-based initiatives,' including community policing, 'weed and seed,' neighborhood revitalization, drug courts, community corrections, community courts and neighborhood prosecution and defense units, prevention and diversion programs, restitution, community service, victim services, and dispute and conflict resolution efforts in schools and neighborhood organizations."[31] Citizens may be involved in these programs, which share an informal nonadversarial approach to sanctioning that is presented as a community-based alternative to court sanctioning, in a variety of ways.[32] Through their engagements, community members maintain a relation to the formal criminal justice system, whether to a judge, prosecutor, or court official with whom they share decision making and authority, or to police and probation officers who are responsible for monitoring and enforcement of the program.

One can compare such community justice programs to traditional models of crime and order. The traditional system "performs as a professional service system of state agents who work in response to criminal events . . . [and are] accountable for a set of professional standards that apply uniformly to all who are engaged in the practice of justice," writes one scholar. The community model, by contrast, "involves professionals who work in response to problems articulated by citizens. . . . Because of the heavy dosage of citizen input and activity in the latter model, professional effort tends to be judged on the basis of citizen satisfaction with justice services."[33]

The citizen takes the place of the fellow professional in judging professional performance. But citizen input does more than simply establish a gauge—satisfaction with services delivered—to judge professionals' performances. Citizens' concerns and desires indicate what problems to address and enable policymakers to develop strategies whose success will in turn depend on the evaluations of citizens. Policymaking uses the information provided by citizens to establish both ends and means.

[30] David R. Karp, *Community Justice: An Emerging Field* (Lanham, MD: Rowman and Littlefield, 1998).

[31] Gordon Bazemore, "The 'Community' in Community Justice: Issues, Themes, and Questions for the New Neighborhood Sanctioning Models," in Karp, *Community Justice*, 330, citing National Institute of Justice, *Communities: Mobilizing Against Crime* (Washington, D.C.: National Institute of Justice, 1996)

[32] One study describes four models of citizen decision-making in neighborhood sanctioning as "circle sentencing," "family group conferencing," "reparative probation," and "victim/offender mediation." Bazemore, "Community."

[33] Todd R. Clear and David R. Karp, "The Community Justice Movement," in Karp, *Community Justice*, 20–21.

Citizens provide information about themselves, their concerns, their neighbors, and their neighborhood to promote public safety, health, and welfare. They register to take tests, learn interactively and give feedback so that they themselves and future generations of test takers, interactive learners, and ballot punchers will be more ably served by colleges, banks, museums, departments of motor vehicles, election boards, and so forth. They constitute the targets of opinion polls and of surveys of customer preferences and consumer satisfaction, the profiles of demographics and the more recent "psychographics" of media research services. Through the strategies of social science, mass media, and market capitalism, in which they participate, they are constituted as a public, which in turn becomes the basis for local and national policies, as well as for less ostensibly political measures, such as dietary recommendations, for instance, which by law will be disseminated via the market.

These engagements—the behavior of a subject who is arguably both empowered citizen and tool of legitimation—are informed by social study and are the objects of it. They point the attentive rhetorician to a new politics—new knowledges and practices—of society in which narrowly "legal realist" social sciences may have had their heyday, but in which postrealism is by no means nonsociological.

Austin Sarat argues that

> [t]he social sciences, and especially sociology (the most social), which had become court sciences at the highest levels in the 1960s and 1970s, are today largely absent from national government and are experiencing their own internal drift and discontent.[34]

Sarat cites Garth and Sterling to the effect that "social science generally and law and society in particular [have] declined in relative prestige." Sarat sees a relaxation of "the confident embrace of social science as the dominant paradigm for work that seeks to chart the social life of law." Like many others, he points to "the decline of the social as a nexus of governing," and to a crisis in the social that he suggests "is being experienced globally today."[35]

The death of the social has been announced prematurely, however, the literal-minded rhetorician would note. The dismantling of "the most florid

[34] Austin Sarat, "Visuality Amidst Fragmentation: On the Emergence of Postrealist Law and Society Scholarship," in *The Blackwell Companion to Law and Society*, ed. Austin Sarat (Oxford: Blackwell, 2004), 5.

[35] Sarat, "Visuality," 4–5. For others, see Jean Baudrillard, *In the Shadow of the Silent Majorities or, The End of the Social and Other Essays* (New York: Semiotext(e), 1983); Austin Sarat and Jonathan Simon, "Cultural Analysis, Cultural Studies, and the Situation of Legal Scholarship," in *Cultural Analysis, Cultural Studies, and Law*, ed. Austin Sarat and Jonathan Simon (Durham, NC: Duke University Press, 2003), 1–34.

forms of the social," as Sarat calls them—social insurance, public transportation and housing, public health and social medicine, as well as socialism—comes in the name of the preferences of society and its ostensibly empowered service users. These preferences may not accord with the liberal reform agenda of many academic social researchers, but they are gathered and known precisely through the techniques of managerial social sciences that pervade the new quasi-public/private networks and relations by which governing occurs. The last decade or so has indeed seen a transformation in the social, but insofar as "society" continues to be both object and subject of government, it is in no danger of disappearing. On the contrary, one sometimes looks in vain for aspects of the world that are exempt from human government.

The "death of the social" then refers only narrowly to particular approches to law and policy. The assumptions and techniques of social research still pervade law and the legal system. Social researchers have complained for decades that their work is not taken seriously enough in legal institutions.[36] Such neglect may indeed characterize the reception of particular studies in particular formal institutions. But it is in the *name* of the social, even the nonrhetorician must grant, that the grand social programs of the twentieth century have come under attack. The social science methods that premeate government and society may not produce tenurable works. A sociological worldview nevertheless predominates in the everyday norms and rules of institutions of modern law and government. This work explores that worldview.

Sociolegal Positivism

If rhetoric discerns in law today a socio-logical worldview, the academic disciplines of society provide a privileged—and generally more articulate—entrée into that worldview and relations within it, than do their managerial cousins. Insofar as law today is a social phenomenon, the academic social sciences—sociology, anthropology, political science—include law within their domain. Even when they do not make positive law their explicit object of study, one often discerns in them the positive law that today is taken to be law. While some sociology is silent about, or does not explicitly concern itself with, justice, some interpretive work turns pointedly to the "justice" of law and provides insight into modern law and its silences.

[36] See Rosemary J. Erickson and Rita J. Simon, *The Use of Social Science Data in Supreme Court Decisions* (Urbana: University of Illinois Press, 1998) and studies cited therein; Jonathan Yovel and Elizabeth Mertz, "The Role of Social Science in Legal Decisions," in Sarat, *Blackwell Companion*, 410–31; Marianne Constable, *The Law of the Other: The Mixed*

In a careful analysis of British colonial administration in Tanganyika, for instance, Sally Falk Moore explores the British conception of "justice" that appears in a colonial directive to officers in charge of African local courts.[37] She looks at what the document states "is the main function of a court—to dispense justice" (18). According to Moore, British commitment to "the rule of law" was grounded in an "ideal of rule standardization" that Moore associates with H.L.A. Hart's positivist model of a legal system (22). The simultaneous British "commitment to discovering and respecting the authentic African legal 'tradition' " that was not simply a set of rules *and* "to writing it down in the form of rules" indicates the ambivalence in and tension of the colonial administration in Tanganyika, she writes. British "aims of empowerment" and "aims of control" were "bound to face in opposite directions" (24, 40).

The tension in British aims vis-à-vis positive law that Moore finds in Tanganyika can be found also in Hart's own positivist conception of law, as well as in sociolegal studies. The most recent theoretical work in legal positivism develops in an explicitly sociolegal fashion from Hart's now-classic sociological and legal positivist account of a modern "municipal legal system."[38] Despite the differences between (and within) contemporary legal theory and sociolegal scholarship, sociolegal studies generally conform to—and share the limitations of—legal positivist conceptions of law. Where Hart argued that there is "no necessary connection" between law and justice, contemporary legal positivism and sociolegal study converge, as we shall see, in affirming that the connection between law and morality is an empirically contingent matter of social factors.[39]

For Hart, the existence of a legal system requires two kinds of rules: first, the rules generally obeyed by citizens, whatever the motive, that are recognized as valid by the system's ultimate criteria of validity; and second, the rules accepted by officials that specify the criteria for validity of the first set of rules (113). The "unification" of rules that Hart associates with the emergence of a modern legal system combines the propositionally articulated customs of what he calls a primitive society with the similarly propositional secondary rules of officials.

The tensions that Moore points out in British incorporation of tradition into rules or into positive law in Tanganyika suggests an instability that characterizes the emergence and existence of any positivist legal system.

Jury and Changing Conceptions of Citizenship, Law, and Knowledge (Chicago: University of Chicago Press, 1994), 49–50.

[37] Sally Falk Moore, "Treating Law as Knowledge: Telling Colonial Officers What to Say to Africans about Running 'Their Own' Native Courts," *Law and Society Review* 26 (1992): 11.

[38] Hart, *The Concept of Law*, v, 17.

[39] Brian Tamanaha, *Realistic Socio-Legal Theory: Pragmatism and a Social Theory of Law* (Oxford: Clarendon Press, 1997).

According to Hart, the first step in the unification of rules (or the establishment of a modern legal system) is the "mere reduction to writing of hitherto unwritten rules" (92). But the "traditions" of which Moore speaks (like the "practices" in Raz's analysis of rules) were not necessarily unwritten "rules" before the British made them so.[40] Furthermore, "what is crucial" for Hart is the second step, "the acknowledgment of reference to the writing or inscription as *authoritative*, i.e. as the *proper* way of disposing of doubts as to the existence of the rule" (92). Moore's analysis points to difficulties not only with writing down tradition in the form of statements of rules, but also with the closure Hart implies is achieved in his "crucial" second step, the acknowledgment of a mark of authority to settle doubts as to the existence of a rule.

Moore implies that there is never a moment in which the Africans in question fully acknowledge the authority of the British, nor of British writings of rules, for determining the validity of British articulations of local custom. "Not only has much of the British-designed structure of the courts been inherited, but so have many of the resistances to it and circumventions of it" (21), she writes. She suggests that, at least in Tanganyika, the emergence of the Hartian positivist legal system of the British directive is—perhaps perpetually—incomplete.

Such incompleteness paradoxically seems to be an attribute of the emergence of any Hartian positivist legal system. The very law that British officials in Tanganyika took as their model of a modern legal system, the common law, also lacks a determinate moment of "acknowledgment of authority." Common-law history is a history of the acknowledgment of the authority of the king's courts over local custom. History locates the acknowledgment of authority, which would mark the emergence of the common law as a properly positivist legal system, in a perpetually receding moment of origin. The shift from custom to law in common-law histories appears as a long continuum, to which no determinate origin can be affixed. Official practice has always already begun to emerge through invasion and the imposition of new ways, even as its power is continually contested.[41] The origin or source of legal positivism thus lies in a perpetual imposition of authoritative will, in an eternal retrospective reenactment of human conquest and command.

The inaccessibility of a singular determinate moment of either "acknowledgment of authority" or of complete conquest in both the future of Tanganyika and in the past of the English common law suggests an

---

[40] See also Joseph Raz, *Practical Reason and Norms* (Princeton: Princeton University Press, 1975, 1990), 49–58. Raz argues in a quite different context that rules are not practices.

[41] Constable, *Law of the Other*, chap. 4, 67–95; Peter Fitzpatrick, *The Mythology of Modern Law* (New York: Routledge, 1992).

eternal deferral of the coming-into-existence of any actual positivist legal system. Either a positivist system of law already exists (and is replaced by or transformed into another) or it is interminably incomplete. Like the oscillation of the origin in Foucault's famous chapter on "man and his doubles" in *The Order of Things*,[42] the emergence of the positivist legal system is not locatable at nor attributable to a determinate moment in chronological time. The acknowledgment of its authority has always already been grounded in the conquering will or else it is not yet. Legal positivism thus cannot acknowledge the prior or continuing existence as law of non-legal-positivist forms of legal authority, without undermining its own claims that law is always positive law.

The genesis of the legal positivist system is admittedly not the focus of Hart's conception of law, nor is it usually of concern for most sociolegal scholars, intent on studying the empirically contingent law (and sometimes justice) that exists. Incompleteness and indeterminacy beset histories of legal positivist systems (and other quests for origins), though. Such histories raise questions about the exhaustiveness of legal positivism as a description of actual law over time. They suggest that faith in the adequacy of socially descriptive accounts of legal systems sustains a belief in the social and empirically contingent character of law and justice. Such faith, manifest in many sociolegal studies, reinforces a sense of the completeness of positive law without recognizing problematic issues of its temporality and coverage. At best, such issues are recognized, as by Moore, as a tension between "empowerment" and "control."

In sociolegal studies (as shall be discussed further in chapter 2), law is foremost a socially powerful system. Power and resistance to law are for sociolegal scholars normal; studies of the everyday and of legal consciousness diffuse the locations of what is still nevertheless human or social power. Even when they do not consider law to be the declarations by state officials of rules of behavior that most people generally obey, whatever their motives most of the time, sociolegal scholars presume that the social practices that constitute the force or power of law are descriptively articulable.

Hart had argued that the first condition for the existence of a modern legal system (as opposed to the first step in its emergence) is that rules of behavior that are valid according to the system's ultimate criteria of validity be generally obeyed.

> [T]he first condition is the only one which private citizens *need* satisfy: they may obey each "for his part only" and from any motive whatever; though in a

---

[42] Michel Foucault, *The Order of Things: An Archaeology of the Human Sciences* (New York: Vintage, 1994).

healthy society they will in fact often accept these rules as common standards of behaviour and acknowledge an obligation to obey them, or even trace this obligation to a more general obligation to respect the constitution. (113)

In discussing obedience, the sociologist of legal consciousness or everyday life displaces this systematicity of Hart's healthy union of rules to the norms and narratives of so-called legal consciousness. Sociological analysis brings to light the obedience or conformity or compliance—or its obverse—that is produced in forums of consciousness or unconsciousness. The turn from the command of the sovereign of Austinian legal positivism to "control by rules" to account for obligation does not amount for Hart to a "necessary connection between law and morality." Neither does legal consciousness amount to such a connection for sociologists.

In other words, for Hart, the rules of a positivist legal system are not necessarily moral or just (202). They are grounded in what he calls "social pressure" (84), a pressure that is ultimately coercive. For the sociolegal scholar, too, behavior of citizens—even when considered an obligation—is also often a matter of social pressure.

Tom R. Tyler's *Why People Obey the Law* provides a case in point. Tyler analyses interviewees' responses to telephone questionnaires to discover citizens' attitudes toward the authority of law.[43] He investigates the influence on compliance "of what people regard as just and moral as opposed to their self-interest" (3). Showing that attitudes toward law fit what Hart would call a "healthy society," Tyler contrasts what he calls normative models of compliance to models that focus on outcomes or instrumental ends. For Tyler, "Normative commitment through personal morality means obeying a law because one feels the law is just; normative commitment through legitimacy means obeying a law because one feels that the authority enforcing the law has the right to dictate behavior" (4). Tyler's conjunction of "normative" and "feeling" here takes the social psyche to be the forum that produces systems of obligation. Tyler concludes that people generally obey law because of its legitimacy or because of their perceptions of the procedural justice or fairness of the legal system. For Tyler, legitimacy is constituted by people's acknowledgment of what Hart would call the authoritativeness of the mark, or of what Tyler calls "the right to dictate behavior" of "the authority enforcing the law."

Even as Tyler affirms that people acknowledge the authoritativeness of law, the "experiences, attitudes, and behavior" that contribute to such affirmation or acknowledgment are, according to Tyler, grounded in a "process of socialization" (168). Tyler and most sociolegal scholars of discourse consider conformity to rules, including rules that establish au-

---

[43] Tom R. Tyler, *Why People Obey the Law* (New Haven: Yale University Press, 1990).

thority, to be the effect of social power. Social power is admittedly not that of classical threatening commanders nor even that of duly constituted officials. It takes the form of socialization or of an often amorphous social production of meaning. For Tyler, socialization involves communication and conformity. Socialization is the way that "a society or organization communicates values within a group concerning the meaning of 'fair' procedures and 'fair' outcomes" (176).

Tyler's grounding of authority in socialization very much resembles the way that Hart grounds the validity or authoritativeness of a legal system in "social pressure."[44] Acknowledgment of authority stems from social power, for Tyler, as authority "dictates" behavior to those who obey. In grasping the authoritativeness of law as dictatorial social power that, through the communication or expression of values, tells members of society what to do, Tyler's work shows the importance of both language and power to contemporary sociolegal conceptions of law (discussed further in chapter 2).

Although Tyler attributes citizens' compliance to socialization, he claims that citizens themselves comply with law as a matter of procedural justice or fairness, much as Moore's British administrators name their *own* conformity to British rules and the rule of law "justice"—not socialization. In transforming justice into a matter of socialization and conformity, Tyler's study affirms the empirically contingent character of connections between positive law and justice or morality.

Even as positive law extends to characterize ostensibly all systems of law, sociolegal studies circumscribe the domain of law. Some set aside justice; some fail to mention it at all; others treat it as does Tyler as the communication of values that are articulable in sociological terms. The latter thereby seem to imply that the justice of the law they study is no other than social power; the others that sociology has nothing to say on the matter, or that, sociologically speaking, "justice" is nonexistent. These claims may in fact all be correct. But their correctness is limited to the frame in which they are asserted: that of sociology. Sociology takes as object only that which is pregiven as social, while extending the social to all. It commits itself to human articulations and determinations of what exists. The chapters that follow challenge the correspondence of sociologically correct knowledge to truth. The claims of sociology are thus the basis on which the chapters that follow suggest that thinking more fruitfully about law and justice requires something other than the sociological and legal positivist frames and limits established through sociolegal studies' assertions.

---

[44] See also Stanley Fish, "Force," in *Doing What Comes Naturally* (Durham, NC: Duke University Press, 1989), 517.

The pervasiveness of sociolegal positivism is a symptom of current conditions, in which "social power" or the power of society threatens to become the sole or unlimited frame of reference for knowing the law—or determining what to do. These conditions constitute a peculiar moment in a history of jurisprudence that has long associated law with matters of justice but threatens to do so no more. This moment marks the convergence of legal positivism and sociological study in a sociolegal positivism that is as important as any natural law/positive law distinction for understanding modern law.

The Problem of Nietzsche

Contemporary sociolegal positivism appears toward the end of the Western tradition that uses reason and truth to attend to questions of law and justice. In its many guises—as modern law, as sociological study, as philosophical legal positivism—it turns a skeptical eye toward the metaphysical truths that have long held sway in the law. Affirming the social and empirical character of law (and of justice, when it takes there to be such a thing), sociolegal positivism grounds itself in a "real world" that has no use for such former transcendental ideals as those of the natural law tradition; it turns, in the very name of truth, away from what it takes as false idols constructed of religion, morality, formal rules.

Sociolegal positivism seldom reflects on itself as standard-bearer of truth; it takes its own truths and its own world, in all sincerity, as the norm for judgment. Friedrich Nietzsche provides a perspective on judgments of truth by sociology. He shows how today's empirical "real" world is a version of the very metaphysics against which sociolegal positivism would turn. (Metaphysics can be thought as the philosophy that addresses the question of what is—of what determines experience or the things that are. Roughly speaking, our experience of the world formerly was founded on truths that were conceived as beyond us. Today, the issue of our experience of the world comes to be posed more locally: is experience determined by human subjectivity or by what objectively exists?) With Martin Heidegger, Nietzsche allows us to see how the issue of the "justice" of the sociologically real world raises profound questions, related to metaphysics, about who or what we are becoming.[45]

[45] Joseph William Singer, "The Player and the Cards: Nihilism and Legal Theory," *Yale Law Journal* 94 (1984): 1; Peter Goodrich, *Reading the Law: A Critical Introduction to Legal Method and Technologies* (Oxford: Blackwell, 1986). Nietzsche's popularity among legal circles has grown recently. See, for instance, "Nietzsche and Legal Theory, Symposium at Cardozo School of Law, New York, Oct. 14–15, 2001," *Cardozo Law Review* 24:2 (2003).

Nietzsche himself recognizes the downfall of a doomed, yet formerly necessary, quest to once and for all establish truth. He celebrates truth's turning back on itself and its creations. For Nietzsche, the end of the tradition of metaphysical truth is the overcoming of the nihilism of a will to truth. Today, one asks to what degree the challenges to metaphysical justice of sociolegal positivism portend a similarly joyous overcoming of nihilism. The answer is not so clear. Nietzsche contrasts the joy of his own free spirits to the "weariness of soul" of false free spirits, whom he describes as preferring a certain nothing to an uncertain something. Could contemporary legal thought correspond to the nihilism of the naysayer— to Nietzsche's false free spirits, that is?

Reading Nietzsche's pithy "History of an Error" or history of metaphysics in *Twilight of the Idols* helps reveal the import of these questions. Nietzsche's "How the 'True World' Became a Fable" traces transformations in metaphysics (*meta-phusis*, after or beyond matter or nature) or the philosophy of what things are.[46] The six moments in Nietzsche's history show how the relations of truth to what appears in the world have changed (see appendix 1). The "true world" of the Greek polis (or of the Platonic idea) is no longer the "true world" of the Christian heaven nor the "true world" of Kantian things-in-themselves nor the "true world" of the empiricists. And yet the truths of these worlds, posited by reason as beyond *this* world, have always judged this—ephemeral, temporal, phenomenal, apparent—world the same way: negatively, as lacking.

Just as reason has constructed metaphysical truths which have served as standards or measures that point to the inadequacies of this world, Nietzsche writes, so too the laws of philosophers, moralists, and priests have judged human beings and their actions in this world to be lacking. They have sought to improve them. From the truths of the Christian divine eternal order to those of the Kantian noumenal world to those of the positivist empirical world, he writes, have issued laws and practices of morality that, in the name of their respective truths, have turned against previous moralities only to cultivate, for the most part, unhealthy human life that does not and cannot flourish.

[46] Friedrich Nietzsche, *Twilight of the Idols*, trans. R. J. Hollingdale (London: Penguin, 1968). Hollingdale translates "Wie die 'wahre welt' endlich zur Fabel wurde" as "How the 'Real World' Became a Myth." "True" is a more fitting translation, as the true world of metaphysics, *meta-phusis* or what "lies beyond matter and nature," becomes today's empirical "real" world. In what follows, I have generally used Hollingdale's translation (and indicated his page numbers within my text), but substituted *true* for *real* in quotations from pages 40 and 41. (I thank Philippe Nonet for emphasizing the significance of this.) Hollingdale does note the connection. For a related reading of these two pages, see Marianne Constable, "Genealogy and Jurisprudence: Nietzsche, Nihilism, and the Social Scientification of Law," *Law and Social Inquiry* 19:3 (1994): 551, and "Rejoinder: Thinking Nonsociologically about Sociological Law," *Law and Social Inquiry* 19:3 (1994): 625.

Many place Socrates at the origin of Western reason and the quest for metaphysical truth and justice. Nietzsche shows how Plato sought to produce virtue, by having the Athenians imitate his teacher Socrates' mastery of his own unruly instincts. In Plato, Nietzsche suggests, truth and action become less events of becoming than matters of correct sight. In Heidegger's terms, truth or *aletheia*, as the unconcealment of beings that man experiences in their appearing to him, withdraws with Plato, in favor of truth as examining and securing—as *eidos* or *idea*—the form of a being. As *eidos*, truth is no longer an event of appearance, but becomes with Plato knowledge of what is unchanging or always present in a being, that without which a being would not be.

So begins the Western quest for supersensible or metaphysical (beyond nature) knowledge that Nietzsche calls the will to truth. This quest culminates with Nietzsche in a new articulation of the question of what determines experience. The will to truth erects successive metaphysical worlds from out of criticisms that destroy, in the name of truth, each preceding world and its respective truth. Nietzsche recognizes that these truths, in some sense, have been needed by man. They have been last-ditch efforts on the part of the will to power of life to stymie the decay and decline characterizing human life at any given moment. Nietzsche now calls on readers to recognize that these truths and their moralities are successful untruths. They can no longer possibly serve strong will to power or flourishing life. Nietzsche thus transforms metaphysics into the determination of will to power. Read as a history of jurisprudence, the history of metaphysics leads into sociolegal positivism.

Nietzsche begins his history:

> 1. The true world, attainable to the wise, the pious, the virtuous man—he dwells in it, *he is it.*
> (Oldest form of the idea, relatively sensible, simple, convincing. Transcription of the proposition "I, Plato, *am* the truth.") (40)

Like Platonic truth and its "true world," the just law of the polis is "relatively sensible." It is known through reason, not simply as an exercise of cognition but as the practice or know-how of the virtuous and wise citizen, Socrates. Perceiving that Socrates suffered evil at the hands of those who knew no better, Plato distinguishes the Athenians from their law. Surrounded by less virtuous Athenians, the Socrates of Plato's early dialogues embodies law and attains justice in his way of life and, ironically, of death (*Apology, Euthyphro*).[47] Plato's failure to distinguish clearly be-

---

[47] Plato, *The Collected Dialogues of Plato*, ed. Edith Hamilton and Huntington Cairns (Princeton: Princeton University Press, 1963).

tween what is (or becomes) and what is true (or is conceived) in the *eidos* or the form suggests to Nietzsche that "I, Plato, *am* the truth." Socrates' impersonation or at least ventriloquization of the laws (in *Crito*) suggests that "I, Socrates, *am*—live and die—the law."

Plato's dialogues, according to Nietzsche, transform just law from the skillful practice—whatever else it is also—of a Socrates who denies he knows into a recipe for virtue. In the middle dialogues, the idea of justice becomes the lawlike truth of a Socratic character *(Republic, Statesman)*. In the late dialogues, a counterfactual exiled Socratic figure—the Athenian Stranger—monologically presents a code of law *(Laws)*.

Plato thus becomes for Nietzsche the bridge to Christianity. Christianity too strives to make sense of the problem of Socrates that Plato bequeaths: the difference between the flawed human law of the Athenians, under which Plato's teacher Socrates suffers in being sentenced to death, and the virtuous law to which Plato would have Socrates subscribe. As in Plato's *Phaedo*, the Christians of Nietzsche's second moment find a solution to the problem of undeserved suffering in this world in eternal life, in the metaphysical hope that constitutes the justice of a divine and perfect order. Although justice is temporally unattainable, it is promised in the Christian heaven of the world beyond.

> 2. The true world, unattainable for the moment, but promised to the wise, the pious, the virtuous man ("to the sinner who repents").
>
> (Progress of the idea: it grows more refined, more enticing, more incomprehensible—*it becomes a woman*, it becomes Christian . . .) (40)

God gives human beings free choice of the will. Human beings owe God a debt of gratitude for this gift. They fulfill their obligation (paradoxically, some argue) by accepting full responsibility for the right or wrong exercise of their God-given wills. God promises divine justice to "the sinner who repents"—to the sinner who accepts that, given the perfection of God's order, suffering evil in this world is just punishment; reward will come in the next (Augustine).[48] *Natural law* names the participation through reason of rational creatures in the eternal order—and still has contemporary adherents.[49]

Kant's categorical imperative or *moral law* emerges in Nietzsche's third moment, when the skeptic Kant (as Nietzsche reads him)[50] forgoes proof

---

[48] Augustine, *On Free Choice*, book 1 and book 3, 100.

[49] Thomas Aquinas, *Treatise on Law: Summa Theologica*, Questions 90–97, in *Political Ideas*.

[50] Nietzsche takes Kant to be a skeptic as to God (see for instance the third moment, *Twilight of the Idols*, 40, cited in my text below). Kant, however, argues only that proofs as to the existence of God are fallacious; he does not express skepticism about God. See for instance, Immanuel Kant, "The Ideal of Pure Reason," in *Critique of Pure Reason* (New

as to the existence of God, but nevertheless seeks to ground the good, which he presumes a person of ordinary intelligence must know, in another version of human will.[51] In Nietzsche's words,

> 3. The true world, unattainable, undemonstrable, cannot be promised, but even when merely thought of a consolation, a duty, an imperative.
> (Fundamentally the same old sun, but shining through mist and skepticism; the idea grown sublime, pale, northerly, Konigsbergian.) (40)

If the justice of the Christian heaven of the second moment is unattainable, according to Kant, the categorical imperative and the kingdom of ends are nevertheless reasoning man's gift to himself. The very thought or "Idea" of freedom and of the intelligible world, a presupposition that cannot be demonstrated, makes one free. Autonomous persons as ends in themselves give themselves the law as the "ought" that binds them when they *think* of themselves as free or as belonging to both an intelligible world of ends in themselves and to a sensible phenomenal world of appearances and experience.[52]

With the realization that a metaphysical moral law cannot be known empirically, utilitarianism, in Nietzsche's fourth moment, brings justice and the true world down to earth.

> 4. The true world—unattainable? Unattained at any rate. And if unattained also *unknown*. Consequently also no consolation, no redemption, no duty: how could we have a duty towards something unknown? (40)

So reasons the empiricist in what Nietzsche calls the "grey morning" of the "first yawnings of reason. Cockcrow of positivism" (40). The principle of utility provides the lawful measure of behavior for human beings, who can rely on their experience of bodily sensations of pleasure and pain to calculate, as rational agents, how to behave. The Benthamite legislator extrapolates from experience to create the human *positive law* that is to improve society and its members in the future.[53] At its most extreme, the

---

York: St. Martin's Press, 1965), 485–572. ("Its [the Supreme Being's] objective reality cannot indeed be proved, but also cannot be disproved, by merely speculative reason" [531].) See also Meyer, "Between Reason and Power," 732 (citing Kant, *Critique of Pure Reason*, 29 [Norman Kemp Smith trans., 1929]): "I have therefore found it necessary to deny *knowledge*, in order to make room for *faith*."

[51] Immanuel Kant, *Groundwork of the Metaphysics of Morals*, trans. H. J. Paton (New York: Harper and Row, 1964), preface, 59.

[52] Neither a being with perfect reason (god) nor a being without reason (beast) would have need or use of obligation, for different reasons. See Kant, *Groundwork*, idea of freedom (115), makes us free, (121), categorical imperative (chaps. 1 and 2), kingdom of ends (100), persons (96); thought of two worlds (119).

[53] Jeremy Bentham, *Introduction to the Principles of Morals and Legislation* (Oxford: Oxford University Press, 1948); J. S. Mill, *Utilitarianism* (New York: Meridian, 1962); Aus-

command of an earthly sovereign backed by threats compels subjects to obey. Strategic rationality replaces reason; law becomes (in Kantian terms) not a categorical but a hypothetical imperative.[54]

Many contemporary legal scholars share the legal realist faith of Nietzsche's fourth moment, the faith that sociological inquiry or empirical knowledge of institutions and practices of society can improve law and that law can improve society.[55] The improvement of society or the clarification of law motivates philosophers such as Bentham and Hart. Like the early law-and-society movement, these philosophers take laws to be phenomena—and law to be a phenomenon—of a real empirical world of experience. They are motivated by a faith that clearer knowledge can conceivably be used to produce a better future: less suffering or greater understanding perhaps, in a more educated, more civilized, society.

The recognition that these hopes of improvement themselves rest on inherited ideals of bygone cultures marks the unfolding of the fourth moment into the fifth, which questions the pragmatism of the very terms that have been used so far. Older ideals of justice, like the concept of the "true world" (placed in quotation marks in Nietzsche's fifth moment), seem "no longer of any use" (40).

> 5. The "true world"—an idea no longer of any use, not even a duty any longer—an idea grown useless, superfluous, *consequently* a refuted idea: let us abolish it. (40)

In the context of a proliferation of social demands and identities, the singular appeal of justice breaks down. Once absolute, ideal and universal, meta-

---

tin, *Province of Jurisprudence Determined*. Mill writes that judgment is by those who are qualified by knowledge of both "higher" and "lower" pleasures, not by those without "nobler feelings," *Utilitarianism*, 261. See also Bentham, chap. 2.

[54] "Hypothetical imperatives declare a possible action to be practically necessary as a means to the attainment of something else that one wills (or that one may will)" (Kant, *Groundwork*, 82). This has a contemporary resonance, in that it reveals something that Brian Bix, in his critique of Anthony Sebok on the legal process school, misses. Bix argues that Sebok confuses the issue of the separability thesis when Sebok maintains that "Hart and Sack's claim that law was instrumental is essentially the same as the separability thesis." But if the separability thesis holds "that questions regarding the existence of law are to be distinguished from questions as to its merit [or morality]," as Bix puts it, then Sebok's reference to the legal process school's understanding of law as instrumental can be read as a claim that law is strategically rational (a hypothetical imperative) and *not* moral. See Anthony Sebok, *Legal Positivism in American Jurisprudence* (Cambridge: Cambridge University Press, 1998); and Brian Bix, "Positively Positivism: Reviewing Legal Positivism in American Jurisprudence," *Virginia Law Review* 85 (1999): 909.

[55] Spokespersons to this effect in the law-and-society movement, for instance, include Friedman, "Law and Society Movement"; and Frank Munger, "Inquiry and Activism in Law and Society," *Law and Society Review* 35:1 (2001): 7.

physical "justice" threatens to become superfluous, subsumed under any number of more relevant socially constructed values. The ability of a single principle or even of the extension of "rational prudence to the system of desires constructed by the impartial spectator" to judge the good of society gives way to the procedural justice-as-fairness of Rawls's abstracted persons-in-the-original-position, whose principles regulate "the basic structure of society." The considered convictions of Rawls's own readers both inform construction of a fair initial position and allow readers to vet the principles of fairness chosen by the parties in the original position. These principles "specify the kinds of social cooperation that can be entered into and the forms of government that can be established."[56]

The positive human law of the fifth moment now becomes public or *social policy*. It grounds itself in social knowledge, in cost-benefit analyses of facts and values, and in socially constructed (and constructing) procedural systems and institutions of principles, rules, and norms.

Contemporary thought about law resonates with the instability of Nietzsche's fifth moment, however. The fifth moment inherits the challenge to metaphysical ideals that characterized the empiricist fourth moment. But its skepticism turns also against the very grounds of the challenge to metaphysics insofar as these grounds lay in a science or knowledge that took the objects and value of knowledge as pregiven.

Legal critics today challenge the former ideals of a "science" of "justice" from all sides. Despite their differences, philosophers, social theorists, and legal commentators and activists alike participate in the task. They fixate on the formalism of norms. "Realistic" work now asserts that Hart's own concept of law was not "sociological" enough. It claims to strip Hart's conception of any remaining "normative" quality and to "demonstrate that a rigorous legal positivism would actually be grounded in the [pragmatic] social theory of law."[57] Realistic sociolegal theory claims to be a "non-political source of knowledge about the nature, function, and effects of legal phenomena. As such it will be the only predominantly descriptive, *non-normative* alternative available among the current schools in legal theory."[58]

---

[56] Rawls, *A Theory of Justice*, 29, 11. Neat categorizations of contemporary work into Nietzsche's moments are difficult. As Unger, *Critical Legal Studies Movement*, 99–102, points out, despite the obvious differences between utilitarianism and Rawls's "subtle contractarianism," both share a notion of "a choosing self whose concerns can be defined in abstraction from the concrete social worlds to which it belongs." To reach concrete results, both methods "define the wants or intuitions that constitute the primary data of the[ir] method restrictively," and both "identify the[ir] ideal method . . . with the existing institutional arrangements of democracy and the market."

[57] Tamanaha, *Realistic Socio-Legal Theory*, 129–52. Compare Brian Bix, "Conceptual Jurisprudence and Socio-Legal Studies," *Rutgers Law Journal* 32 (2000): 227.

[58] Tamanaha, *Realistic Socio-Legal Theory*, 8.

Philosophical work too severs the remaining connections between formal law and justice. As long as the possibility of a society of law without justice exists, Jules Coleman writes, legal positivism correctly denies, conceptually speaking, that there is a necessary connection between law and justice.[59] Frederick Schauer (see chapter 5) sets aside debates about both the normative desirability and the conceptual validity of legal positivism. He limits his descriptive account of law to a presumptive positivism in which law is one social system of rules among others.[60]

The turn against metaphysics is not limited to philosophical legal positivism and positivist sociology. Joined by critical legal scholars, feminist jurisprudes, and critical race and postcolonial theorists, the soft social sciences also imply that what was formerly known as "justice" is a discredited carryover from an oppressive past. The turn to the study of everyday life and legal consciousness challenges the usefulness of universals to diverse or flourishing life today.[61]

What now? The free spirits of Nietzsche's fifth moment *call for* the abolition of justice and the true world; in the sixth moment, justice and the true world *have been* abolished. For Nietzsche and his free spirits, this is cause for celebration, the end of the error of reason. With Zarathustra, Nietzsche hails a new world of becoming, in which metaphysical truth no longer holds sway.

> 6. We have abolished the true world: what world is left? The apparent world perhaps. . . . But no! *with the true world we have also abolished the apparent world!* (41)

The end of the nihilistic (in the sense of its negative judgment as to the world) metaphysical tradition, for Nietzsche, is an overcoming of nihilism. Insofar as reason invented the true world and produced distinctions between truth and appearance, the apparent world is abolished with the true world. Distinctions between truth and appearance, ideal and actual, ought and is, collapse. A revaluation of values accompanies the entrance of Zarathustra, who serves as the bridge to a new nonhuman species that has no human need for either the solace or judgments of metaphysics. *Amor fati*, or love of fate, for Nietzsche, means that one is neither ac-

---

[59] Jules Coleman, "Negative and Positive Positivism," in *Markets, Morals and the Law* (Cambridge: Cambridge University Press, 1988).

[60] Schauer, *Playing by the Rules.*

[61] In addition to work cited elsewhere in this chapter and in chapter 2, see for instance, Pheng Cheah, "The Law of/as Rape: Poststructuralism and the Framing of the Legal Text," in *Legal Education and Legal Knowledge*, ed. Ian Duncanson (Bundoora, Victoria, Australia: La Trobe University Press, 1991–92), 117–29 (situating the legal discourse of rape within the social text of patriarchy); Vicki Schultz, "The Sanitized Workplace," *Yale Law Journal* 112 (2003): 2061.

countable for oneself nor determined from outside of oneself. One is part of a whole, a piece of fate.[62]

But Zarathustra's moment does not happen until the modern world has perished. At the beginning of the twenty-first century, the question of the future of the just law—and of the modern world—remains. It confronts us as the chasm between the fifth and sixth moments, in which we have already called for the abolition of metaphysical justice but a Zarathustrian revaluation has yet to come. It is the issue of what happens at the "end" of our tradition of jurisprudence.

Can calls for the abolition of metaphysical justice from law provide a bridge to a glorious new law and society in which former unjust ideals of "justice" give way? New values proliferate. Some do so in the name of reason, suggesting returns to earlier moments. Some valorize unreason; others emerge from unidentifiable places.[63] A few give us pause to think. Might the deviationist doctrines and solidarity rights of Roberto Unger's perpetually transformative "superliberalism," for instance, fulfill the promise of modern society to be "made and not given"? Could social imagination remove the obstacles to justice by identifying justice with society's own creative powers?[64] Can empire, the "new global form of sovereignty" identified by Hardt and Negri that "creates the very world it inhabits," be successfully resisted by the "creative forces" that also sustain it?[65] Can society constitute itself by determining its own law? Would unimpeded and infinite social self-constitution represent an overcoming of the nihilistic judgments of a former metaphysics?

And if so, would such ostensible overcoming of metaphysics—the erasure of the judgmental divide between truth and appearance, the disappearance of the split between objective truth and subjective experience— be cause for celebration? Would unceasing recognition of the successful untruth of truth and of the abysmal ground of justice become our heaviest burden or our greatest liberation? Nietzsche himself asks this.

Heidegger goes further. The very posing of the nihilism of metaphysics as a problem we must solve, he writes, points not to its overcoming, but to the threat of its completion. The arrogance of Nietzschean will to power to determine experience is matched only by that of the society

[62] Nietzsche, *Twilight of the Idols*, "The Four Great Errors," sec. 8.

[63] See Mariana Valverde, *Law's Dream of a Common Knowledge* (Princeton: Princeton University Press, 2003), arguing that the popular and hybrid knowledges on which law draws are not properly grasped as either science or counterscience.

[64] Unger, *Critical Legal Studies Movement*, chap. 2.

[65] Michael Hardt and Tony Negri, *Empire* (Cambridge: Harvard University Press, 2001), xv.

of sociological positivism, which arrogates to itself the voice of law and justice.[66]

For Heidegger, truth is not a variation on a theme of higher worlds that judge this one. Metaphysics is not a choice between human or world as controlling subject. Rather, truth is an opening or clearing in which human and world—only today conceived strictly on the order of subject and object—give rise to one another. Reason has indeed tried and failed to secure a true world of being, Heidegger claims. But the will to power in the name of which Nietzsche judges life and truth, according to Heidegger, is even more extreme. Will to power, he argues, forgets the impossibility of mastering being and ultimately recognizes no limit to its own powers to determine (and to having determined) the world. With Nietzsche, according to Heidegger, the nihilistic quest to secure truth again manifests itself, this time in the absolute mastery asserted in the will to power's inability to let the problem of nihilism be.[67]

Could the new sociological law be another manifestation—like the just law of earlier moments—of continuing human attachments to values and judgments antithetical not only to flourishing life but to being? Could social policy become a social mastery grown forgetful of all value that is not of society's own making? Could the law of sociolegal positivism be absolute will to power, a refusal to accept any bounds on its power that come from outside of itself?

To wonder about law this way is to wonder about the limits and possibilities of sociolegal positivism and of the skepticism about justice that characterizes the current age. Justice no longer instantiates itself in the virtuous way of life of a Socrates, nor in the natural law of Christianity, nor even in the moral law of Kant, nor simply in the utility of social policy and the norms of society. It lies in silences of positive law.

The chapters that follow constitute neither apologia nor condemnation of existing positive law and current scholarship. They suggest that modern law is silent about justice in a new way. They seek to talk about contemporary law and justice in ways other than those of social and sociological evaluation. They aim neither to justify nor to dismiss particular laws or legal systems, but to think of law on the (ungrounded) ground of what it (already) is. To the extent that readers feel that the chapters more directly on law (3, 4, 7) minimize issues of power, readers are reminded that

[66] For arrogation of voice in another (yet related) context, see Stanley Cavell, *A Pitch of Philosophy: Autobiographical Exercises* (Cambridge: Harvard University Press, 1994).

[67] Martin Heidegger, *Nietzsche*, vol. 3, *Will to Power*, trans. Joan Stambaugh et al. (New York: Harper and Row, 1987).

part of the point of the other chapters (2, 5, 6) is to show how completely embedded in power is current thinking about law. To the extent that readers feel that the chapters on sociolegal and philosophical texts are overly pessimistic, they are reminded that the point has been precisely to speak of what that work—as sophisticated articulations of our modern ways of understanding law—overlooks or is strangely (if not always literally) silent about: justice. Finding what has been overlooked may offer new—paradoxically preexisting—possibilities for thought. The justice that many contemporary legal texts overlook may offer possibilities not only of thought, but also of law.

Chapter 2 ⸺

The Naming of Law:
Sociolegal Studies and Political Voice

> The Naming of Cats is a difficult matter,
> It isn't just one of your holiday games;
> You may think at first I'm as mad as a hatter
> When I tell you, a cat must have THREE DIFFERENT NAMES.
> —T. S. Eliot, "The Naming of Cats," *Old Possum's Book of Practical Cats*

THE PROLOGUE TO THIS BOOK suggested that law may be silent about justice. Chapter 1 explained the implications of the claim: the silence of modern law raises the question of nihilism. Chapter 1 went further than the prologue and suggested that sociology too may be silent about justice in a particular way. The present chapter takes a step back from chapter 1 to address a possible response to the prologue. If the silence of law is taken to mean that law does not talk much about justice, then one response is that although law doesn't talk much about justice, it nevertheless does justice. This chapter thus returns to sociology, because sociology today tells us what law does. The chapter reconsiders and refines the preceding chapter's suggestion that sociology is silent about justice today by showing *how* sociology is silent about justice.

The first section, "Everyday Names: Social Power and Discourse," shows how social power functions as an "everyday name" that sociolegal studies almost unanimously attribute to language and law. While the power of language is neither uniform nor conceptually consistent in sociolegal studies, recognition of discursive power—whether as control or as empowerment—is explicit. Sociolegal studies' focus on the social power of discourse fails to address what is particular to words or to speech, however: their saying. And sociolegal studies' concern for the social power of language contrasts noticeably with the studies' pronouncements—or rather lack of pronouncements—about justice, whether the justice of law or of language. The ostensible inattention to justice in sociolegal studies of language and discourse seems to underscore an unbridgeable distance between law, of which the studies do speak and whose words and power they analyze, and justice, for which and of which no word appears.

At the same time however, the invocation of "voice" in some sociolegal studies and elsewhere to counter the social power that is perceived as domination suggests a "more dignified" approach to law and language that recognizes the way that words appeal to an oft-unnamed justice. Even as appeals to voice from across the political spectrum are conceived in terms of empowerment or counter-power and fail to mention justice explicitly, the second section, "More Dignified Names," argues, they may implicitly seek justice. If the justice to which voice calls in some senses lies in silence, the final section, "One Name Left Over," continues, then the ineffable silences required for the hearing of voices and words may offer ways of thinking about relations between law and justice.

Everyday Names: Social Power and Discourse

> First of all, there's the name that the family use
>   daily,
> Such as Peter, Augustus, Alonzo or James,
> Such as Victor or Jonathan, George or Bill Bailey—
> All of them sensible everyday names.
> There are fancier names if you think they sound
>   sweeter,
> Some for the gentlemen, some for the dames:
> Such as Plato, Admetus, Electra, Demeter—
> But all of them sensible everyday names.

There are many versions of sociology, especially in the broad sense in which it is used in this work. For decades, sociolegal scholars have studied law in action, often counterposing it to what they have called "law on the books." In its earlier incarnations, sociology of law made a strong distinction between language and action. Taking their cues from legal realism, sociolegal studies of law criticized what they perceived as narrow approaches to law that restricted it to doctrine or to ostensibly problem-solving rules. Lawrence Friedman, for instance, contrasts law-and-society scholarship to an understanding of law as "norms, or language or ideology, or rhetoric or 'consciousness,' or discourse—anything but behavior." He argues for values of "clarity, honesty and rigor," which he claims the social scientific study of institutions and behavior offers to both speculative law school law and lawyers' instrumentally rational policymaking.[1]

---

[1] Friedman, "Law and Society Movement," 775.

During the past two or three decades, however, sociolegal scholars, like scholars in other fields, have come to recognize that the uniqueness of law as phenomenon cannot be captured without some acknowledgment of law's discursive character. They have approached law accordingly, seeking to incorporate, as subject matter in their largely empirical analyses of society and power, the language of law.

Thus there have emerged various approaches to legal language, both the language of official law and the nonofficial language of law. On the whole these studies treat language in one way or another as social power. Some view language as more-or-less in the control of a speaker; others view language as itself a cause of effects; still others combine the two approaches in understanding language as an instrument or tool. Many identify language with domination. In attributing causal power to speaker-actors' manipulations of tools of language, to aspects of language itself, or to the social contexts that shape linguistic possibilities and interactions, scholars suggest a dynamic between the social formation of language and the linguistic construction of social reality that points to a fundamental capacity of language, like law in their view, to oppress and resist.

In turning to language, then, sociolegal studies have fit language into a sociolegal frame. Such treatment is not a fault for which researchers are to blame. The very grammar of the English language, with its identification of complete sentences with subjects and predicates, reinforces ways of talking that frame things in terms of power.

Here again, Nietzsche leads the way. He shows how the grammar of subject and predicate, of nouns that verb, shares with Western metaphysics a division of the world into primary doers that derivatively deed. A grammatical world consists of fundamental objects with secondary attributes. Grammar grasps its subject—whether God, man, author, agent, or other noun—as that which "verbs" (i.e., acts as a verb) or as a controlling cause on the model of sovereign power. God creates; man acts; authors write; agents behave: all produce subsequent effects.[2] Nietzsche notes

> our bad habit of taking a mnemonic, an abbreviative formula, to be an entity, finally as a cause, e.g., to say of lightning "it flashes." Or the little word "I."

---

[2] "I fear we are not getting rid of God because we still believe in grammar," Nietzsche writes (*Twilight of the Idols*, 48). See also Martin Heidegger, "The Origin of the Work of Art," regarding the simple assertive sentence and the undecidability of a question in the form of what comes first, the sentence-structure or the thing-structure. I am relying here on an unpublished translation by Roger Berkowitz and Philippe Nonet, 2003, quoted with permission, referring to *Holzwege* (Frankfurt am Main: Vittorio Klosterman, 1950), 13–14.

To make a perspective in seeing [into] the cause of seeing: that was what happened in the invention of the "subject," the "I"![3]

The lightning *is* the flash flashing. My "perspective" is the seeing from which language separates the "I" who sees, making "I" into a subject who sees and in whose control seeing is placed. "I" become the cause of seeing.

In attributing agency alternately to human beings and to language, sociolegal studies accord power to humans and their speech.[4] Susan Berk-Seligson, for instance, shows how language may be a tool or instrument by which the "power" of a speaker affects an independently ascertainable world. The bilingual courtroom interpreter, claims Berk-Seligson, "plays a far more active verbal role than the [American legal] system could ever imagine, [which role] is very much tied to the [interpreter's] linguistic control of 'legitimate' [noninterpreter] participants in judicial proceedings, a degree of control that often is tantamount to linguistic coercion."[5]

Others attribute power less to a speaker or an interpreter than to some aspect of language itself. Control in studies of institutional rules and practices in legal or judicial proceedings often belongs to the studies' subject matter: the object of study seems to serve as the subject or agent with power, as its status as grammatical subject of a sentence indicates. Narrative, story, or style, for instance, may be granted a power that escapes the control of any determinate agent. "Narrative forms," for

[3] Friedrich Nietzsche, *Will to Power*, ed. Walter Kaufmann, trans. Walter Kaufmann and R. J. Hollingdale (New York: Random House, 1968), 294. I thank Scott Barnes for bringing this passage to my attention.

[4] Bibliographies and review essays on sociolegal studies of language and discourse make it unnecessary to rehearse more conventional classifications of approaches here. See Brenda Danet, "Language in the Legal Process," *Law and Society Review* 14 (1980): 445; Peter Goodrich, "Law and Language: An Historical and Critical Introduction," *Journal of Law and Society* 11 (1984): 173; Judith N. Levi, *Linguistics, Language and the Law: A Topical Bibliography* (Bloomington: Indiana University Linguistics Club, 1982), and *Language and Law: A Bibliographic Guide to Social Science Research in U.S.A.*, Teaching Resource Bulletin no. 4 (Chicago: American Bar Association Committee on College and University Legal Studies, 1994); see also Donald Brenneis, "Language and Disputing," *Annual Review of Anthropology* 17 (1988): 221; William O'Barr and John Conley, "Litigant Satisfaction versus Legal Adequacy in Small Claims Court Narratives," *Law and Society Review* 19 (1985): 61. Elizabeth Mertz's "Language, Law, and Social Meanings: Linguistic/Anthropological Contributions to the Study of Law," *Law and Society Review* 26 (1992): 413, in particular, provides an overview of anthropological and linguistic approaches to language and reviews work on legal language that focuses on its contextual or social character.

[5] Susan Berk-Seligson, "Bilingual Court Proceedings: The Role of the Court Interpreter," in *Language in the Legal Process*, ed. Judith N. Levi and Anne Graffan Walker (New York: Plenum Press, 1990), 156; see also Susan Berk-Seligson, *The Bilingual Courtroom: Court Interpreters in the Judicial Process* (Chicago: University of Chicago Press, 1990).

Douglas W. Maynard, "shape and narrow the range of what kinds of truths can be told."[6]

> Case characteristics and legal matters . . . are not irrelevant, but neither are they self-invoking or self-evident features of the negotiational process. . . . [T]hey are "talked into being" by way of narrative and narrative structure. As an aspect of the interaction order, this structure shapes the content of the case and clearly *effects* the course of negotiations. The exact ways in which it also *affects* outcomes cannot be ascertained until more is known.[7]

In a search for "some underlying judgment scheme" that makes it possible "for different people with different relationships to the law to communicate meaningfully about the issues in legal cases," Bennett and Feldman are led to the view that "stories *produce* a clear definition of an action and the conditions surrounding it."[8] The seminal work of O'Barr and his colleagues on "speech styles" in the courtroom focuses on the effects of the particular dimension of style considered "powerful" and "powerless" on the perceptions of legal actors.[9] Experimental and ethnographic research on the effects of style or of what some call "the power of language" extends such work beyond its original courtroom context to, for instance, adjudication and mediation[10] or the assessment of waivers of the right to remain silent in in-custody interrogations.[11]

Many studies of institutional legal discourse affirm a speaker-agent's control at the same time that they treat the speaker-agent as him/herself determinable: Berk-Seligson accords to the court interpreter both the status of "actor" and of "variable" or "intrusive element."[12] Maynard suggests that "narratives and their components may be devices for 'doing' the identities by which principal actors in the discourse are known" (87).

[6] M. Schudson, "The Politics of Narrative Form," *Daedalus* 111 (1982): 98, quoted in Douglas W. Maynard, "Narratives and Narrative Structure in Plea Bargaining," in Levi and Walker, *Language in Judicial Process*, 89.

[7] Maynard, "Narratives and Narrative Structure," 92, citing John Heritage, *Garfinkel and Ethnomethodology* (Cambridge: Polity Press, 1984).

[8] W. Lance Bennett and Martha Feldman, *Reconstructing Reality in the Courtroom* (New Brunswick, NJ: Rutgers University Press, 1981), 11, 10; emphasis added.

[9] B. E. Erickson, E. A. Lind, B. C. Johnson, and W. M. O'Barr, "Speech Style and Impression Formation in a Court Setting: The Effects of 'Powerful' and 'Powerless' Speech," *Journal of Experimental and Social Psychology* 14 (1978): 226; William O'Barr, *Linguistic Evidence: Language, Power, and Strategy in the Courtroom* (New York: Academic Press, 1982).

[10] Calvin Morrill and Peter C. Facciola, "The Power of Language in Adjudication and Mediation: Institutional Contexts as Predictors of Social Evaluation," *Law and Social Inquiry* 17 (1992): 191.

[11] Janet E. Ainsworth, "In a Different Register: The Pragmatics of Powerlessness in Police Interrogation," *Yale Law Journal* 103 (1993): 259.

[12] Berk-Seligson, "Bilingual Court Proceedings," 198.

Bennett and Feldman's "ordinary people in criminal trials" transform evidence into stories that themselves establish the contexts for "social action" or frameworks for judgment (3, 7). Some studies minimize the role of motives and intentions of particular individuals, while nevertheless attributing power to the actions of particular human group entities. Thus Edelman, Abraham, and Erlanger argue that in conveying ideas about wrongful discharge law, legal and personnel professionals and their journals help shape employment law and construct a particular legal environment.[13]

Other work moves even further away from human agent-centered accounts of language, however. Concerned with the authority and legitimation of law, some scholars turn to the interstitial space in which "law" interacts with "society." Their work explores, for instance, everyday language or the conversations between those belonging to the legal profession and those ostensibly outside of it for societal conceptions of law and justice. At issue in this work are the linkages that lie in what earlier law and society scholars took to be the "gap" between law in action and law on the books. Now the "gap" between the everyday and official law is filled with legitimating discourse, made manifest to the observant sociolegal scholar who renders such discourses coherent and investigates their effectiveness in producing meaning. Yngvesson thus attributes power to "exchanges" and "interaction."[14] She shows how

> exchanges between [the court] clerk and citizens produce legal and moral frameworks that justify a decision to handle a case in a particular way. The clerk plays a dominant role by controlling the language in which the issues are framed. . . . But the definition of events during a hearing is also shaped by these working, middle, and lower class people. (410)

Sarat and Felstiner show how divorce lawyers' explanations justify their authority and invite client dependence as well as dissatisfaction; they go on to view the interactions of lawyers and clients as a site for the generation and conveyance of "meaning," where "power" is present: "Power is seen in the effort to negotiate shared understandings, and in the evasions, resistances, and inventions that inevitably accompany such negotiations."[15] The "meaning-making power" of law is not unidirectional, how-

[13] Lauren B. Edelman, Steven E. Abraham, and Howard Erlanger, "Professional Construction of Law: The Inflated Threat of Wrongful Discharge," *Law and Society Review* 26 (1993): 785.
[14] Barbara Yngvesson, "Making Law at the Doorway: The Clerk, the Court, and the Construction of Community in a New England Town," *Law and Society Review* 22 (1988): 409.
[15] Austin Sarat and William L. F. Felstiner, "Law and Social Relations: Vocabularies of Motive in Lawyer/Client Interaction, *Law and Society Review* 22 (1988): 738.

ever; it is "interactive, dynamic, and strategic" and invites "adaptation and change in the practices of judges, lawyers and other officials."[16]

Social meaning itself is conceived as manipulable, as many law review articles attest. Lawrence Lessig writes of the construction of social meaning as a goal of law. Dan Kahan and Cass Sunstein write about how to manipulate social meaning. Paul H. Robinson argues that the best utilitarian theory of punishment is retributive because of its social meaning.[17]

The dynamic of the shaping of law through linguistic interactions that are themselves to some degree shaped by law and in all cases social is the focus of scholarship that adopts reflexive interpretive approaches. Acknowledging and self-consciously reflecting on their own language and complicity in worlds of particular sorts of language, some scholars dwell on the constitutive aspect of legal discourse and its capacity or potential to both oppress and resist. Taking to heart that one cannot get outside either language or society, their exploration of the interaction between discourse and social world leads scholars such as Harrington and Yngvesson, and lawyers such as White, to consider explicitly their own positions as actors and speakers.[18]

While such reflexivity at first seems promising as an opening to something other than social power, it too treats language as fundamentally a matter of social power. Critical race theorists, for instance, whose stated aim is admittedly less the analysis of discourse than the pursuit of "racial justice," have adopted a self-consciously "subjective" stance. Since Patricia Williams' *Alchemy of Race and Rights* appeared,[19] critical race theory has drawn on "personal histories," as well as "parables, chronicles, dreams, stories, poetry, fiction, and revisionist histories"[20] to reveal the

[16] Austin Sarat and William L. F. Felstiner, *Divorce Lawyers and Their Clients* (New York: Oxford University Press, 1995), 13, citations omitted.

[17] Lawrence Lessig, "The Regulation of Social Meaning," *University of Chicago Law Review* 62 (1995): 943; Dan M. Kahan, "Social Influence, Social Meaning, and Deterrence," *Virginia Law Review* 83 (1997): 349; Cass R. Sunstein, "Law, Economics, and Norms: On the Expressive Function of Law," *University of Pennsylvania Law Review* 144 (1996): 2021; Paul H. Robinson, "The Criminal-Civil Distinction and the Utility of Desert," *Boston University Law Review* 76 (1996): 201. Linda Meyer brought these articles to my attention.

[18] Christine B. Harrington and Barbara Yngvesson, "Interpretive Sociolegal Research," *Law and Social Inquiry* 15 (1990): 135; Lucie E. White, "Subordination, Rhetorical Survival Skills, and Sunday Shoes: Notes on the Hearing of Mrs. G," in *At the Boundaries of Law*, ed. Martha Albertson Fineman and Nancy Sweet Thomadsen (New York: Routledge, 1991).

[19] Patricia Williams, *The Alchemy of Race and Rights* (Cambridge: Harvard University Press, 1991).

[20] Mari J. Matsuda, Charles R. Lawrence III, Richard Delgado, and Kimberlé Crenshaw, *Words that Wound: Critical Race Theory, Assaultive Speech and the First Amendment* (Boulder: Westview Press, 1993), 5.

"dominant narratives" and "liberal premises" that shape the problem of race.[21] In critical race theory's challenge to "assaultive speech" as well as in its turn to "the words of law and politics to fight the words that wound and exclude," language becomes an issue of power.[22]

Legal language is also an issue of power for feminists such as Mary Joe Frug:

> Identifying the gendered character of the discourses [of law] can . . . be a feminist strategy for challenging the extensive and complicated network of social and cultural practices which legitimate the subordination of women. The assumption underlying this strategy is that language is a mechanism of power, that there is always more at stake in the relationship of gender and language than "just" a question of literary style—indeed that style itself can constitute a powerful socializing apparatus.[23]

Likewise, Catherine MacKinnon in *Only Words* criticizes pornography as a kind of hate speech that reduces women to sexual objects and subordinates them to men.[24]

All of the studies mentioned so far conceive of language and power together, as somehow social, even when they do not go so far as to construct what, for instance, Patricia Ewick and Susan S. Silbey call a "sociology of narrative."[25] Ewick and Silbey's sociology "recognizes that narratives are social acts performed within specific contexts that organize their meanings and consequences" (205). According to Ewick and Silbey, the stories that people tell about "trouble" in their lives reveal three types of stories told about law and experiences with, before, or against law. These stories

> do more than simply reflect or express existing structures and ideologies. Through their telling, people's stories help constitute whatever hegemony may in turn shape social lives and conduct. The taken-for-granted world of legality—in all its forms and experiences—gets produced and reproduced within individual, seemingly unique and discrete personal narratives. Thus by telling stories

---

[21] Richard Delgado, ed., *Critical Race Theory: The Cutting Edge* (Philadelphia: Temple University Press, 1995), xiii, citation omitted.

[22] Matsuda et al., *Words that Wound*, 15. For a critique of these views of language that maintains yet transforms the issue as one of power, see Judith Butler, *Excitable Speech: A Politics of the Performative* (New York: Routledge, 1997).

[23] Mary Joe Frug, *Postmodern Legal Feminism* (New York: Routledge, 1992), 112.

[24] Catharine MacKinnon, *Only Words* (Cambridge: Harvard University Press, 1993). See also *Feminism Unmodified: Discourse on Life and Law* (Cambridge: Harvard University Press, 1987) and *Toward a Feminist Theory of the State* (Cambridge: Harvard University Press, 1989).

[25] Patricia Ewick and Susan Silbey, "Subversive Stories and Hegemonic Tales: Toward a Sociology of Narrative," *Law and Society Review* 29 (1995): 197.

of our lives, we not only report, account for, and relive portions of those lives, we participate in the production of legality.[26]

Ewick and Silbey's conjunction of teller and telling fits nicely with what Mertz calls "an integrative approach" to language and social context.[27] Using Sally Engle Merry's *Getting Justice and Getting Even* (1990) and John M. Conley and William M. O'Barr's *Rules versus Relationships* (1990) as examples, Mertz describes a recent move to view language as neither simply "reflectionist" (language mirrors society) nor "instrumentalist" (language as transparent instrument of social actor).[28] This ostensibly new approach acknowledges what Mertz calls "a moment of linguistic creativity."

The "resistance or unpredictability" Mertz identifies still belongs, however, to a language that is primarily *social*. Language in these studies, Mertz writes, is both a "process whereby cultural understandings are enacted, created, and transformed in interaction with social structure" and itself "structured in crucial ways by its social context," such that "social power is implicated at every level of contextual influence on language" (423). Or, as Mertz puts it in her own work:

> The approach taken here views language as a key mediator in human interaction, and as socially-grounded. In both respects, language is ideological. As work by linguists and semioticians has demonstrated, language filters and channels the stories speakers tell. Language is also the medium through which much of our social interaction is accomplished. Thus language is socially grounded, structuring and being structured by social context.[29]

Mertz's return to an account of language that does not exceed the social extinguishes the promise of linguistic creativity—the flickering possibility of unpredictability—that Mertz briefly raises. For language to speak in a way that belongs to it as language and not just as socially constructed and socially constructing sign, however complex, its speaking cannot be limited to what can be grasped as social. Speaking requires not only the possibility of repetition and social creativity, but also the possibility of the emergence of a non-preordained "creativity" or difference.

---

[26] Patricia Ewick and Susan Silbey, *The Common Place of Law: Stories from Everyday Life* (Chicago: University of Chicago Press, 1998), 30.

[27] Mertz, "Language, Law," 413.

[28] Mertz, "Language, Law," 418, 417. See Sally Merry, *Getting Justice and Getting Even: Legal Consciousness among Working-Class Americans* (Chicago: University of Chicago Press, 1990); John Conley and William M. O'Barr, *Rules versus Relationships: The Ethnography of Legal Discourse* (Chicago: University of Chicago Press, 1990).

[29] Elizabeth Mertz, "The Uses of History: Language, Ideology, and Law in the United States and South Africa," *Law and Society Review* 22 (1988): 662, citation omitted.

At stake in understanding language as reducible to the social—to social behavior, meanings, functions, creation and creativity—is a particular worldview. This worldview insists on the primacy of a social framework from which there is no escape or outside. In this worldview, language and law function as dynamic social processes that are simultaneously subjects or structures, producing effects and modeled on traditional grammars of agency and control, and objects or resources, subject to human mastery. Captured and held within the terms of social power, language like law becomes the object of social knowledges whose reach is potentially limitless. Such knowledge takes the socially constructed and constructing world to be the extent of the world and of language. In its assertion of mastery over language, sociology accepts no limits to itself beyond those of the "society" that is its own object and subjected to it.

Sociology thus sets the terms for the reform of language and law. Peter Tiersma, for instance, looks at how aspects of legal language promote particular goals (e.g. clear and precise communication) and fulfill particular social functions (e.g. solidifying lawyer-group cohesion) that may conflict. He concludes that "understanding the competing goals and interests of the profession with respect to its language can help us decide which aspects of legal language are worth preserving and which should be set aside," as, from the point of view of the public, "legal language can and should be much less arcane and ponderous, and be much more understandable, than it is now."[30] Judith Levi makes the justice of jury instructions a question of what society desires: "One question in this context is just what a 'desirable' level of comprehensibility would be in the setting of a jury trial—and how such a level might be decided."[31] Judgment as to the ostensible justice of jury instructions involves the evaluation of desire. It becomes a matter for social policy and research: "This question is patently not one for psycholinguists alone but rather is an issue of public policy that must be addressed by the legal profession *in the light* of relevant empirical research" (22).

In sociolegal scholarship about language then, social power is key. As Conley and O'Barr say of their work analyzing transcripts of legal practices, "This research looks at the law's language in order to understand the law's power. Its premise is that power is not a distant abstraction but rather an everyday reality." And, they conclude, "language is not merely the vehicle through which legal power operates: in many vital respects, language *is* legal power."[32] Cutting across varieties of power in their work

[30] Peter Tiersma, *Legal Language* (Chicago: University of Chicago Press, 1999), 244, 6.

[31] Judith N. Levi, "Study of Language in the Judicial Process," in Levi and Walker, *Language in Judicial Process*, 22.

[32] John M. Conley and William M. O'Barr, *Just Words: Law, Language and Power* (Chicago: University of Chicago Press, 1998), 2, 14.

as well as in the studies they cite, the presence or absence of power gauges the efficacy of language and the condition of a legal subject whom the studies consider within some framework of power. Subjects' silence in the face of powerful (or obfuscating) official institutions and texts or silence in the face of a powerful and discursive law indicates the absence of power. Absence of words—the absence of stories and voice, the absence of history as articulation of a past, the absence of a tradition that knows itself—constitutes absence of power. Implicitly or explicitly identifying law with only-sometimes-authoritative declarations, sociolegal studies characterize silence as an absence of power that is given various names— hegemony and hierarchy (Messick),[33] repression and domination (Kessler),[34] subordination (White, Frug), oppression.[35] These names for an absence of power give rise to calls for "further action" (White, "Subordination," 58), "resistance" (Engel),[36] and "empowerment" (Merry).[37] Meanwhile "justice" remains largely unspoken.

Most sociolegal studies of discourse lack explicit reference to justice. The sociological worldview they adopt transforms justice into power and into human or social power at that. In the same way that sociology of religion transforms faith,[38] these studies transform justice into empirical terms of social power, social pressure, or socialization (as chapter 1's "Sociological Positivism" discussed) or into the terms of social policy explored in later chapters.

Scholars rarely use cognates of the term *justice* in its own terms; when they do, such references are noteworthy. Mertz, for instance, refers to South Africa's Homeland apartheid policy as "this unjust system."[39] Injustice in this context indicates exclusion or lack—of voice: "the power behind the imposition of law was evident in its summary treatment of indigenous people's history and rights—indeed in its exclusion of their voices and stories," writes Mertz (668).

[33] Brinkley Messick, "Kissing Hands and Knees: Hegemony and Hierarchy in Shari'a Discourse," *Law and Society Review* 22 (1988): 637.

[34] Mark Kessler, "Legal Discourse and Political Intolerance: The Ideology of Clear and Present Danger," *Law and Society Review* 27 (1993): 559.

[35] Mertz, "The Uses of History," 684.

[36] David Engel, "Origin Myths: Narratives of Authority, Resistance, Disability and Law," *Law and Society Review* 27 (1993): 785.

[37] Sally Engle Merry, "Law and Colonialism, Review Essay," *Law and Society Review* 25 (1991): 889, and "Wife Battering and the Ambiguities of Rights," in *Identities, Politics, and Rights*, ed. Austin Sarat and Thomas R. Kearns (Ann Arbor: University of Michigan Press, 1995).

[38] Michel de Certeau, *The Writing of History*, trans. Tom Conley (New York: Columbia University Press, 1988).

[39] Mertz, "The Uses of History," 661.

It is to voice then—and to the possibilities of relating it to issues of justice—that the chapter now turns.

More Dignified Names: Political Voice

> But I tell you a cat needs a name that's particular,
> A name that's peculiar and more dignified,
> Else how can he keep up his tail perpendicular,
> Or spread out his whiskers, or cherish his pride?
> Of names of this kind, I can give you a quorum,
> Such as Munkustrap, Quaxo, or Coricopat,
> Such as Bombalurina, or else Jellylorum—
> Names that never belong to more than one cat.

The section "Everyday Names" above reveals the prevalence of socially powerful law and language in sociolegal studies of language. The identification of law with powerful language is not unique to sociolegal study, however. Legal positivism long ago identified law with the powerful declarations or commands of a sovereign.[40] The Austinian relation in which the speech of master or state dominates subjects "bound to the silence of respect, reverence or terror" has given way to a classical liberal paradigm in which citizens, as minisovereigns, demand to speak.[41] But while more sophisticated versions of speech and of legal positivism have indeed emerged, they still generally accord speech to power as right and privilege.

Liberal theory complements sociolegal understandings of law as social control and of speech correlative to power, by emphasizing the citizen

---

[40] Austin, *Province of Jurisprudence Determined.*

[41] Pierre Clastres, *Society Against the State* (New York: Zone, 1987), 151. Clastres provides a fascinating alternative to conventional Western relations between speech and power in the inversion of those relations that he finds in Indian tribes in South America. "If in societies with a State speech is power's right, in societies without a State speech is power's duty. Or, to put it differently, Indian societies do not recognize the chief's right to speak because he is the chief: they require that the man destined to be chief prove his command over words. Speech is an imperative obligation for the chief. The tribe demands to hear him: a silent chief is no longer a chief" (153). Clastres writes further that the word of the chief, a ritualized act, "is not spoken in order to be listened to. . . . The chief, for all his prolixity, literally says nothing. His discourse consists of a celebration, repeated many times, of the norms of traditional life: 'Our ancestors got on well living as they lived. Let us follow their example and in this way we will lead a peaceful existence together' " (153–54). According to Clastres, "[T]he discourse of the chief is empty precisely because it is not a discourse of power. . . . An order? Now there is something the chief would be unable to give; that is the kind of fullness his speech is denied. A chief forgetful of his duty who attempted such a thing as an order would be met by a sure refusal of obedience, and a denial of recognition

who speaks rather than the language with which s/he does so. Recall that in Hart's second condition for a minimal legal system, officials accept, rather than simply obey, secondary rules. Under the rule of law, officials as citizens are bound to their own rules. In social theories of democracy, citizens conversely function to some degree as their own officials or rulers. They are minisovereigns, entitled to speak and demanding of voice. Although the proverbial silence may be golden, silence in contemporary politics "equals death," as it was put in campaigns for gay rights and increased funding for AIDS research in the 1990s.

The minisovereigns of contemporary liberal accounts of politics are not only free and equal individuals capable of owning things and bearing rights, but also speaking subjects. According to liberal political theory, legitimate government, or government whose authority society acknowledges, requires speech—or at least general public participation and individual opportunity to participate.[42] Liberal theorists thus invent speech forums (Habermas); they project speech onto silence and name it "consent" (Locke). Liberal politicians take mixed messages, the results of surveys of what pollsters warn are transitory public opinions, as clear mandates.[43] Liberal scholars strive to find consistency over incoherence to such a degree that almost any public expression is read as acquiescence or resistance.

Critiques of liberal theory generally rely also on appeals to the reality of social power. Despite the importance of speech to liberalism, critics tend to dwell on the liberal construction of autonomous rights-bearing subjects, rather than on liberalism's construction of speaking subjects. Standard critiques of liberalism claim either that liberalism disregards the social embeddedness of persons (e.g., Sandel on Rawls,[44] Kymlicka,[45] communitarians, liberal feminism) or that liberalism disregards the way that as a theory it

---

would not be far behind. . . . Primitive society is the place where separate power [based on the division masters/slaves, lords/subjects, leaders/citizens, etc. (151)] is refused, because the society itself, and not the chief, is the real locus of power" (154).

[42] See the extensive recent political theoretical literature on deliberative democracy.

[43] But see Louis Uchitelle, "Consumer Confidence Index Goes from an Aha to a Hmm," *New York Times*, June 8, 2002, A1 ("now a growing number of researchers and economists say that consumer confidence may be a phantom concept, an attempt to quantify a state of mind that does not exist. The much-watched indexes may not capture mood swings that lead to more or less spending, they argue, but only such down-to-earth concerns as how much the next pay check will be and whether it will still be arriving six months from now").

[44] Michael J. Sandel, *Liberalism and the Limits of Justice* (Cambridge: Cambridge University Press, 1982).

[45] Will Kymlicka, *Multicultural Citizenship: A Liberal Theory of Minority Rights* (Oxford: Clarendon Press; New York: Oxford University Press, 1995).

is itself implicated in existing structures of power (e.g., Marx,[46] critical legal studies,[47] critical race theory,[48] feminists such as MacKinnon[49]). Both these critiques challenge the neutrality of the liberal rights-bearing subject by grounding themselves, like the sociolegal studies of discourse discussed earlier in this chapter, in a reality that privileges social power: sociologically determinable characteristics or social structures constitute the frame from which both sorts of critiques of liberalism are launched.[50]

Political demands for voice, like sociolegal appeals to it, complicate this frame. They suggest that relations between law and social power may not be so simple: voice corresponds neither to actual power nor to submission nor resistance to it. But more to the point, appeals to voice bring into view the limited scope of the social, revealing the limitations of the linear temporality that sociolegal and legal positivist accounts take for granted. The empowerment that is to come with voice is a power that cannot be conjured without *first* being asserted; but the voice that asserts or demands power must in some sense be *already* empowered.

Others have also pointed out this paradox. Judith Butler, for instance, claims that "The temporal paradox of the subject is such that, of necessity, we must lose the perspective of a subject already formed in order to account for our own becoming." She describes the paradox in terms of "submission" and "subordination" to a world that is not one's own, however, to account for how one becomes oneself as "social being."[51] Somewhat similar insights have led Jed Rubenfeld to criticize what he calls the "presentism" of voice. He turns to written constitutionalism to stabilize the conditions of voice.[52] What follows takes a different tack from either of these works. First, it attempts to move away from the terminology of social power. Second, it focuses on the inability of voice to ground itself or to state or stipulate the conditions of its own emergence, not to establish ostensibly determinate foundations such as writing, but to explore the weird temporality of claim and response that is the very condition, not only of voice,

[46] See, for instance, Piers Bierne and Richard Quinney, eds., *Marxism and Law* (New York: John Wiley and Sons, 1982).

[47] Unger, *Critical Legal Studies Movement*; Peter Fitzpatrick and Alan Hunt, eds., *Critical Legal Studies* (Oxford: Basil Blackwell, 1987).

[48] See, for instance, Derrick A. Bell, *And We Are Not Saved: The Elusive Quest for Racial Justice* (New York: Basic Books, 1987); and texts cited at notes 18–20.

[49] MacKinnon, *Feminist Theory of the State*.

[50] Wendy Brown, *States of Injury: Power and Freedom in Late Modernity* (Princeton: Princeton University Press, 1995) is in some ways an exception, insofar as Brown associates her critique with Nietzsche's critique of *ressentiment*.

[51] Judith Butler, *The Psychic Life of Power* (Stanford: Stanford University Press, 1997), 28, 30.

[52] Jed Rubenfeld, *Freedom and Time: A Theory of Constitutional Self-Government* (New Haven: Yale University Press, 2001).

but also of law. The appeal to what is at once beyond and not beyond oneself opens the possibility of the unpredictable in language and law.

Voice is neither monolithic nor single-minded. "Voice" is appealed to today from across the political spectrum. Both Left and Right equate voice with their own understandings of both empowerment and justice. They usually equate an absence of voice with an absence of power and an absence of justice.

Silence is not always an absence of voice, of course. It may be heard as a voice of consent—to the legitimacy of power, for instance. Within the current democratic politics of voice, however, silence is almost always taken up as an absence of power, as an issue to be raised on behalf of the less powerful to contest their marginalization, exclusion, or domination. Silence in this context marks those who have not been properly heard, who are not listened to, or who have yet to come into their own voices. In this context, voice is asserted as empowerment and right.

More interesting than the reference voice makes to power, whether legitimating or challenging, however, is its appeal or assertion of right. Voice makes its demand for recognition—and admittedly power—in the name of justice. This demand or appeal comes from within the world yet reaches beyond itself. In the call for recognition, a demand that cannot even be recognized as a demand without some previous possible recognition of this voice as a voice, voice asserts the need that is its claim for justice. On the one hand, justice is not there, in the sense that it is needed and claimed or called for. Yet justice must also be there for it to respond when called to. If justice were not within earshot, no acknowledgment that what was heard was indeed a voice and a call, no recognition or response to the call, would be possible. An unsayable silence marks the way in which justice is and is not there for the voice that calls its need for something other than itself. In a silent stillness that waits, justice is the responsiveness to which and for which voice appeals.

In an essay published in 1944, Eugen Rosenstock-Huessy writes of the imperative,

> [W]e are mistaken when we ascribe to the imperative the content of being "in the second person." As the six persons in search of an author in the play of Pirandello, the imperative is in search of a subject. It is said to "whom it may concern." "Go" does not contain the second person "you" or "thou"; what it does is to create this person. For this reason, the imperative is pure verb without an ending. He who does just this, becomes the second person by answering the first person. The listener, who says "I will do it," becomes the person to whom "go" was addressed.[53]

[53] Eugen Rosenstock-Huessy, "The Listener's Tract," in *Speech and Reality* (Norwich, VT: Argo, 1970), 149.

The imperative creates the second person of the listener who does just this and *becomes* the one who will have been addressed by the imperative. The person who now has a voice was once both already and not yet the speaker who will have been heard. (Recall Walter Benjamin: "A man . . . who died at thirty-five will appear to *remembrance* at every point in his life as a man who dies at the age of thirty-five.")[54] For Rosenstock-Huessy, in saying, "I will do it," the listener indicates that he was selected and that reason requires the coming into being of the act (149–50).

As "reason" for Rosenstock-Huessy both retrospectively and prospectively enables the one whom the imperative concerns to act and to be as the person who will have been addressed, so "justice" recognizes voice. Law is the necessity of the strange temporal structure of recognition needed for action and voice. It constitutes the repeated insight of twentieth-century thought, articulated through and despite myriad variations, differences, and disputes, about identity, history, and language.[55] The four analyses below begin to explore this law in the silences surrounding voice. These silences are not always the same. But they disclose the need out of which voice calls and the stillness to which voice appeals—even when the voice fails to articulate "justice" or when there is no response.

Ahern: The Voice of the "Innocent Child"

In "Letter: On Abortion" to the New York Times, the (Most Rev.) Patrick V. Ahern declares that "The pro-life movement exists to be the voice of [the] innocent child."[56] (See Appendix 2.) What voice is this?

The statement appears in Ahern's response to critics of the first President Bush's 1989 veto of Medicaid funding for abortion in cases of rape and incest. Ahern argues that such a veto is "quite reasonable if we believe in the equality of all human beings." Ahern's defense of "the pro-life position" shows his position to be grounded not simply in notions of equality, but also in the possibilities and limitations of voice.

Ahern begins by distinguishing between the viewpoint of "the pregnant woman" and that of "the child in the womb." The viewpoint "of the child in the womb" is the viewpoint of one who

has done no wrong to anyone. He or she is the most innocent of bystanders, who has been called into existence and finds him or herself washed up on the

[54] Walter Benjamin, "The Storyteller," in *Illuminations*, ed. Hannah Arendt, trans. Harry Zohn (New York: Schocken, 1968), 100.

[55] Heidegger, of course; but also Derrida on language, Freud on the joke, Benjamin on art, Cavell on voice.

[56] Patrick V. Ahern, "The Child Has a Right to Be Born," October 25, 1989, letter to the editor, *New York Times*, National Edition, November 3, 1989, A14.

shores of the world not knowing where he came from or why he was created, and having done nothing to bring himself into existence—the same as the rest of us.

That child, Ahern continues, "has offended no one, has caused nobody pain, is asking only what all of us ask: to be allowed to live."

The child, according to Ahern, is "innocent." As a "bystander called into existence," the child (no longer referred to by Ahern as the child "in the womb") has "done no wrong to anyone." Indeed, the child has "done" nothing and has had no chance to do wrong—as Ahern acknowledges. But if the child has never had the opportunity to *do* anything, on what grounds does one judge the child as "innocent"? How are right and wrong, innocence and guilt, posited of a "child" who is a nonactor, a nonchooser, a nonagent? What sense does it make to use right and wrong in the absence of a context of possible actions and will?

Ahern's "child" constitutes an amorphous subject, whom Ahern nevertheless treats as distinct. Such a subject is *of* a pregnant woman, *in* the womb, "called into existence," and yet Ahern suggests this subject can "find" and "know" and hold a "viewpoint" distinguishable from that of the pregnant woman. In some sense, Ahern's subject does not will, but has a will; its innocence is the innocence of powerless will.

Ahern identifies this ostensibly innocent child with "all the rest of us." "That child is as good and as valuable as any one of us, for 'all are created equal.' " Not only are we all the same in original existence—"innocent"—but all are equal, all are of the same value in that innocence. This is shown for Ahern by our all asking the same thing: "The child is asking only what all of us ask: to be allowed to live." Indeed, "life is all we ask": " 'Please don't kill me' is all the child could say if he could speak."

Taking the child's point of view prompts "an interesting point" to come to Ahern's mind. That point is a distrust of the mother:

[N]one of us know for sure who his or her father is. That is a matter of trust. Ultimately it is an act of implicit confidence in our mother. She is the only one who really knows who our father is. Even her husband does not know with absolute certitude.

Such distrust of the mother "leads" to Ahern's question: suppose we were to discover, "at the age, say, of 50," that "the man we had supposed to be our father was not our father at all." Instead, we learn that "our father was, in reality, our grandfather, or that we were conceived by an act of violent rape: would we—he, I, or any one of us—wish that we were killed in the womb?" Ahern thinks not.

Before turning to Ahern's response, one must note the situation from which Ahern now calls on the innocent child (who, if speaking, could say only, "Please don't kill me") to speak. The child in the womb has become a collectivity of fifty-year-olds. The "he or she" by which Ahern initially characterized the child in the womb (paragraph 3), has gone from the "he" of "that innocent child" (paragraph 4), to the "we" who take "his" or "her" point of view and who distrust our mothers (paragraph 5), to the "we—he, I, or any one of us" whose distrust has been borne out by a discovery of our origins (paragraph 6).

In a context of betrayal by a lying mother, then, Ahern thinks that, given a choice, we—sharing in both the "imperfect world" and the choices of such grand men as "Beethoven, Dante, Thomas Edison, Irving Berlin [and] Francis of Assisi"—would choose to be born. Ahern fails to consider that we might consider asking *not* to be born into a world of betrayal—a world of betrayal not only of the child by the mother, but of the mother by the father. The absence of such consideration on Ahern's part reveals the limitations of Ahern's speaking subject. Ahern's collectivity discovers "she betrayed me" and thinks, "That has nothing to do with my asking to live." It does not occur to Ahern's subject to ask, "How can one live in such a world?"

The foreclosure of even the possibility of considering how one can live with betrayal (whether of oneself or of the mother) stems from Ahern's earlier distinction of the child from the mother and his characterization of the child as like "any one of us," all of whom ask, and ask only, to live. The exception to "any one of us," for Ahern, is the mother, who wants to kill. The radical separation of innocent child (and all who are created equal) from (guilty) mother precludes the possibility of a free response by the child-subject to the mother's betrayal (in either sense). For the child, like all of us, according to Ahern, can *only* ask for life. The possibility of asking—nay, of even considering—otherwise, the possibility of choosing, willing, forgiving, of reconciliation between mother and child, is blocked from the start.

The "child" who "responds" to Ahern's hypothetical and asks for life forgets not only the betrayal by the father of the mother, but also by the mother who has deceived the growing child. For Ahern's child asks for life, regardless of, and indifferent to, betrayal. Ahern's child is unaware of betrayal, for betrayal can be only of prior obligation in a context of relation between a choosing self and an other. Ahern's child knows neither betrayal nor obligation.

The point is not that some of us, in the situation constructed by Ahern where we have been betrayed by a lying mother, would ask not to be born. The point, rather, is that Ahern's characterization of the lack of possibilities of choice in such situation reveal the "voice" of his impossible subject to be pre- or amoral. Ahern ignores that bare life alone is neither moral nor meaningful, that for voice to mean anything requires having entered a preexisting world of relationships.

Morality—like the equal rights with which Ahern would endow the child and the voice that he would have represent it—requires not only separation, but also relation—a relation between self and other, who are, in some sense, the same. Absent any separation, the equality that moral theory grants to persons as actors, the rights that liberal theory grants to "distinct individuals," and the voice that political liberalism accords speaking subjects, are unnecessary. Absent any relation, on the other hand, equality, rights, and voice are nonsensical, empty forms. In Ahern's radical separation of mother and child, the possibility of relation, of non-separate existence, and hence of equality and rights and voice, is denied.

Ahern's argument thus depends on a separation of mother from child far more radical than that condoned by the pro-life movement's opponents. Ahern's argument creates a separation between mother and child that precludes the possibility of relation and of morality. The absence of morality that lies in such separation cannot be overcome by simply requiring a woman to carry a child to term, as the voice of the powerless child demands, in the name of life.

Ahern concludes by claiming that the abortion issue turns upon the child—the child's right, and the equality of all human beings. His argument thus appears to draw on conventional distinctions between persons and traditional claims about equal rights. But the argument is more complex. Ahern believes that "our" choice of life affirms "the most fundamental right of all, the right not to be killed for no reason except that we have begun to exist through no choice of our own." The "choice" that Ahern has the "pro-life position" voice on behalf of the "innocent child" replaces appeal to a just life—to a godly life or a moral life—with appeal to a bare "life" that is unaware and neglectful of possibilities of—indeed incapable of—any sort of life other than its own. That voice repeats without differentiation the only thing it has to say: "Please don't kill me."

The voice of the pro-life movement, like that of the ostensibly innocent unborn child, cannot say otherwise. Its reiterations point simultaneously to themselves and to the limits of what they say. What is otherwise for the voice that insists only on life—the conditions that make life meaningful; the possibility of morality, of obligation, of connection; the context that must matter for voice to speak—is for it unsayable. Nothing other than bare life is possible in the homogeneity of its past, present, and future.

Hirschman: Exit, Voice, and Loyalty

Albert O. Hirschman's now-classic 1970 book, *Exit, Voice, and Loyalty: Responses to Decline in Firms, Organizations, and States,* provides a more thematized account of "voice," in both economics and politics, than that found in Ahern's letter.[57] Hirschman identifies "two alternative routes" by which management "finds out about its failings." Customers may stop buying a firm's products or members may leave an organization: "this is the *exit option*," favored by economic analysis (4). Or members may "express their dissatisfaction directly to management or to some other authority to which management is subordinate or through general protest addressed to anyone who cares to listen: this is the *voice option*," favored by political scientists' analyses (4).

In many respects, Hirschman suggests, voice is the opposite of exit. Loyalty complicates the relation, though. Loyalty "holds exit at bay and activates voice" (78). Although some loyalists "may simply refuse to exit and suffer in silence, confident that things will get better soon" (38), the presence of loyalty means that "the *effectiveness* of the voice mechanism is strengthened by the possibility of exit" (83).

Hirschman argues, in a chapter titled "Exit and Voice in American Ideology and Practice" that in the American political tradition, "exit has been accorded an extraordinarily privileged position. . . , but then, suddenly it is wholly proscribed, sometimes for better, sometimes for worse, from a few key situations" (106). From its origins, Hirschman writes, "the United States owes its very existence and growth . . . to millions of decisions favoring exit over voice" (106). He quotes Louis Hartz's acclaimed 1955 book, *The Liberal Tradition in America*:

> It is one thing to stay at home and fight the "canon and feudal law," and it is another to leave it far behind. It is one thing to try to establish liberalism in the Old World, and it is another to establish it in the New. Revolution, to borrow the words of T. S. Eliot, means to murder and create, but the American experience has been projected strangely in the realm of creation alone. The destruction of forests and Indian tribes—heroic, bloody, legendary as it was—cannot be compared with the destruction of a social order to which one belongs oneself. (106)

Hartz continues: "The first experience [the destruction of forests and Indian tribes] is wholly external and, being external can actually be completed; the second experience [destruction of a social order to which one belongs oneself] is an inner struggle as well as an outer struggle, like the slaying of a Freudian father, and goes on in a sense forever" (106).[58]

Hirschman at first claims that the "preference for the neatness of exit over the messiness and heartbreak of voice has then 'persisted throughout

---

[57] Albert O. Hirschman, *Exit, Voice, and Loyalty: Responses to Decline in Firms, Organizations, and States* (Cambridge: Harvard University Press, 1970).

[58] Citing Louis Hartz, *The Liberal Tradition in America: An Interpretation of American Political Thought Since the Revolution* (New York: Harcourt, Brace, 1955), 64–65.

our national history' " (107, again quoting Hartz). There are what he calls exceptions: "the case of a minority that has been discriminated against" for whom exit is "bound to be unsatisfactory and unsuccessful even from the point of view of the individuals who practice it" (110). But apart from "latter-day dissonant voices," such as that of the black power movement, "the ideology of exit has been powerful in America" (112).

At the same time, however, Hirschman writes, the "national infatuation" with exit—from the old country—can give way to "emergence of its opposite"—loyalty or attachment to the United States as "the country of last resort." Hence, "to most of its citizens—with the important exception of those whose forefathers came as slaves—exit from the country has long been peculiarly unthinkable" (113). But the "love" in "love it or leave it," may become as much a matter of voice as of loyalty. When adjustment to American conditions does not occur, voice may "come into its own with unusual force" (114).

> It will be animated by the typically American conviction that human institutions can be perfected and that problems can be solved. The compulsion to be happy [in the new country of the United States] is replaced by the compulsion to use voice for the purpose of making the country live up to its image. It is, in fact, to this compulsion that the country owes some of its greatest achievements just as it owes its origin to exit. (114)

What Hirschman calls the compulsion to use voice to make the country live up to its image manifests itself in part in the United States' fierce commitment to various freedoms. One of the United States' greatest achievements, for instance, has certainly been the extension of freedom of speech, discussed further below, to precisely those who had no voice in the old country from which they exited.

Hirschman concludes though by acknowledging some of the complications of a democratic politics of voice. He discusses the instability of an "optimally efficient" mix of exit and voice and refers to the "invigorating effects" of suddenly injecting voice or exit into politics when the other has been the norm. He asks why exit can be galvanizing in such conditions. And he answers:

> Exit is unsettling to those who stay behind as there can be no "talking" back to those who have exited. By exiting one renders his arguments unanswerable. The remarkable influence wielded by martyrs throughout history can be understood in those terms, for the martyr's death is exit at its most irreversible and argument at its most irrefutable. (126)

Although under Hirschman's schema, silence is most often taken as loyalty (under conditions of dissatisfaction, or as satisfaction or indifference), the silence of the martyr's death appears now as active, as both "exit" and "argument." Hirschman's neat distinction between exit and voice breaks down in the silence of death. Such silence reminds those who remain—irrefutably—of the conditions that make life worth living. Without "voice," the silence of the martyr tells of the need for justice in this world in a way that words alone cannot. Such silence again invokes the unsayable, this time as the justice without which voice itself is meaningless.

Mill: The "Real Morality of Public Discussion"

Today, Hartz's account seems somewhat dated. The American polity now usually claims or aspires to be politically inclusive and gestures toward accepting descendants of non-Europeans as full members. Insofar as one takes these claims seriously, one cannot rest with an account of the creation of a new United States that is grounded simply at its origin in external struggle and exit. The establishment of the nation, contra Hartz (and implicitly Hirschman) has not been "completed." Native Americans and blacks did not *decide* to exit to the United States to create a New World. From the point of view of Indian tribes at least, the American destruction of forests and tribes is not an external affair, but precisely "the destruction of a social order to which one belongs oneself." The history of Native Americans and blacks (as Hirschman acknowledges) in America suggests that the ongoing creation of a liberal and pluralist United States is more properly understood as, in Hartz's words, "an inner struggle as well as an outer struggle," a struggle in which the very terms of recognition and of extension of voice are at issue.

Neither Hirschman's dead martyr nor Ahern's repetitive child has language to name the conditions of voice: the justice or responsiveness that makes voice meaningful and to which voice appeals. John Stuart Mill, by contrast, seems to have no qualms as to his ability to name conditions of voice—or, rather, of freedom of speech.[59] For even Mill distinguishes freedom of speech from political voice. At the end of the famous second chapter of On Liberty, "Of the Liberty of Thought and Discussion," Mill informs his readers what "the real morality of public discussion" requires.[60]

Mill has just taken notice of those who would qualify his argument for freedom of speech. They would object that "the free expression of all opinions should be permitted, *on condition* that the manner be temperate,

---

[59] Mill's lack of subtlety in this and other regards leads Nietzsche to include Mill among "My impossibles." Nietzsche writes, "*John Stuart Mill*: or offensive clarity." *Twilight of the Idols*, 67 ("Expeditions," 1).

[60] John Stuart Mill, *On Liberty* (New York: Pelican, 1985).

and do not pass the bounds of fair discussion" (59; emphasis added). Mill defends *un*qualified freedom of expression in a variety of ways. He begins with the difficulty of identifying misconduct in argument and emphasizes that such misconduct may occur in good faith. He then concedes:

> With regard to what is commonly meant by intemperate discussion, namely invective, sarcasm, personality, and the like, the denunciation of these weapons would deserve more sympathy if it were ever proposed to interdict them equally to both sides; but it is only desired to restrain the employment of them against the prevailing opinion: against the unprevailing they may not only be used without general disapproval, but will be likely to obtain for him who uses them the praise of honest zeal and righteous indignation. (117)

As he continues, Mill identifies the "unprevailing" or "unpopular" opinion with that of "the comparatively defenceless," with, for example, "infidelity" rather than "religion." He distinguishes the effects of moderate and intemperate speech on "prevailing" or "received" or "common" opinion from their effects on unprevailing opinion.

> Unfair advantage . . . accrues almost exclusively to received opinions. The worst offence of this kind which can be committed by a polemic, is to stigmatize those who hold the contrary opinion as bad and immoral men. To calumny of this sort, those who hold any unpopular opinion are peculiarly exposed, because they are in general few and uninfluential, and nobody but themselves feels much interested in seeing justice done them; but this weapon is, for the nature of the case, denied to those who attack a prevailing opinion: they can neither use it with safety to themselves, nor, if they could, would it do anything but recoil on their own cause. In general, opinions contrary to those commonly received can only obtain a hearing by studied moderation of language, and the most cautious avoidance of unnecessary offence, from which they hardly ever deviate even in a slight degree without losing ground: while unmeasured vituperation employed on the side of the prevailing opinion, really does deter people from professing contrary opinions, and from listening to those who profess them. (117)

For Mill, law and authority "have no business restraining" attacks on either commonly accepted or unpopular opinion, but it is "obvious" to Mill that

> opinion ought, in every instance, to determine its verdict by the circumstances of the individual case; condemning everyone, on whichever side of the argument he places himself, in whose mode of advocacy either want of candour, or malignity, bigotry, or intolerance of feeling manifest themselves; but not inferring these vices from the side which a person takes, though it be the contrary side of the question to our own; and giving merited honour to every one, whatever opinion he may hold, who has calmness to see and honesty to state what his

opponents and their opinions really are, exaggerating nothing to their discredit, keeping nothing back which tells, or can be supposed to tell, in their favour. (118)

"This," he adds, "is the real morality of public discussion," and, he concludes, "if often violated, I am happy to think that there are many controversialists who to a great extent observe it, and a still greater number who conscientiously strive towards it" (118).

Despite his early comment that it is difficult to assess when offense is properly taken by the manner of an argument, Mill clearly considers the "calmness to see" and "honesty to state" opponents' opinions, the open disclosure of the weaknesses of one's own position, objectivity of sorts, and respect rather than "calumny, invective, etc." to be the virtues of good discussion. He does so even in the context of his overall argument against the silencing of opinions. Opinions are not to be silenced because, if right, they are deprived of exchanging error for truth; if wrong, they lose the clearer perception of truth that is produced by collision with error (21). Mill believes in a particular sort of truth, a truth that is not immediately apparent but that emerges from rational discussion. Silencing of opinions is evil insofar as this truth is Mill's goal.

If, according to Mill, law must permit everything to be said as freedom of speech, it is nevertheless still the case for Mill that some voices are more virtuous or more equal than others. (In *Representative Government*, Mill goes so far as to propose a pluralistic system of votes, in which those who are more qualified would vote multiply and in multiple jurisdictions.)[61] Even Mill—the champion of freedom of speech—does not confuse freedom of speech under the law with equality of voice. He analyzes freedom of speech in terms of removing constraints and the relative power of prevailing and unprevailing, dominant and offensive, opinion. Voice for Mill, on the other hand, however much he thinks he may have it in the grip of his explanations, nevertheless remains a matter the quality of which lies beyond the regulation of positive law.

Hate Speech

Through statutes and rules, U.S. law shapes the environment of speech. U.S. federal, state, and local governments create a space of "free speech" by regulating language explicitly and implicitly. They do so through, for instance, official English laws, laws concerning bilingual education, rules about who is authorized to speak with what effect, rules governing disclo-

[61] John Stuart Mill, *Considerations on Representative Government* (New York: Bobbs-Merrill, 1958).

sure of information and confidentiality. In principle, all that is "speak-able" may be "spoken" in this (configured) space, although some things of course remain unspoken or unsaid. Deliberately excluded from this space is only the "unspeakable," that to which words are inadequate. "Fighting words," for instance, are banned from the public space of free speech, insofar as they incite to violence and thus introduce an element—violence or force—that escapes the bounds of speech.

The United States has developed protections against hate speech quite slowly, compared to Europe. The United States has even attached reserva-tions to its ratification of international covenants that might otherwise call on it to restrict offensive or discriminatory speech. Policies to protect offensive speech emerged in the 1940s to 1970s and were only challenged in the last decades of the twentieth century.[62] Court cases now protect the rights of vilified minorities to speak (and offend) the majority—hence "offensive" speech by a Jehovah's Witness, for instance, is protected.[63]

In the context of cultural pluralism, however, the speech of normally prevailing majorities offends normally unprevailing minorities. Tables are turned and new issues arise. Mill's power-oriented distinctions between what generally prevails and what does not become less useful. Critical race theorists operating within a framework of "domination" and "sub-ordination" seek to reverse or invert these power relations. But the issue holds more interesting possibilities than reversals of power.

Critics of American free speech law approach it two ways. The first way concerns what is speakable but not spoken within the ostensibly free space of speech. Critics argue that actual silences reveal that the configur-ing of the environment works to privilege and marginalize (or exclude) particular voices or opinions. These are the silences imposed by law. Thus Owen Fiss, for instance, argues that the judiciary should ask itself whether a given regulation would enhance the quality of public debate.[64] In effect arguing for greater (or different) access to the "power" of speech on the parts of those who are silenced, these critics hearken to a "voice equals power equals justice" equation that characterizes the liberal ideology of democratic participation.

A second set of critics—some critical race theorists, for instance—make a more interesting criticism. They argue that some spoken things *ought* to be excluded from the space of free speech or, in the language of the First Amendment, ought not be protected speech. This argument itself can be taken in a couple of ways.

---

[62] Samuel Walker, *Hate Speech: The History of an American Controversy* (Lincoln: Uni-versity of Nebraska Press, 1994).

[63] *Chaplinsky v. New Hampshire*, 315 U.S. 568, 62 S.Ct. 766 (1942).

[64] Owen M. Fiss, *The Irony of Free Speech* (Cambridge: Harvard University Press, 1996).

First, their argument is sometimes mistakenly characterized as an argument for silencing. As such, the argument is doomed to fail in the terms of Millian First Amendment free speech theory insofar as it argues, in the context of hate speech regulation, that some of what is speakable and even spoken ought not be said. The argument comes directly into conflict with absolutist interpretations of First Amendment law, which, with J. S. Mill, maintain that if something is speakable, it may be said—or at least the positive law must allow it to be said.

In First Amendment interpretation of speech as what is speakable by a speaker, language is a weapon (like the symbol of the flag, as shall be seen in chapter 4) that may be used equally by both (or all) sides. In this interpretation, protecting the use of the speech or weapon of one party at one time entails protecting the ability of other parties to use the same weapon in the future. U.S. law may agree with Mill and critical race theorists that "unmeasured vituperation employed on the side of prevailing opinion, really does deter people from professing contrary opinions, and from listening to those who profess them." But more like Mill than critical race theory, the U.S. Court insists on identifying speech with ideas and concepts. It maintains (in the flag-burning cases and elsewhere) that "the Government may not prohibit the expression of an idea simply because society finds the idea itself offensive or disagreeable." Potentially offensive expressions must take their challenges in a "marketplace of ideas" among the "joust of principles protected by the First Amendment."[65] Or as Mill would put it, "law and authority have no business restraining" such attacks; restraint is a matter best left to "opinion" or what Mill calls "the real morality of public discussion."[66]

But there is (second) another more interesting way of understanding the argument made by those who would restrict offensive or hate speech. This understanding relies on the ambiguity or double meaning of the word *unspeakable*. First Amendment law, we have seen, takes the "unspeakable" or what is excluded from the protections of the space of free speech to be nonspeech—either conduct without expressive content or violence. It takes the "speakable" or "speech" to refer to what is in the control of speakers in the regulated space of free speech. Proponents of hate speech regulation, however, take the "unspeakable" to mean what is unutterably horrible—that to which words, though they may exist, do not belong. This latter unspeakability contrasts to the unspeakability that lies outside the terms of First Amendment law as well as to the unnameable conditions of voice. It draws attention not so much to what a speaker

---

[65] *Texas v. Johnson*, 491 U.S. 414, 109 S.Ct. 2533 (1989), at 418.
[66] Mill, *On Liberty*, 59–61.

cannot say, but to what is utterable but cannot properly be *heard*. Proponents of hate speech regulation, in this interpretation, imply a rethinking of the space of free speech as a space for proper hearing, at whose boundaries words may exist but do not belong.

Many commentators have taken the call by critical race theorists and others to explore this space as a need to turn to the subjective experience of the listener (and the "personal voice" and narrative approaches of some critical race theory indeed imply this). But just as speech or language is not purely within the control of the one who speaks, neither is it to be judged entirely by the experience of its addressee, much less by that which the speech excludes.

Any judgment of language and speech requires knowledge of the world in which particular words are spoken. It requires knowledge too of the world in which those words are heard. Judgment requires hearing what is spoken and how it is spoken. As in the old blasphemy cases, so too in judging hate speech, a legal hearing responds to a call to judge language as to its unspeakability. Hearing an issue becomes a response to a call for justice that was itself a hearing of what was claimed unspeakable.

The unspeakable, as what is unutterably horrible, is not the same as the unsayable. But a hearing is the coming to speech not only of the unspeakable, but also of the unsayable out of which all speech comes. In blasphemy trials of earlier centuries, the unspeakable became a matter of law. A legal *issue*—like hate speech, whether it is the subject matter of public discussion or of more formal legislative or judicial debate—both joins and divides parties over a legal matter. When as in the blasphemy cases, a hearing culminates in a judgment of the matter, that judgment emerges from the issues. It issues from out of the unsayable, as does recognition of voice.

The judgment may not be just, of course. The issue of the justice of the judgment though will in every case be a matter of responding from out of the unsayable to claims made by voices that are to be heard.

The valorization of voice in liberal theory and politics raises interesting possibilities that problematize society's understanding of language as fundamentally a matter of social power. As we have seen, political appeals to voice sometimes assert, and even more often imply, that they are making claims to or about justice. Although "justice" often remains unsaid, appeals to voice draw on unsayable conditions of meaningful life that are not reducible to sociological terms: the relatedness of persons in and to a world through speech and silences that can be heard. When sociolegal scholars and others point to an absence of power as an absence of voice whose rectification lies in empowerment, do their calls for empowered voice—despite their emphasis on power—also call for justice? Might others too call for justice without using the word?

One Name Left Over

But above and beyond there's still one name
   left over,
And that is the name that you never will guess;
The name that no human research can discover—
But the cat himself knows, and will never confess.

Reflecting on voice allows us to think about the calling of words. How is one to hear the call of words to justice? To listen to such calling is to hear words differently than do either the texts of sociolegal studies of language and discourse or, as we shall see, the positive laws of a liberal state. In contrast to the focus of sociolegal studies and of liberalism on the power of speech—whether as control or empowerment—such listening attends to the limits of speech.

It hearkens to spaces empty of power where sociolegal and positivist texts have nothing to say. It goes to the unspeakable places where texts fall silent. It ponders the silences out of which political appeals to voice and sociolegal studies, like all speech, emerge. It inhabits the paradoxical temporality of coming to voice. It hears claims and appeals to justice not so much in the explicit articulations of liberal sociolegal positivism and its positive law, but in their silences.

In hearing the silences of political voice and modern law, one encounters complications in the equation of voice with power and justice. One encounters, as the following chapters show, the limits of liberalism and of sociolegal study: the justice of and about which they do not or cannot explicitly speak. One encounters speech that is other than the deployment of tools for social communication by autonomous liberal subjects. One encounters the silences that surround the speech of loquacious modern law. And one encounters in the inextricability of law with the unspoken, the unspeakable, and the unsayable, what remains, if anything, of the "necessary" connection between law and justice that legal positivism would deny.

Sociolegal studies' simultaneous garrulousness about power and silence about "justice" lead one to wonder about the silence of justice. They lead one to ponder the limits of legal texts. Those limits beckon and call: they mark the place where silences surround the powerful articulated and propositional declarations of the law of sociolegal study and legal positivism. They mark the poetry and possibility of law.

When you notice a cat in profound meditation,
The reason, I tell you, is always the same:
His mind is engaged in a rapt contemplation
Of the thought, of the thought, of the thought of his name:
His ineffable effable
Effanineffable
Deep and inscrutable singular Name.

Chapter 3

What Voice Is This?

Good friend, for Jesus sake, forbeare
To digge the dust enclosed here
Blest be ye man yt spares thes stones
And cursed be he yt moves my bones
—Shakespeare's grave

Language, like religion and other traditional practices, must be fostered if the culture is to survive.
—Senate Report No. 102–343

THE TWO PRECEDING CHAPTERS have suggested a "sociologization" of
contemporary law. The sociologization of law involves, first, an insistence
that law is a social and empirical, and hence sociologically knowable—a
socio-logical—phenomenon. It involves, second, a privileging, in accounts of law, of efficacious power or control, however indirect or variously attributed. This chapter turns to a third aspect of the sociologization
of law: the pervasive privileging *at law* of the kind of discourse that corresponds to a sociological worldview. Analyses of the Native American Languages Acts and the Native American Graves Protection and Repatriation
Act reveal the sociologically discursive and rulelike character of American
law. They show how language and religion, speech and the sacred, become the objects of well-intentioned social studies that articulate the conditions for preserving cultures. At least in the United States, the articulations of modern law—like the speaking of the truths of modern society—
cover over and render inaccessible the nonarticulated truths and laws of
those for whom law consists neither of social scientific realities nor of
propositional truths. In the silences that U.S. law does not hear, there lie
possibilities of law—as of language and of religion and of justice—that
positivist jurisprudence and sociological society do not acknowledge and
whose truths they cannot accept.

As an analysis of texts, this chapter focuses on what is said in U.S.
law, in particular in official articulations of U.S. policy regarding Native
Americans: the Native American Languages Acts of 1990 and 1992 and
the Native American Graves Protection and Repatriation Act of 1990.[1] If

[1] Indian Education Programs and Native American Languages Act, Public Law 101–477
(October 30, 1990); Native American Languages Act of 1992 and Native Americans Educa-

any practice is privileged more than language in discussions of cultural identity and preservation, that practice is religion. The debates around language and religion provide a wealth of textual material about issues of culture and identity, preservation and loss, speech and silence. This material shows how U.S. law states concerns about language and culture.

The chapter also concerns what is not said in U.S. law. Native silences[2] highlight the unsaid and the unspeakable. The chapter does not attempt to speak for some or all Native Americans, nor even to interpret their speech. Neither does the chapter seek to pry open Native American silences or practices through empirical investigation or other means. Rather it tries to hear some Native silences or, better, to let them be heard. Problematic as this project may be, it is somewhat akin to what Michael Wood attributes to Edward Said in another context:

> Said doesn't want to speak for the silenced or the ignored—he thinks the Orientalists are already doing that—he wants their silence to be heard. . . . the story, as a story, concerns a group or groups of people who are unable to represent themselves not because they cannot speak or have no stories, and not even because they have been repressed, although that is also often the case. It is not even chiefly a question of their access to the means of distribution of narrative, although that too is of course important. They cannot represent themselves, Said is saying, because they are already represented.[3]

U.S. law already represents Native Americans, their identities and their cultures, in a particular way—as do, ironically, this chapter and the poet Gary Snyder in what follows, although in different ways. What U.S. law grasps as Native silences, the chapter shows, highlights the loquaciousness of a powerful U.S. law that is deaf to all that cannot be rendered in its own—sociological—terms.

The Native American Languages Acts of 1990 and 1992

In the context of the history of U.S. federal and state actions vis-à-vis Native Americans and their languages, the Native American Languages Act (NALA) of 1990 is an astounding document. Passed without fanfare

---

tional Assistance Act, Public Law 102–524 (October 25, 1992); Native American Graves Protection and Repatriation Act, Public Law 101–601 (November 16, 1990).

[2] I use *Native* and *Native American* synonymously and for lack of better terms. Just as the term *Native American* groups different peoples together, so too the practices of any particular Native people have changed over time, adapting and adapting to the practices of others. See James Clifford, "Identity in Mashpee," *The Predicament of Culture: Twentieth-Century Ethnography, Literature, and Art* (Cambridge: Harvard University Press, 1988).

[3] Michael Wood, *Children of Silence: On Contemporary Fiction* (New York: Columbia Press, 1998), 167–68.

as a rider to a bill reauthorizing tribally controlled community colleges, NALA announces U.S. policy regarding Native American languages. Finding that "the United States has the responsibility to act together with Native Americans to ensure the survival of [the] unique cultures and languages [of Native Americans]" (102.1), the act declares the "policy" of the United States to be to "preserve, protect, and promote the rights and freedom of Native Americans to use, practice, and develop their languages" (104 (1); 25 USC 2903). The 1990 act states further that the right of Native Americans "to express themselves through the use of Native American languages shall not be restricted in any public proceeding" (105). The 1992 NALA provides some mechanisms and funding to support the aims of the 1990 act. Outside of the grant program and a few articles, little attention seems to have been paid to the 1990 statute.

The 1990 act sets out to establish "policy" in an area where it suggests there has been none. Without attributing agency to any particular subject, it recognizes that "acts" to suppress Native American languages have occurred.[4] It attributes the causality to a "lack" from which the earlier "acts" resulted. The act states: "there is a lack of clear, comprehensive, and consistent Federal policy on treatment of Native American languages which has often resulted in acts of suppression and extermination of Native American languages and cultures" (101 (5)). The Senate report on the 1990 bill attributes responsibility or at least agency to the U.S. government and its "unwritten policy":

> It was once the unwritten policy of the United States government to reprimand children for speaking their own languages in school. They were made to feel like foreigners in their classrooms, and, worse, in their own homelands.[5]

According to the 1990 law, a language preservation policy now furthers "the United States policy of self-determination for Native American peoples" (102 (8)), as well as furthering other U.S. interests. U.S., state, and territorial "interests" include encouragement of "the full academic and human potential achievements of all students and citizens" (102 (7)). The act

> encourages and supports the use of Native American languages as a medium of instruction in order to encourage and support—
>
> (A) Native American language survival,
>
> (B) educational opportunity,

[4] For more about these acts and resistance to them, see Allison M. Dussias, "Waging War with Words: Native Americans' Continuing Struggle Against the Suppression of Their Languages," *Ohio State Law Journal* 60 (1999): 901.

[5] Senate Report No. 101–250, on S. 1781, Select Committee on Indian Affairs, March 7, 1990, 2, as reproduced in Senate Report 101–371 (on S. 2167, into which S. 1781 was incorporated), in *Congressional Record*, vol. 136, 1841 (1990).

(C) increased student success and performance,
(D) increased student awareness and knowledge of their culture
and history, and
(E) increased student and community pride. (104 (3))

Language preservation is a matter of "policy" not simply because of its relevance to U.S. interests, though, but because of the importance of language survival to "culture." The Senate report continues:

> Yet Native Americans resisted giving up their cultures. The result is that today, some indigenous cultures are still very traditional and intact while others have nearly lost their identities. With the change of policy by the United States government in the 1970's to one of self-determination, Native Americans have been able to begin to reverse the trends that have been so destructive to their cultures. Yet the low socioeconomic and health status of Native Americans underscores the fact that many Native Americans are still lost between two cultures and there are not assurances that native cultures are still not in danger of extinction. (1841)

Although loss, destruction, and extinction, of languages, cultures, and identities are clearly linked in these texts, their precise relations remain unclear. The "result," presumably of the unwritten policy of language suppression, not simply of resistance to it, is that cultures have "nearly lost" their identities. Their members are "lost between two cultures." Languages are key to culture, although exactly how varies in the report and the legislation. Languages may be part of a whole of culture, or language may be the basic medium for the transmission of culture or, again, the means of communication that safeguards the integrity of a culture. "The traditional languages of Native Americans are an integral part of their cultures and identities." They also "form the basic medium for the transmission, and thus survival, of Native American cultures, literatures, histories, religions, political institutions, and values" (102 (3)). They are "the means of communication for the full range of human experiences and are critical to the survival of cultural and political integrity of any people" (102 (9)) and also "provide a direct and powerful means of promoting international communication by people who share languages" (102 (10)). Native Americans "express themselves" through the medium of Native American languages, which are "direct and powerful means" of communication.

The Senate report on the 1992 NALA cites a 1989 select committee report on an Alaskan languages act approvingly to reinforce its claim as to the value of language to culture:

> Language is the basis of culture. . . . History, religion, values, feelings, ideas and the way of seeing and interpreting events are expressed and understood through

language. When others place meanings and definitions on words that are from a language that is not their culture, the original meanings of the words and the concepts they represent become lost. When a language is lost or forgotten, the integrity and identity of the group is diminished.[6]

Making language the "basis" of culture and words the representation of concepts, the 1992 Senate report again notes the diminution of group integrity and identity that corresponds to loss of the group's language. The manner in which such dual loss occurs is not explained. But the 1992 report—unlike the 1990 and 1992 acts—provides a clue as to the per- ceived relation between language and culture. It draws on the work of "a noted linguist" to explain what is at stake in language loss:

> In an essay entitled, "The World's Languages in Crisis," [Michael] Krauss de- clared that "Language endangerment is significantly comparable to . . . endan- germent of biological species in the natural world. . . . Languages no longer being learned as mother-tongue by children are beyond mere endangerment, for, unless the course is somehow dramatically reversed, they are already doomed to extinction, like species lacking reproductive capacity." (2955)

In the final sentence of the passage immediately above, "they" who "like species lacking reproductive capacity" are "doomed to extinction" may refer to "languages" unspoken by children or to "children" without mother-languages. The ambiguity here is telling. In conflating language with children, speech with biology, the 1992 report insists on a necessity and functionality of spoken language that makes language the link be- tween the natural and biological and the cultural.[7]

The 1992 report notes that the 1990 NALA had provided that the presi- dent direct the heads of the various federal departments, agencies, and

---

[6] Senate Report No. 103–343, Select Committee on Indian Affairs, Report to accompany S.2044, July 27, 1992; included in Legislative History of P.L. 102–524; in *Congressional Record*, vol. 138, 2956 (1992).

[7] Language here functions like "environment" in wildlife preservation, where naturalists battle for the preservation of, for instance, native plant species against encroachment by "escaped exotics" and other "aliens." See Ron Brean and Laura Svendsgaard-Brean, "Aliens in our Midst: A Perspective on Non-Native Species," in California State Parks Foundation, *Parklands* newsletter, 1998. See also Jean Comaroff and John Comaroff, "Naturing the Nation: Aliens, Apocalypse and the Postcolonial State," *International Social Science Review* 1 (2000): 7; also published in *Journal of Southern African Studies* 27 (2001): 627, and in *Social Identities* 7 (2001): 233. Despite his invocation in the report, Michael Krauss else- where speaks of himself both as a linguist "who is supposed to view languages as objects of scientific study" and as one who believes "speaking of the sacredness of things . . . that somehow or other [languages] elude us, because every language has its own divine spark of life." "Status of Native American Language Endangerment," *Stabilizing Indigenous Lan- guages*, ed. Gina Canatoni (Flagstaff: Northern Arizona University, Center for Excellence in Education, Monograph Series, 1997), 16.

instrumentalities to evaluate their policies and procedures and to bring them into compliance with the act. "The President shall submit a report to Congress on these within a year" (106 (a)). President Bush apparently made clear, in his signing of the bill, that he considered the directive advisory.[8] Despite what the 1992 Senate report called "repeated requests" from the chairman of the Select Committee on Indian Affairs for a government-wide report, the only report to appear in response to the 1990 NALA was that of the Bureau of Indian Affairs (2957).[9] The 1992 act itself then authorized a grant program to support language preservation activities, such as "language training programs, development of materials, purchase of recording equipment and computers, compilation, transcription, and analysis of oral testimony, and conversion of existing facilities when necessary for the conduct of language programs."

The Native American Graves Protection and Repatriation Act

Native Americans silences are often perceived as incompatible with U.S. law—or with the "compliance" and "cooperation" that legal officials today associate with law. The Native American Free Exercise of Religion Act of 1993 (NAFERA) aims to "protect and preserve the inherent right of any Native American to believe, express, and exercise his or her traditional religion" (103 § 1021) or, in the words of its sponsor, "to assure religious freedom to native Americans."[10] A response to the perceived inadequacies of the 1978 American Indian Religious Freedom Act (AIRFA), whose more narrow purpose was "ensuring that the management of Federal lands does not undermine and frustrate traditional native American religious practices,"[11] NAFERA has proved quite controversial, precisely over its "secrecy" provisions.

One of NAFERA's provisions accords protection in the consultation process to Native American religions that forbid the disclosure of information relating to beliefs and practices, including the locations of religious places. A published comment on that portion of NAFERA

[8] Dussias, "Waging War with Words," 945.

[9] See, however, Scott Ellis Ferrin, "Reasserting Language Rights of Native American Students in the Face of Proposition 227 and Other Language-Based Referenda," *Journal of Law & Education* 28 (1999): 4, mentioning (without reference), President Bush's delivery of a report of "only one slender page—a page that asserted that no Federal laws needed to be amended to comply with the provisions of the Act."

[10] Senator Inouye, quoted in Comment, "Sacred Sites and Federal Land Management: An Analysis of the Proposed Native American Free Exercise of Religion Act of 1993," *Natural Resources Journal* 34 (1994): 450.

[11] "Sacred Sites," 449–50.

states, "From the perspective of land managers, the secrecy section is of major difficulty, and perhaps entirely unworkable."[12] The comment continues,

> Under § 105(a)(1), an aggrieved party has the burden of proving that an undertaking "is positing [sic, posing] or will pose a substantial threat of undermining or frustrating a Native American religious practice." In contrast, when a tribe has certified under § 104(b) that their religion requires secrecy, the burden of proof shifts to the government to demonstrate a compelling interest under § 105(b)(1) in pursuing the proposed undertaking as originally proposed.
>
> This shifting of burdens based on secrecy implies that religious practices requiring secrecy are somehow more deserving of statutory deference than religious practices not similarly restricted. (461–62)

The comment proposes an alternative for dealing with burden of proof when Native American religions prohibit disclosure of information related to beliefs and practices. The solution lies in speech:

> Many land managers and Native American groups have learned to work creatively together throughout the years. The impetus has often been a requirement for legal compliance, but the basis, when cooperation has occurred, has always been a willingness to listen to each other and to learn to see something of another world view. (463)

Mutual "willingness to listen" is not necessarily an explicitly spoken exchange, although the comment treats it as such. Such treatment underscores that some U.S. officials take "legal compliance" and "cooperation" at law to be incompatible with religious silence, secrecy, or confidentiality.[13] Official solutions to problems of secrecy and silence involve disclosure through formal or informal speech. They make of Native American silences "no longer a phenomenon on its own," as Max Picard says of silence, but a "word that has not yet been spoken."

> Just as there is no difference today between silence and language (silence is no longer a phenomenon on its own, but merely the word that has not yet been spoken), so there is today no longer any difference between what has and what has not yet been investigated. What has not yet been investigated, what is still hidden and mysterious, is no longer a phenomenon in itself but simply that which has not yet been investigated.[14]

---

[12] "Sacred Sites," 461.

[13] See Lloyd Burton, *Worship and Wilderness: Culture, Religion, and Law in Public Lands Management* (Madison: University of Wisconsin Press, 2002), for examples of what may be interpreted as compromises on these points, however.

[14] Max Picard, *The World of Silence*, trans. Stanley Godman (Chicago: H. Regnery, 1952), 75.

The approach of U.S. law to Native religions bears out Picard's point. The most sacred and mysterious matters are unburied, exposed as objects of social scientific investigation. The Native American Graves Protection and Repatriation Act of 1990 (NAGPRA) provides an example.[15] It touches on one of the most sacred matters of many religions: death and the treatment of the dead. Characterized by some as an issue on which all Native Americans could agree, the Repatriation Act is ostensibly grounded in unassailable values of cultural pluralism that are formulated in terms supported by social research. But at least some Native Americans would not speak on the issue, and others explicitly limited what they did say. In the context of a debate that is framed in terms of both the values of cultural preservation and those of science or the pursuit of knowledge, the silence of some Native Americans around the issue speaks to the loudness and limits of the words of official law today.

The Repatriation Act requires museums and agencies (including universities) receiving federal funding to compile an inventory of their "holdings or collections of Native American human remains and associated funerary objects" and to identify their "geographical and cultural affiliation." Once such affiliation is established, request by "a known lineal descendant of the Native American or of the tribal organization" requires the "expeditious return" of the remains.[16]

Reports of congressional testimony and public debate about the Repatriation Act often characterize the issue as two-sided: on the one hand, a matter of scientific pursuit and academic freedom; on the other, a matter of human rights and religious freedom. Yet things are clearly more complicated. Museum and university experts—mainly anthropologists and archaeologists—indeed appeal to the usefulness of the bones in their collections for medical research and for learning about the past. Bones are "sources" of knowledge; one can learn tribal social structure, for instance, by analyzing the age, sex, stature, diseases, injuries of skeletons in their collections—or rather, as Native Americans charged, in their closets. For many outspoken Native Americans did not object to science as such. Rather they invoked scientific standards to accuse scientists of shoddy storage of unused artifacts in roomfuls of unlabeled cardboard boxes, for instance, or of retention of bones beyond the period needed for study. Anthropologists responded that, "Just as in a library, there might be a book that is not used all the time but which is necessary to

---

[15] *Public Law 101–601.*

[16] Arizona State Law Journal 24:1 (1992) contains an invaluable collection of articles on repatriation.

keep as a resource in the event that someone needs it—bones work in the same way."[17]

Some Native Americans did note that "remains are classified as 'resources' rather than as human remains" by scientists[18] or claimed that social scientists' appeals were based on "the non-Indian value that is placed on scientific research and public education."[19] Seeking respect for Native American religions and culture and dignity for the remains of their ancestors, Native Americans did not appeal to their own religions, however. This is in some sense not surprising, given that the dichotomy between "sacred" and "secular" is apparently Western in origin and foreign to many Native peoples.[20] Native Americans instead turned to "internationally understood human rights principles"[21] and to standards "in a Christian nation."[22]

Museums accepted the value of respecting other cultures. They asserted that the motivations and effects of their collections of "Native American material" were sympathetic to the Native American cause.[23] Museums claimed to counter

> policies and practices of our government . . . effecting rapid deterioration or outright disappearance of traditional Native American society and cultural practices.
>
> At a time when Native American art and cultural material was widely considered to be nothing more than "curios" by the general public, museums exercised social leadership by collecting objects they recognized as art and important and significant cultural material.

[17] Steve Heimoff, "Angle of Repose," *East Bay Express*, July 21, 1989, citing interview with Dr. Tim White, UC Berkeley's Lowie Museum of Anthropology. (The new user-oriented approach that many research libraries have adopted during the budget-shrinking era of the 1990s suggests that print collections may no longer be the resources to be kept in the event of need that White suggests they are.)

[18] United Indian Nations in Oklahoma, Resolution passed by Inter-Tribal Council, December 20, 1989.

[19] Testimony presented by Edward Lone Fight, National Congress of American Indians, before the Select Committee on Indian Affairs, U.S. Senate, December 1989. See also Renee M. Kosslak, Comment: "The NAGPRA: The Death Knell of Scientific Study," *American Indian Law Review* 24:1 (1999–2000): 142–46, regarding the tension between Indian beliefs and archaeology.

[20] Richard Keeling, "The Sources of Indian Music: An Introduction and Overview," in *World of Music* 34:2 (1992): 3, 4.

[21] Statement of Suzan Shown Harjo, president and executive director of the Morning Star Foundation, on the NAGPRA, S.1980, before the Select Committee on Indian Affairs, U.S. Senate, May 14, 1990.

[22] Edward Lone Fight, Testimony.

[23] Statement of Thomas A. Livesay, director, Museum of New Mexico, on behalf of American Association of Museums, before the Select Committee on Indian Affairs, U.S. Senate, May 14, 1990, 2.

In a statement that seems somewhat schizophrenic as to whether things or persons are the objects of their respect,[24] museums acknowledged that they had not always been so enlightened:

> For years our museum had collected Native American material without a social conscience or only an occasional nod to the tribes that were responsible for producing these goods. There are museums that have been guilty of viewing these Native Americans as curiosities or resources. We must learn to educate ourselves; to respect the purpose of the object as much as we appreciate the aesthetic results. And logically, this respect must extend itself to people—to Native Americans and to the tribes.[25]

The "human rights" concern for Native Americans rested on a shared perception of the widespread inequity with which a dominant culture had treated Native Americans, their land, and their values. A spokesperson for the Panel for a National Dialogue on Museum/Native American Relations (organized by the Heard Museum's Barry M. Goldwater Center for Cross-Cultural Communication) "put it bluntly":

> [M]useums and similar institutions would not now have possession of most of these materials if Native Americans had been accorded full citizenship rights, full rights of equal protection and full and equal human respect during the period of America's dynamic expansion across the continent. The retention by museums, against a tribe's will, of sensitive materials that are part of the tribe's heritage or religion, and that were taken from that tribe without its freely given consent, constitutes not only a bitter reminder, but also a contemporary perpetuation, of acts of discrimination and injustice.[26]

All parties thus acknowledged their commitment to a "humanist" position that called for recognizing religious, tribal, and cultural values and for abstaining whenever possible from interfering with their expression. This tolerant stance toward tribal cultures characterized both the Native American position and that of museum administrators.

Those both for and against the Repatriation Act also expressed their positions in terms of, or at least compatible with, social science. Parties

---

[24] See also the American Association of Museums' "Comparison of Repatriation Legislation," which charts the meaning of particular provisions in several bills. In an embarrassing Freudian slip, the memo describes the meaning of "Indian Tribe" under the Smithsonian bill (National American Indian Museum Act) as "a tribe, band, nation, or other organized group or *commodity* of Indians recognized by the United States, and such terms include an Alaska Native" (emphasis added).

[25] Livesay, statement, 2–3, 10.

[26] Testimony presented by Paul Bender, facilitator, Panel for a National Dialogue on Museum/Native American Relations, before the Select Committee on Indian Affairs, U.S. Senate, May 14, 1990, 3–4.

generally agreed that bones serve as sources of knowledge, that scientific standards must be met, that attention must be paid to preserving cultural values. Although Native Americans argued that the remains were important for Native American religious reasons, they did not make their own religious arguments. They did not argue why or how particular artifacts were important from *within* religious traditions, but explained the religion from outside. For them, as for the anthropologist, as in the legislation, "sacred" objects meant "specific ceremonial objects which are needed by traditional Native American religious leaders for the practice of traditional Native American religions by their present day adherents." Native American establishment of "cultural affiliation" or lineage and descent from particular bones in the act turns not on Native American religious assertions, but on factors accessible to sociology and biology. As a University of California policy implementing the Repatriation Act indicated:

> Cultural affiliation refers to a relationship of shared group identity which can be reasonably traced historically or prehistorically between a present day Indian tribe and an identifiable earlier group. Evidence to establish cultural affiliation may include biological, geographical, kinship, archeological, anthropological, linguistic, folkloric, oral tradition, historical, or other relevant information or expert opinion. In the inventory, specific and direct biological continuity shall be given priority in establishing cultural affiliation.[27]

Like the Native American Languages Acts' concern for language, then, the Repatriation Act's concern for religion grounds itself in both biological and social scientific knowledge. Both the Repatriation Act and the languages acts, as well as the disputes surrounding them, presume that persons and things in the world can be articulated in terms of biological and social sciences. Native Americans' bones are objects of religious practice just as their languages are instruments of communication. Religion and language constitute cultural resources in what Heidegger would call an age of "technique" (usually translated "technology," as in William Lovitt's translation of Heidegger's "The Question concerning Technology"). In such an age, the world is raw material for exploitation; everything becomes object to the subject that is modern man. Through precise methods, modern man develops the concepts that allow him to master and mold the universe to his own ends. "Nature and spirit" alike become objects for this self-conscious subject whose power compels from these objects a uniformity that respects neither identity nor difference. Such

---

[27] University of California, Office of the President, "Policy and Procedures on Repatriation of Human Remains and Cultural Items," April 1, 1991, 2. I thank Betty Lou Bradshaw in the University of California Office of the President for generous help in orienting me to relevant issues and materials.

"technique" attributes autonomy and the right of domination over all objects of the world to human—social—action.

Even as NAGPRA affirms the religion of Native Americans, then, it reveals—unsurprisingly in a secular state—the articulation at law of the issue of what to do with skeletal remains in language that belongs to scientific rather than religious discourse. The laws and those engaged in the debates around them propositionally describe not only Native American religions and practices, however, but also the U.S. policy. As legislation, law takes the form of statements of rules accompanying definitions and findings of facts and values about social objects.

Telling Silences

The silences of some Native Americans around their rites and rituals, in contrast to and in the context of the loquacious legislation of the United States, remind one of what at times may seem commonplace—that practices and knowledges of what to do need not be articulated and may not be articulable. Practices need not be articulated in the sense that they can be transmitted without words (through example or custom, as rules rather than rule formulations, and so forth). Practices are not articulable, in two senses. First, actions cannot be entirely grasped in statements and propositions.[28] Second, some practices refer to what is to be kept in mystery. Native American silences suggest the potential destructiveness of particular sorts of exposure and articulation of practices; in so doing, they disclose the doubly unspeakable in and to U.S. law. What is unspeakable here is not only that which cannot be spoken, but also that which in its speaking is destructive in that it cannot properly be heard.

Stories of Native American silences—of refusals to speak, of secrets kept, of tales untold but not forgotten—abound. Botanists locate only eight individual Kearney's blue-stars and declare the species practically extinct. The Tohono O'odham (Desert People) then lead botanists to a "secret refuge" of hundreds of the plants.[29] When he was young, a Hopi clanmember learned that certain teachings, traditions, and prophecies were only to be told when a gourd of ashes fell from the sky. He interprets the 1945 atomic bombs as such a gourd.[30]

[28] See Hubert L. Dreyfus and Stuart E. Dreyfus, "From Socrates to Expert Systems: The Limits of Calculative Rationality," in *Interpretive Social Science: A Second Look*, ed. Paul Rabinow and William M. Sullivan (1987).

[29] William Stolzenberg, "Sacred Peaks, Common Grounds," *Nature Conservancy*, September–October 1992, 17–23.

[30] Richard O. Clemmer, "The Hopi Traditionalist Movement," *American Indian Culture and Research Journal* 18:3 (1994): 125.

These particular stories concern what ultimately is said. What is said in these stories, though, is what has long been unsaid. The unsaid can become said. As in many stories, its silence may open into speech. But some silences are not simply unsaid.

Reading silence is of course problematic, taken by some as just short of random or arbitrary divination.[31] Contemporary law and politics do interpret silence, however, as do social sciences more broadly, if only, as Ron Scollon puts it, through the metaphor of the malfunction of a speech machine.[32] Liberal political institutions, supported by liberal political and constitutional theory, as chapter 2 noted, continually assert the need for citizens to speak, to participate, to have input into governmental and public decisions. In the context of political speech, dialogue, participation, surveys, voice, and vote, silence often appears either as a lack to be remedied or as itself a form of "voice" that signifies acquiescence or consent. James C. Scott, in *Domination and the Arts of Resistance*, transforms silence into speech within an excluded group, which is then used to resist the dominant group.[33]

Reading the silences of Native Americans need not transform silence into power/resistance, however, nor revert to the stereotype of the silent Indian that Keith H. Basso and others have set out to combat. Basso in 1970 challenged the common portrayal of American Indian silence as "the outgrowth of such dubious causes as 'instinctive dignity,' an 'impoverished language' or, perhaps worst of all, the Indians' 'lack of personal warmth.' "[34] Basso classified "situations" in which the Western Apache keep silent. He turned to "acts of silence" and their interpretations (68) to suggest that keeping silent among the Western Apache is a response to ambiguity, uncertainty, or unpredictability in social relations (83). Since Basso's groundbreaking work, others too have argued against the view of the "Silent Indian" as passive, sullen, withdrawn, unresponsive, lazy, backward, destructive, hostile, uncooperative, antisocial, or stupid.[35]

Basso suggests that his work may help explain silence behavior beyond Apache cultures. Certainly, the history of encounters between Native Americans and non-Native Americans in what is now the United States has been a history of ambiguous and uncertain (if now retrospectively

[31] See, by contrast, Peter Tiersma, "The Language of Silence," *Rutgers Law Review* 38 (1995): 1.

[32] Ron Scollon, "The Machine Stops: Silence in the Metaphor of Malfunction," in *Perspectives on Silence*, ed. Deborah Tannen and Muriel Saville-Troike (Norwood, NJ: Ablex, 1985), 21–30.

[33] James C. Scott, *Domination and the Arts of Resistance: Hidden Transcripts* (New Haven: Yale University Press, 1990).

[34] Keith. H. Basso, " 'To Give Up on Words': Silence in Western Apache Culture," in *Language and Social Context*, ed. Pier Paolo Giglioli (Baltimore: Penguin, 1972), 67.

[35] Scollon, "The Machine Stops," 21–30.

predictable) situations in which Basso's account of Native Americans' silence behavior seems apt. But the character of the situation in which a
participant responds by being silent need not be what the silence of the
participant says. Even when silence is a response to ambiguity, for instance, it need not express ambiguity. It may express fear, hatred, caution,
love, respect; it may be a habit or decision or choice; it might say nothing
and it might say much more.[36]

The secrecy and silence of at least some Native Americans suggests
that the very speaking or articulating in the American public forum of
the truths of their religions or of their own ways concerning death and
the body may constitute a betrayal of those very truths. Just as social
science transforms or translates "religion" and the "sacred" into its
own terms, that is, Native silences suggest that so too does law. The
articulations of U.S. law—the procedures of the Repatriation Act, the
wording of the languages acts—translate other law, the ways of Native
Americans speaking in the first-person plural, into the sociological terms
of the third person, which are then spoken back to Native Americans.[37]
In the transformation of the first person, who may not have spoken,
into a third person about whom facts are known, and thence into a
presumed second-person "you" who will have been presumed to be
addressed as such, lies the legal positivist and social scientific misrecogni-
tion of other ways.

In the context of belated efforts to preserve Native American language
and culture, the relation of silence to culture becomes increasingly problematic. Many identify not speaking a particular language with the silence
that indicates the end or the death of that culture.[38] Those who stop speak-

---

[36] On cross-cultural comparison, see William J. Samarin, "Language of Silence," *Practical Anthropology* 12 (1965): 115.

[37] One is reminded of Eugen Rosenstock-Huessy's argument that Alexandrinian lists of
grammatical forms cauterize the social sensibilities of the objects of our educational system
(114). Using the table "*amo, amas, amat*, . . ." Rosenstock-Huessy shows how each would
work as an utterance. "Whereas *amat* is debatable as to truth, *amas* is debatable as to
authority, *amo* is debatable as to wisdom. . . . In grouping our three sentences as modes of
behavior, *amat* stands disclosed as a dualism of our power to know, *amas* as the evaluation
of our power of authority, *amo* as our power to reveal our secrets. Hence, knowledge (third
person); authority (second person); communion (first person) are faced with three different
hurdles . . . knowledge faces problems of fact, of truth or falsity, of information or observation . . . authority faces the dilemma between the listener's freedom and his necessity . . .
communion faces the decision between being silent and speaking out." "Grammar as Social
Science" (1970), in *Speech and Reality*, 107.

[38] See "With World Opening Up, Languages Are Losers," *New York Times*, Sunday, May
16, 1999, Late Edition–Final, section 1, 17, describing the situation of the last fluent speaker
of Chamicuro in the Peruvian Amazon. "[L]inguists say when Sangama dies, the language
will die with her."

　　Many of the world's languages are disappearing as modern communications, migra-
　　tion and population growth end the isolation of ethnic groups. Linguists warn that

ing a language are often thought to be young or upwardly mobile, leaving
the indigenous language or old culture behind to move into a mainstream
language and culture that provides desirable benefits, resources, and status. Compulsory or universal public education, linguists claim, weans indigenous speakers from their cultures as language substitutions occur. As
the old language no longer supplies usable words, they claim, its terminology and rules fail to develop. Not speaking the old language, according
to this view, is to reject or forget the old ways and to do so rationally.

The silences of Native Americans (like the best of language programs,
one suspects),[39] raise another possibility: that of "ways" that cannot be
spoken in the terminology of U.S. law and the social study of language.
Native silences remind us of ways of knowing the world other than through
Western rationality. They remind us that not all law need tell its addressees
what to do through utterances. Today, official "declarations" tell persons
subject to the law what to do in the language of concepts and of ends-
means thinking that Heidegger calls technique. (Chapter 4 will explore
further what technique means for language; chapters 5 and 6, for law.) To
think of a law that is inaccessible to propositional articulations of policies
grounded in findings and definitions strikes one as odd. But the "telling
what to do" that is law, as Native American silences remind us, need not
only be the declarations of officials or the statements of regulations that
show up as propositional articulations of legislation and court opinions.

The law of nonpositivist custom or tradition may tell one what to do
without regard for social science or its worldview and without the sorts
of utterances associated with modern law. Today custom appears in social
science as the behavioral norms of others. It appears in legislation as rules
about the cultures of others. Just as custom is never completely susceptible
to social scientific description, though, neither is it completely within the
grasp of U.S. law (or of positive law; recall "Sociolegal Positivism" in
chapter 1). Some laws cannot be heard in the language of American law
and social science: they cannot be said in its terms or they are not spoken
or speakable at all.

The silences of Native Americans bring into relief not only the loquaciousness of modern American law, but also the way that positive law
grounds itself in what it takes to be relevant social knowledge of cultural
facts and values. Modern U.S. law conforms to social scientific discourse
and to a legal positivist conception of itself. Like legal positivism, it partakes in a particular regime of truth—an *episteme*—in which the speaking

---

one result is a "crash" in cultural and intellectual diversity similar to what many biolo-
gists say is happening in animal and plant species as wilderness areas are cleared.

Each language contains words that uniquely capture ideas, and when the words
are lost, so are the ideas, linguists say.

[39] See Mark Abley, "The Words that Come Before All Else: Mohawk," in *Spoken Here:
Travels Among Threatened Languages* (Boston: Houston Mifflin, 2003), 163–89.

of truth—including the telling what to do of law—is the utterance of propositions about what exists in the present, what has existed in the past, and what will exist in the future of society. The propositions of modern law are compatible with a legal positivism that, again, takes law to be the official declarations or descriptive statements of rules that members of a society generally obey.[40]

Modern law is a matter of fact. It is grounded in empirical investigation and informed by sociological knowledge of values and preferences. Its very existence corresponds to empirically verifiable procedural norms or to public attitudes. Its authority, like its validity or existence, is a verifiable matter that itself turns on propositionally articulable (and social psychological—recall discussion of Tyler, in chapter 1) facts of belief in the legitimacy of the system. Within this context, the silence of citizens becomes obedience that, interpreted as the loyalty or consent of a silent majority, bolsters the system.

When law accepts the discourse of social science as its own, law becomes indistinguishable, as in Nietzsche's fifth moment, from social policy. Here lies the oft-unrecognized crux of debates as to the place of social research at law.[41] The issue is less how or whether social research affects the law that should be. It is rather how the sociological worldview adopted in law—admittedly articulated there in a less sophisticated manner than much of the research itself—takes law to be the social means to produce social ends. In starkest terms, is law other than a tool of social self-constitution, a social policy produced by social knowledges that gauge the social options in, and social preferences of, a society governed by social policy? What else could law be?

Against a background of possibilities of law that cannot be said in the language of—or, what comes to the same, heard in—American political forums, appears the significance of the nineteenth- and twentieth-century development of the currently pervasive human or social sciences that presume that practices are propositionally knowable and explicitly articulable: such *savoirs* readily ally themselves with an understanding of law as propositions or statements of rules. To those for whom practices are law, the social scientific translation of actions or deeds into knowledge of words and facts itself may betray truth, as it seems to do for some Native

[40] Recall from chapter 1 that H.L.A. Hart maintains that the existence of a legal system requires two types of rules: the primary rules that citizens generally obey, which are marked as valid through secondary rules that officials accept as rules of practice (*The Concept of Law*, 113). For Hart, both types of rules are statements of rules. Rules are discussed further in chapter 5.

[41] Austin Sarat and Susan Silbey, "The Pull of the Policy Audience," *Law and Policy* 8:1 (1986): 7; Erickson and Simon, *Social Science Data*; Patricia Ewick, Robert A. Kagan, and Austin Sarat, *Social Science, Social Policy and the Law* (New York: Russell Sage Foundation, 1999).

Americans. From this perspective, U.S. law, in its readiness to declare what to do propositionally in terms of "facts" and "values" that together are thought to exhaust possibilities of knowledge about the world, swallows the truths of social science.

The Shell of a World?

The poet Gary Snyder tells of a friend of his, a student of California Native languages, who visits an old Indian man, Louie, one of "perhaps no more than three" surviving speakers of Nisenan. The linguist tells Louie of another person he has found who speaks Nisenan. "I know her from way back," Louie replies. "She wouldn't want to come over here. I don't think I should see her. Besides, her family and mine never did get along."

"That took my breath away," writes Snyder:

> Here was a man who would not let the mere threat of cultural extinction stand in the way of his (and her) values. To well-meaning sympathetic white people this response is almost incomprehensible. In the world of his people, never over-populated, rich in acorn, deer, salmon, and flicker feathers, to cleave to such purity, to be perfectionists about matters of family or clan, were affordable luxuries. Louie and his fellow Nisenan had more important business with each other than conversations. I think he saw it as a matter of keeping their dignity, their pride, and their own ways—regardless of what straits they had fallen upon—until the end.[42]

What is one to make of Louie's reluctance to converse with a fellow Nisenan? of Snyder's breathless celebration of it? of the incomprehensibility of Louie's response to "well-meaning white people"? What is cultural extinction? What is a culture's relation to language? To speech? What is the relation of language to a people? To its "own ways"?

These are not simple questions. At a time when multiculturalism and diversity are all the rage, Louie's silence —or, perhaps, Snyder's story— raises prickly issues about relations between white people, the good intentions of cultural preservation, and the Native ways in which "cultural preservation" as such seemingly has no place. Who is responsible for a culture? For its preservation or loss? For whom are cultures preserved? At what cost? And, again, to whom? As English historian Gillian Tindall puts it in another context, writing of a French village in which she has passed twenty summers:

> I feel divided in my mind about the dancers in smocks at the *fetes* and the loving reconstruction of Sarzay. On the one hand, there is the simple perception that

---

[42] Gary Snyder, *The Practice of the Wild* (San Francisco: North Point Press, 1990), 3–4.

if places, objects and customs are not preserved, then we are lost, and that therefore preservation efforts must on balance be a good thing. But there is the more sophisticated knowledge that to preserve things deliberately, for the sake of doing so, is to lose them in another way, and to risk keeping the shell of a world at the expense of its meaning.[43]

Not everyone will agree, given a choice between preservation and loss, that preserving "the shell of a world" constitutes a loss of its own. Nor will everyone call such knowledge sophisticated nor consider Louie's silence dignified. For many, critique of or resistance to cultural preservation flies in the face of pluralism and aspirations of multicultural democracy. To them, Louie's not-speaking is a willful refusal. What is unsaid in it no more points to the unsayable than do the everyday words of sociolegal studies.

The reluctance of a Native American to speak his language before the linguist who would preserve it, like the testimony of the poet as to the event of such a silence, can say something else, however. It highlights the way that so-called well-meaning white people take particular ways of knowing for granted. Louie's silence not only raises questions about cultural preservation and extinction but points toward what some linguists and lawyers forget: that one lives in one's language and that language is not an item to be collected or an object to be displayed.[44]

Snyder suggests that for Louie, turning from the ways of his people would lie in speaking Nisenan for well-meaning white people, rather than in not speaking Nisenan at all. For Snyder, Louie's silence gestures to a speech that is other than linguistic knowledge of terminology and application of the rules of language, whether in structure or performance, *langue* or *parole*, grammar or use. To Snyder, Louie's silence suggests that the loss of Louie's "own ways" and those of the Nisenan may accompany the linguist's very effort to preserve Nisenan language. In Snyder's terms, Louie's silence draws attention to what is lost in a people's culture that a preservation effort alone will not save—the relations of language and the world one inhabits. Louie lives in his language; it is true speech.[45]

The silences of Native Americans about their religions in American political and legal forums may point to possibilities of laws and of ways of

[43] Gillian Tindall, *Celestine: Voices from a French Village* (New York: Henry Holt, 1996), 269.

[44] See Leeann Hinton, *Flutes of Fire: Essays on California Indian Languages* (Berkeley: Heyday, 1994) and others as examples of linguists who may not forget.

[45] "Often Native American groups have no particular name for their language other than something equivalent to 'our language,' 'the language,' or 'the true speech.'" Lyle Campbell, *American Indian Languages: The Historical Linguistics of Native America* (New York: Oxford University Press, 1997), 57.

knowing what to do that differ from those of contemporary American politics and law. Some may ask: what exactly lies in Native American silences? How might Native ways be brought to bear on modern law? These are not the questions of this work, however. They call for empirical investigation into the ways of ostensibly silent others and for more accurate representations of a silent—or silenced—other. It suffices here that Native silences may hold not only what is unsaid in U.S. law, but also what U.S. law in some sense cannot hear.

Chapter 4 _____

Flags, Words, Laws, and Things

Law is a profession of words.
—David Mellinkoff, *The Language of the Law*

IN RESPONSE TO THE PROLOGUE's suggestion that modern law doesn't say much about justice, chapter 2 considered what (sociology says) law does. It found that sociology doesn't say much about law doing justice either, although (like other voices) sociology may call to justice. Chapter 3 claimed that modern law, like much sociology, may not hear certain things. This chapter now turns to what law does say and hear, by focusing on the American flag-burning cases that extend First Amendment protection of freedom of speech to symbolic speech.

The chapter again proceeds on two registers. First, the Supreme Court opinions show the pervasiveness in law of conceptions of language described in chapter 3 that belong to what Heidegger calls an age of technique. Second, the cases and public and legislative responses to them illustrate the peculiarity of the "profession of words" that is law. In law, as in the sociolegal studies and political voice of chapter 2, justice may go without saying. This chapter now shows how law names the profession—in the sense of "vocation" or "calling"—of words to justice.

Profession has at least three meanings: an open declaration or public avowal; an avowal in appearance only or a pretense; and an occupation, vocation, calling, or business in which proficiency or expertise is claimed. While the training and practices of lawyers, judges, paralegals, and other legal professionals most obviously draw the third definition into play, chapters 1 and 2 showed that many scholars at least take the "profession of words" that is law to be less an open declaration or public avowal than an avowal in appearance only or a pretense, insofar as whatever law claims, it is actually about social power. This chapter by contrast shows how law names avowals or declarations made in the name of justice.

The first section, "The Concept of Language," looks at construals of the U.S. flag in *Texas v. Johnson* to see how the Supreme Court understands language.[1] All of the opinions, including the dissents, consider the

---

[1] *Texas v. Johnson*, 491 U.S. 397; 109 S.Ct. 2533 (1989). Page references that follow refer to the Supreme Court Reporter.

flag to be a symbol. The majority treats burning the flag as akin to a performative utterance or speech act. It takes the symbol of the flag in this
case to be like the words of a language and declares the distinction between
word and symbol to be irrelevant. The second section, "Politics, Speech,
or Property?" turns to the responses—public, legislative, and judicial—that
follow *Texas v. Johnson*. Although the dissents in *Texas v. Johnson* argue
against First Amendment protection for flag burning, their ready acceptance of the symbolic character of the flag means that they are unable to
distinguish Texas's interest in the flag as a thing from its interest in a flag's
use as means of expression. The third section, "The Calling of Words,"
turns to the prevalence of characterizations of flags, words, and things as
strategic resources. It asks whether claims and declarations of law, conceived and articulated as strategic avowals, can still appeal to justice.

The Concept of Language

In 1984, while the Republican National Convention was taking place in
Dallas, Gregory Lee Johnson burned a U.S. flag in front of City Hall as
part of a protest against Reagan administration policies and certain Dal-
las-based corporations. Johnson was convicted of burning the American
flag under a Texas statute making desecration of venerated objects a
crime. In June 1989, a divided Supreme Court overturned Johnson's conviction. It ruled in *Texas v. Johnson* that applying the statute to Johnson
violated the First Amendment prohibition against government abridge-
ment of "speech."

The Supreme Court held, in a five-to-four decision with two written
opinions on each side, that Johnson's burning of the U.S. flag was "expressive conduct" protected under the First Amendment (2538–40). Brennan
wrote the majority opinion, in which Marshall, Blackmun, Scalia, and
Kennedy concurred. Kennedy also wrote his own opinion. O'Connor and
White joined Chief Justice Rehnquist's dissent. Stevens wrote a separate
dissent.

The majority first claimed that since Johnson's burning of the flag was
"expressive conduct," its regulation implicated—although could not yet
be said to violate—the First Amendment (2538). The majority then considered whether Texas's interest was in regulating the *nonspeech* element of
Johnson's conduct because, if so, this might justify "incidental limitations
of First Amendment freedoms."[2] It then argued that because Texas as-

[2] If not, then Texas's interest would be "related to the suppression of expression" and
"content-based," subject to standards of "strict scrutiny." *Texas v. Johnson*, 2540, citing
O'Brien; 2541–43, citing *Boos v. Barry*.

serted an interest "in preserving the flag as a symbol of nationhood and national unity," Texas's interest was indeed "related to expression" (2542) and that Johnson's conviction "depended on the likely communicative impact of his expressive conduct" (2543).[3] Using a standard of "strict scrutiny," then, the majority argued that the state's interest did not justify infringement of Johnson's First Amendment rights. The involvement of the flag in Johnson's case, it maintained, created no exception to the principle that the government cannot prohibit an idea just because society finds it offensive or disagreeable (2544–48).

The majority's argument relies on two facets of "expression," in both of which the flag functions linguistically or at least in the way that the majority believes words of a language operate. The first aspect of expression concerns communication; the second, signification. The first focuses attention on the activity of burning the flag; the second on the flag itself.

The majority first associates expression with communicating. Johnson's conduct, like the utterance of spoken or written word, it finds, is expressive. Johnson's conduct "possesses sufficient communicative elements to bring the First Amendment into play" because there is "intent to convey a particularized message" and "likelihood . . . that the message would be understood by those who viewed it." Characterizing expression as transmitting a message from a speaker with intent to a receiver who understands, the majority has "little difficulty" in "identifying an expressive element in conduct relating to flags" because "the very purpose of a national flag is to serve as a symbol of our country." It cites the flag salute cases: "Symbolism is a primitive but effective way of communicating ideas. The use of an emblem or flag to symbolize some system, idea, institution, or personality, is a short cut from mind to mind." Johnson's flag-burning conduct implicates the First Amendment, the majority continues, because "the expressive, overtly political nature of such conduct was both intentional and overwhelmingly apparent" (2539–40).

The majority rejects the State of Texas's claims that its interests are unrelated to the expressive aspect of Johnson's conduct. The majority rejects the state's distinction between nonverbal conduct (which the state claims it would be able to regulate) and written or spoken words. The distinction between nonverbal conduct and the use of words "is of no moment," writes the majority, "where the nonverbal conduct is expressive, as it is here, and where the regulation of that conduct is related to expression, as it is here" (2545). For the majority, the use of symbols,

---

[3] Texas also asserted an interest in preventing breaches of the peace that the Court found not to be implicated on the facts of Johnson's case, *Texas v. Johnson*, 2541–42.

expressive conduct, and linguistic "communication" function in the same way: a message is transparently transmitted via symbols from an intending speaker, a willing actor, or an active will to a receptive (in the sense of being able to understand) audience, an other mind.

The majority's insistence that the state's interest is "content-based" relates also to the second aspect of the majority's understanding of expression, the capacity of symbols or signs to signify. The majority affirms that the First Amendment ban on government prohibition of expression "is not dependent on the particular mode in which one chooses to express an idea" (2546). The majority here treats the flag itself as the "mode" chosen to express an idea, or as a symbol that, like the words of a language, serves as the communicative instrument by means of which a message is transmitted. The majority argues that as instrument or means of communication, the flag must be kept neutral or accessible to all. As an instrument or means, the flag is not already partial to particular ends or message-contents nor, the majority insists, must it become so. The majority maintains that the state's position implies that flag burning would be forbidden where it endangers the flag's symbolic role, but would be allowed where it promotes that symbolic role.[4] This would be as problematic, claims the majority, as "saying that when it comes to impairing the flag's physical integrity, the flag itself may be used as a symbol—as a substitute for the written or spoken word or a 'short cut from mind to mind'—only in one direction" (2546).

The majority considers the government's "interest in making efforts to preserve the national flag as an unalloyed symbol of our country"[5] to involve the flag's ability to "reflect . . . concepts." In the majority view, Texas is concerned that burning the flag "will lead people to believe either that the flag does not stand for nationhood and national unity, but instead reflects other, less positive concepts, or that the concepts reflected in the flag do not in fact exist, that is, we do not enjoy unity as a nation." Here the meaning of the flag for the majority consists in a relation of signifier to signified (something like word to concept), which itself depends on structures of relations to other signifiers and signifieds, respectively. *What* is signified is a concept, a mental representation of a thing, not a thing. "Pregnant with expressive content," writes the majority, "the flag as readily signifies this Nation as does the combination of letters found in 'America' " (2540).

---

[4] The state's position actually seems to be that in order to safeguard the symbolic power of the flag all flag-burning may be prohibited, whether it is in the service of a message for or against or neutral as to the nation. See Randall P. Bezanson, *Speech Stories: How Free Can Speech Be?* (New York: New York University Press, 1998), 187–205.

[5] *Texas v. Johnson*, 2547, citing *Spence*.

All languages have their dangers, as James Boyd White points out in a chapter on the language of concepts.[6] The language of concepts—and the language of the concept of language—is especially fraught. White argues, drawing on Wittgenstein, that the word *concept* draws attention away from language and what it says, or words and what they name, to internal or intellectual phenomena (28).

> To talk about concepts is . . . to take a step in the direction of talking as if words had no force of their own, as if they were in fact transparent or discardable once the idea or concept is apprehended. On this view, in its extreme form, the function of words is either to identify external phenomena that can be observed without the use of language—that rock, or tree, or person—or to define or clarify concepts, which are also thought to exist outside language and beyond culture. (29)

To White, utterances have meanings, not reducible to definition or rule. "Much of the meaning of words," he writes, "lies in silence, in the un-stated but accepted background against which they have their meaning" (34). J. L. Austin, as chapter 7 discusses further, would not use "meaning" the same way, but would share White's concern with what is unstated in utterances. Austin writes rather of the locutionary and illocutionary import of utterances. As a locutionary act or something said, an utterance cannot be reduced to its propositional content; neither, as an illocutionary act, can an utterance be reduced to satisfaction of required conventions. The point is that for both White and Austin, speaking draws something out of both language and silence, and in its saying something new arises. White continues, "It is not the words themselves but their various uses—or the ways they have been used—that have meaning. . . . It is an abuse of language to try to reduce its meaning to the restatable, the proposi-tional" (34), as talk of the "concept" of something tends to do.

When the majority writes that the flag, like "other concepts virtually sacred to our Nation as a whole," may not go "unquestioned in the mar-ketplace of ideas" (2546), it partakes in the kind of discourse that White describes. "One form of the kind of discourse that talk about concepts invites," he writes,

> is definitional, deductive, and empirical in nature, and in this sense fashioned on a certain model of science. In this way of talking, we define our terms on the assumption that they can be reduced to phrases that could substitute for them.

This understanding of "discourse," as White describes it, perfectly suits J. S. Mill. In White's understanding of this view,

---

[6] White, *Justice as Translation*, 26.

Rationality consists of manipulating these definitions in patterns of deductive coherence or hypothetical description that will be tested by reference to extra-linguistic phenomena, which will in turn establish whether they are true or false. Rational discourse, so conceived, is propositional in character; and knowledge, whether factual or conceptual, is of necessity propositional too. . . . At its center is an image of language that is transparent: our talk is about what is "out there" in the natural or conceptual world, to which it is the function of language to point. (29)

In the majority's talk of "concepts," then, protection of the flag, like protection of transparent language, accrues to a capacity to serve as a neutral instrument, to be kept accessible in all directions, and to a character that signifies "idea" or even "principle." The lack of "a separate juridical category" for the American flag means that the majority declines "to create for the flag an exception to the joust of principles protected by the First Amendment."

In sum, the majority looks to the use of the flag as a symbol to communicate, whose neutrality must be protected and whose instrumentality must be kept accessible to all, and to its form as a signifier of concepts or principles that, in the name of free speech, must take their challenges like any others. Implicitly taking language to be communicative symbol and sign, the majority sees no need to distinguish between expressive nonverbal conduct, symbolic or communicative speech, and use of the flag.

Meanwhile, like the State of Texas, the dissents attempt to dissociate the flag from this linguistic framework, referring instead to the more tangible visible embodiment that they take the American flag to be. Grounding their claims as to the importance of the flag on its character as a symbol undermines their own cause, however, since the majority takes symbolicity to be in the very nature of language.

Rehnquist's dissent, for instance, at first seems to reject the representational function of the flag and to affirm it as a tangible body. He writes, "The flag is not simply another 'idea' or 'point of view' competing for recognition in the marketplace of ideas," he writes. Immediately, though, his dissent imbues the flag with an intangible (although still nonlinguistic) aspect: "Millions and millions of American regard it with an almost mystical reverence regardless of what sort of social, political or philosophical beliefs they may have" (2552). The dissent then acknowledges that flag burning is expressive conduct (2553), while explaining that flag burning "is the equivalent of an inarticulate grunt or roar that, it seems fair to say, is most likely to be indulged in not to express any particular idea, but to antagonize others" (2553). The implication is that antagonizing others or conveying dislike, as such, not necessarily articulately nor in a manner expressing ideas, may properly be called "expression," although it would not be protected speech. (In J. L. Austin's terms, Rehnquist says in effect that although burning the flag is not a locutionary act or utterance [and hence is undeserving of the protection that the First Amendment presumably accords to illocutionary speech], burning the flag has a perlocutionary effect. The majority in effect takes the expressiveness of the burning of the flag to imply that burning the flag must be like a Searlian propositional statement or perhaps an Austinian locutionary act and hence deserving of protection.) Sharing neither the majority's view that flag-burning conduct involves an intent to convey a message, nor its view that the flag reflects "concepts," Rehnquist's dissent at first seems to view the "expression" that flag burning produces as nonlinguistic.

In arguing for the constitutionality of flag-burning prohibitions, however, the dissent's use of the vocabulary of symbol and expression implies that the flag functions the same way that the majority thinks language does. Discussing the flag's symbolic value, for instance, the dissent adopts "expression" not only to refer to the *effect* of flag burning, but also to refer to the burning of the flag as one of several *methods* of communication. Flag burning is a "relatively inarticulate form of protest," it claims, a mode or means of expression admittedly "profoundly offensive to many." The prohibition of flag burning leaves a flag burner "with a full panoply of other symbols and every conceivable form of verbal expression to express his deep disapproval of national policy" (2554). Although the dissent seeks to argue against the extension of First Amendment protection of speech to flag burning, it nevertheless accepts that the flag operates in the same ways as the majority thinks language works: as a symbol that communicates and as a signifier of ideas.

Speech is clearly at stake in *Texas v. Johnson*. All members of the Court understand the flag at least in part as a symbol that communicates and signifies in the same way as they take language to do. But discussions of the decision seem to focus less on speech than on politics.

Politics, Speech, or Property?

The announcement of the *Texas v. Johnson* decision, according to one law review article, "precipitated a tidal wave of adverse reaction."[7] Some characterized the decision as an "exercise of raw judicial power and the evasion of faithful constitutional and statutory interpretation."[8] State-

[7] R. Neill Taylor III, "The Protection of Flag Burning as Symbolic Speech and the Congressional Attempt to Overturn the Decision," *Cincinnati Law Review* 58 (1990): 1499.

[8] Douglas W. Kmiec, "In the Aftermath of *Johnson* and *Eichman*: The Constitution Need Not Be Mutilated to Preserve the Government's Speech and Property Interests in the Flag," *Brigham Young University Law Review* 1990: 638.

ments from the *New York Times* and the *Congressional Quarterly* immediately characterized the responses to *Texas v. Johnson* as partisan politics. Being "far from immune to this reaction," according to one
commentator, Congress and the president "busied themselves with attempts to overturn the decision."[9] Thirty-nine separate resolutions for a
constitutional amendment prohibiting flag desecration were introduced
in the House,[10] where hearings began July 13. By July 15, the "battle
lines" drawn in Congress concerned not whether to take action but
"whether to adopt a statutory or a constitutional solution."[11]

Media described proposals for flag-protection measures in strategic
terms, as attempts to "circumvent"[12] the Court or to "get around" the First
Amendment.[13] After two weeks of hearings and two days of debate, the
House Judiciary Committee passed a bill out of committee outlawing flag
burning and other physical desecration of the flag. Two similar proposals
had been introduced in the Senate—one as a bill; another, adopted by voice
vote, as an amendment to an unrelated bill. In October, after the Senate
failed to approve a constitutional amendment prohibiting flag desecration,
President Bush allowed the Flag Protection Act of 1989 to become law
without his signature.[14] The act criminalized the conduct of one who
"knowingly mutilates, defaces, physically defiles, burns, maintains on the
floor or ground, or tramples upon any flag of the United States."

Journalists attributed passage of the Flag Protection Act of 1989 to
political tides or political battles, both of which occurred against a background of opinion poll findings and the strategic mustering (or nonmus-
tering) of votes by elected officials. Not only journalists, but also witnesses
testifying at congressional hearings on the measures seemed to accept the
journalistic description of their position as instrumentally "political."
They spoke, for instance, of proposed measures as attempts to "avoid"
the second "prong" of the second part of the Court's argument or to
avoid judicial scrutiny while regulating speech they found offensive.

[9] Taylor, "Protection of Flag Burning," 1499.

[10] Joan Biskupic, "Flag-Burning Ruling Sparks Cries for Action on Hill," *Congressional Quarterly*, July 1, 1989, 1623.

[11] Joan Biskupic, "Critics of Flag-Burning Ruling Debate Next Step to Take," *Congressional Quarterly*, July 15, 1989, 1790.

[12] Bernard Weinraub, "Bush Seeking Way to Circumvent Court's Decision on Flag Burning," *New York Times*, June 27, 1989, I-1; Biskupic, "Flag-Burning Ruling," 1623; Frank Michelman, "Saving Old Glory: On Constitutional Iconography," *Stanford Law Review* 42 (1990): 1337.

[13] Joan Biskupic, "House Committee OKs Measure to Outlaw Flag Desecration," *Congressional Quarterly*, July 29, 1989, 1963.

[14] Passed House, September 12, 1989; the Senate amended and passed it October 5, 1989; House passed Senate version October 12, 1989; it became Public Law No. 101-131, 103 Stat. 777 (1989).

But some critics did suggest that flag protection measures need not be understood as politically instrumental attempts to evade the First Amendment or to change the law declared by or to rein in the power exercised by the Court. As one law professor testified before a House subcommittee, "the Supreme Court has never held . . . that there is a general 'right to burn the American flag.' " The Supreme Court had found the "flaw" in the Texas statute to be that the statute made "communication of an idea . . . essential to the commission of the crime. The 'governmental interest' is thus directly related to the message being communicated," he claimed. It would still be consistent with the Supreme Court opinion, this witness continued, for "the government [to] prohibit and punish flag-burning—even flag-burning done as part of a political protest—as long as the government has an interest that is unrelated to the message being conveyed."[15]

From this perspective, critics of the *Texas v. Johnson* decision appear concerned not with circumventing the law, but with articulating, in written law, what they take to be *already* implicit but unsaid in the Court's own articulations of constitutional law: the absence of an affirmative right to burn the flag. Viewed this way, the issue joining critics of *Texas v. Johnson* who favored legislation and those who favored constitutional amendment is neither patriotism, vote gathering, nor evasion of law, as journalists would have it, but law—or perhaps the silences of the law. Those favoring legislation sought to articulate in writing (as legislation) what they conceived to be compatible with the constitutional law articulated by the Court and not incompatible with the constitutional law that the Court had not articulated. Those favoring constitutional amendment sought to articulate in writing (as constitutional amendment), what they conceived to be constitutional law as it ought to be—although was not yet—articulated by the Court. As a critic of *Texas v. Johnson* said of those who favored constitutional amendment, "Many who have voiced their disagreement with the Supreme Court's decision in *Texas v. Johnson* first did so within minutes of hearing about that ruling in the most general terms. They are, in my view, disagreeing not with what the Court actually held, but with what they think it held."[16] Both those who favored constitutional amendment and those who favored statutory flag-protection could be said to be challenging not what they thought the Court actually held,

[15] Walter Dellinger, Duke University Law School, testimony, July 18, 1989, before Civil and Constitutional Rights Subcommittee of the House Judiciary Committee, 101st Congress, 1st Sess., *Congressional Record* (1989), reprinted in "Flag Desecration Legislation: Should a Constitutional Amendment to Prevent Flag Desecration Be Approved?" *Congressional Digest*, August–September 1989, 209.

[16] Lawrence H. Tribe, testimony, July 18, 1989, reprinted in "Flag Desecration Legislation," 215.

but what they feared others might think its silences held—an invitation to burn the flag.

In this reading, those who favored legislation and those who favored constitutional amendment appear concerned with articulation of law rather than its circumvention. Insofar as their concern is not to circumvent the law, the issue for them consists in a double problem of language and law: how to articulate as-yet-unspoken law; and how to affirm proper conduct toward the flag without regulating "expression."

Proponents of flag-protection measures took their cues about the problem and its solution in part from the *Texas v. Johnson* dissenting opinions. They noted, in particular, Rehnquist's claim in the dissent that an "entity constitutionally may obtain a limited property right in the word (or symbol)" (2552) and Stevens's suggestion that the flag may be a valuable "national asset."[17] Proponents of flag protection reasoned that treating the flag as *property* would entail an interest in the flag as a thing, whose integrity could then be protected irrespective of its expressive functions or use.[18]

Shortly after passage of the act, Shawn Eichman, Gregory Johnson (of *Texas v. Johnson* fame), and two others burned three flags on the steps of the Capitol to test the act's constitutionality. The Supreme Court agreed to a Bush administration request to rule quickly. In June 1990, in *United States v. Eichman*,[19] the Court held the Flag Protection Act, too, to be unconstitutional under the First Amendment.

Unfortunately for flag protection proponents, they had asserted an ostensible property interest in the flag as a thing in the same terms as those used to protect the flag's expressive function: in terms of symbolism. Thus an insuperable difficulty emerged for those favoring flag protection. The *Eichman* decision that followed less than a year after the Flag Protection Act turned on the issue. Insofar as the flag as thing was nevertheless a symbolic thing, the flag carried with it all the linguistic connotations associated with the communicative and significative functions of language. Because the *Eichman* majority still took symbols to function as language, associating the flag with symbolism necessarily aroused "governmental interests" related to expression or speech. Because the majority under-

---

[17] See Kmiec, "Aftermath," 580 n. 11, for instance, discussing proposed bill criminalizing defilement of an American flag belonging to the federal government. Kmiec maintains, though, that the asserted property interest "would have been confined to an overly narrow class of public property—focused on the tangible 'thing'—rather than its intellectual property design component of the flag."

[18] Again, this may indeed be what the State of Texas was trying to argue at oral argument. See Bezanson, *Speech Stories*, 87–205.

[19] *United States v. Eichman*, 496 U.S. 310, 110 S.Ct. 2404 (1990).

stood symbols to be forms of expression comparable to words, the flag as symbol necessarily held expressive content.

Although the *Texas v. Johnson* dissents had indeed opened the possibility of asserting a property interest in the flag, they had also accepted the characterization of flag as symbol. Their characterization of the flag thus invited property rather than speech analysis only insofar as one could distinguish claims about the flag from claims about flag burning as expressive or symbolic conduct. The *Texas v. Johnson* dissents could have acknowledged that flag burning was communicative or even "expressive," while insisting that the flag itself was used *improperly* (in Johnson's burning of it) as an instrument or mode of expression. Indeed the Rehnquist dissent stated: "It was Johnson's use of this particular symbol, and not the idea that he sought to convey by it or by his many other expressions, for which he was punished" (2554). (There is some evidence in the transcript of the oral argument to suggest that this is indeed what the State of Texas meant to argue.)[20] In such a reading, the dissent's claim about the improper use as an instrument of expression, of the thing-that-is-the-flag, would be about "property" or the proper use of a thing, rather than about symbol or "speech."[21]

In this reading of the dissent, improper use endangers or harms the flag as, in some sense, a sacred thing. The sacredness of a thing lies not in its distinctiveness, but in proper use in worship. The language of veneration, present in the first half of Rehnquist's dissent, suggests that to some, the flag is sacred. For the *Texas v. Johnson* majority, though, use of the flag refers only to its "special role" as symbol. The majority sees no need to consider anything beyond the flag as symbol and the "Nation" it symbolizes. The majority's response to the dissent's concern for the danger created by Johnson's improper use of the flag comes at the end of its opinion. The majority is convinced that "forbidding criminal punishment for conduct such as Johnson's will not endanger the special role played by our flag or the feeling it inspires." The "serious offense" that onlookers may feel toward "physical mistreatment of the flag" does not suggest to the majority a danger that must be dealt with through criminal law. On the contrary, the majority claims, taking offense confirms "that the flag's special role is not in danger; if it were, no one would riot or take offense because a flag had been burned" (2547). On this basis, then, the majority calls for "more speech, not enforced silence," for education or "persuasion," and for exposure of "falsehood and fallacies" through discussion,

---

[20] Bezanson, *Speech Stories*, 192, refers to putting out a barbecue that's on fire, as an example of improper use, according to Texas.

[21] See Jill Frank, *A Democracy of Distinction* (Chicago: University of Chicago Press, 2005), on property as proper use.

as a response to flag burning and the offense it causes. The majority is even "tempted to say" that "the flag's deservedly cherished place in our community will be strengthened, not weakened, by our holding today." Knowledge of the "cherished place" of the flag will be strengthened, the use of the flag as symbol reaffirmed, the majority reasons, when improper use leads not only to taking offense but also to *discussing* proper use.

The likelihood of such a reasonable—speech—reaction is precisely what those concerned primarily with the flag as (sacred) thing rather than conceptual object—the dissenters and Kennedy in his concurrence—would dispute. The danger of allowing "public desecration of the flag" is that the flag's value (as a thing) will "tarnish" (2556), that Johnson's improper use of the flag will lead not to learning proper use but, instead, to furthering improper use—desacralization or desecration. Appeals such as the majority's to speech and discussion seem inappropriate to the dissents in the context of an inability to learn what to do with or how to use the thing. It is as such that the dissents and Kennedy articulate their concerns. According to the Rehnquist dissent, the appropriate response, like the response to "murder, embezzlement, pollution," or other conduct "regarded as evil and profoundly offensive to the majority of the people," is neither education nor the sort of "patronizing civics lecture" it finds in the majority opinion, but "legislation" and punishment (2555). As Kennedy puts it: "this respondent was not a philosopher and perhaps did not even possess the ability to comprehend how repellent his statements must be to the Republic itself" (2548).

For Kennedy, though, in contrast to the dissents, Johnson's acts are protected, "whether or not [Johnson] could appreciate the enormity of the offense he gave," because "his acts were speech, in both the technical and fundamental meaning of the Constitution" (2548). In his dissent, Stevens confronts Kennedy directly on this point. He takes the flag to be neither speech nor sacred thing, but an object of property: "the case has nothing to do with 'disagreeable ideas,' . . . It involves disagreeable conduct that, in my opinion, diminishes the value of an important national asset." As in the Rehnquist dissent, Stevens mixes the relatively concrete with the intangible, claiming this time not that the flag is a sacred symbol, but that "the asset at stake in this case is intangible." The value of the "asset," a term that suggests a financial instrument or property resource, lies once more in its value as "symbol" though, for Stevens as well. He concurs with Rehnquist that the flag is a symbol that both "signifies the ideas that characterize the society that has chosen that emblem" and "carries its message . . . both at home and abroad" (2556).

Throughout their disagreements, then, the entire *Texas v. Johnson* Court and all of the parties, including the State of Texas, understand the flag as a symbol that functions expressively, through communication and signification. Although the dissents' concern for proper use—whether as sacred thing or asset—would make property the issue, the dissents accept the symbolic character of the flag. Their failure to extricate or distinguish their concern for the proper use of a thing from symbolic expression character-izes also the efforts of flag-protection advocates after *Texas v. Johnson.*

Advocates of flag-protection spoke of protecting the sacredness of the thing they took the flag to be in the paradoxical terms of the physical integrity of a symbolic object. On the one hand, the Flag Protection Act of 1989 aimed for "blanket protection"[22] against "physical desecration" and amotivational destruction of a tangible "cloth flag."[23] On the other hand, legislation was warranted, advocates argued, precisely because the flag is "not simply 'another idea,' " as Rehnquist had put it, but *more* than an idea. The flag is a "unique national symbol" in Bush's words,[24] "a national symbol of unique reverence to Americans"[25] a "single symbol that is the embodiment of the country,"[26] "the one symbol that expresses our existence as a community, the one symbol that stands above all others as an expression of our nationhood, . . . the one symbol that stands above political and partisan ideological dispute,"[27] a "primary symbol of our American freedom"[28]—whose destruction threatens "the fabric of na-tional unity."[29]

In reviewing the constitutionality of the Flag Protection Act in *U.S. v. Eichman,* then, the Supreme Court declined to reconsider the first part of the *Johnson* opinion, that flag burning was expressive conduct. The Court held that, under the First Amendment, the Flag Protection Act could not constitutionally be applied to appellees who had "knowingly set[] fire to several United States flags on the steps of the United States Capitol while

[22] Tribe, testimony, in "Flag Desecration Legislation," 215.

[23] Sen. Howard Metzenbaum, testimony, July 13, 1989, reprinted in "Flag Desecration Legislation," 203.

[24] "For the Record. Presidential News Conference [June 27]. Flag Burning, HUD Scandal Dominate Press Queries," *Congressional Quarterly,* July 1, 1989, 1650. See also Bernard Weinraub, "Bush Seeking Way to Circumvent Court's Decision on Flag Burning," *New York Times,* June 27, 1989, I-1 and I-21, quoting the president as saying, "I think the flag is very special. And there's only one."

[25] Hon. Robert Michel, testimony, July 13, 1989, reprinted in "Flag Desecration Legisla-tion," 204.

[26] Hon. Phil Gramm, testimony, July 18, 1989, reprinted in "Flag Desecration Legisla-tion," 212.

[27] Hon. Robert H. Bork, testimony, July 19, 1989, reprinted in "Flag Desecration Legisla-tion," 212.

[28] H. F "Sparky" Gierke, National Commander of the American Legion, testimony, July 20, 1989, reprinted in "Flag Desecration Legislation," 222.

[29] Hon. Robert Michel, testimony, July 13, 1989, reprinted in "Flag Desecration Legisla-tion," 206.

protesting various aspects of the Government's domestic and foreign policy" (2406).

This time there were two opinions. Brennan again wrote the opinion of the Court; Stevens wrote the dissent, which Rehnquist, White, and O'Connor joined. The majority argued that the government's asserted interest in the Flag Protection Act, " 'protect[ing] the physical integrity of the flag under all circumstances' in order to safeguard the flag's identity 'as the unique and unalloyed symbol of the Nation' " again was related to the suppression of free expression and concerned with the content of expression (2408; citations and some internal quotation marks omitted). Because the government's interest in protecting privately owned flags "rests upon a perceived need to preserve the flag's status as a symbol of our Nation and certain national ideals" and "is implicated 'only when a person's treatment of the flag communicates [a] message to others that is inconsistent with those ideals,' " the majority found the government's interest to be concerned with suppressing expression relating to "its likely communicative impact" (2409, citing *Texas v. Johnson*). The majority supported its claims by reference to the language of the act.[30]

In other words, although the *Eichman* majority acknowledged that the act proscribed conduct "without regard to the actor's motive, his intended message, or the likely effects of his conduct on onlookers," and "contain[ed] no explicit content-based limitation on the scope of prohibited conduct," it took the government's interest in the flag as a "symbol" to mean that its interest was related to expression or likely communicative impact. Although the government had explicitly denied its concern with the elements of a communicative model of symbolic speech—a willing agent, transmitting a message, to a receptive audience—the government's appeal to the symbolic value of the flag reinstated a similar model at the level of conduct—a knowing agent, producing through use of the flag, an impact on society. The majority could thus rely on the point that it had made in *Johnson*: the distinction between written or spoken words and nonverbal conduct—speech and action—is "of no moment" where both concern symbols, since any deployment of symbols transmits expressive effects or produces expressive impacts.

Stevens, though grasping the flag as an "object" having "value" in a "marketplace," also links symbolism with communication, like the rest of the Court. The damage to the symbol that has already occurred as a result of *Texas v. Johnson*, means for Stevens that

---

[30] "[E]ach of the specified terms ['knowingly mutilates, defaces, physically defiles, burns, maintains on the floor or ground, or tramples upon any flag']—with the possible exception of 'burns'—unmistakably connotes disrespectful treatment of the flag and suggests a focus on those acts likely to damage the flag's symbolic value" (2409). Further, "the explicit ex-

a formerly dramatic expression of protest is now rather commonplace. In to-day's marketplace of ideas, . . . burning of a Vietnam draft card is probably less provocative than lighting a cigarette. Tomorrow flag burning may produce a similar reaction. There is surely a direct relationship between the communica-tive value of the act of flag burning and the symbolic value of the object being burned. (2412)

Stevens fails to distinguish property from speech "interests": there is a "direct relationship," for him, between the communicative (speech) value of the act of flag burning and the symbolic value of the object (property) being burned.

The marketplace of ideas for Stevens is in effect an economy of "govern-ment resources."[31] When speech and conduct, action and expression, all concern symbolically caused or instrumentally produced effects, distinc-tions between intention (or persons' willing of actions for which they are responsible) and motivation (or production of behavior determined by factors outside individual's control) breaks down. In the undifferentiated expressive environment of symbolic use, the Kantian distinction between a noumenal or true world of ideas and things-in-themselves and a phe-nomenal world of the appearances of objects of empirical investigation becomes "of no moment." The flag-burning decisions show in part how modern law turns, in the name of reason, against its own constructions. Law finds itself sharing in the predicament of modern metaphysics that Heidegger calls technique. Technique for Heidegger refers not just to the set of machines and instruments that help us reach our goals more effi-ciently and completely, as Linda Meyer explains.

[T]he mindset that thinks in terms of means and ends, causes and effects, is not itself a mere tool. Its way of looking at nature, the world, and even human talent as raw material for achieving human goals is itself what opens the possibility of building and using machines. As Heidegger says, "[o]ur age is not a technologi-cal age because it is the age of the machine; it is an age of the machine because it is the technological age." . . . Technology, he says, is the way of being in the world in which everything appears as a stockpile of fungible stuff to be ordered and used, managed and regulated, as we will.[32]

Not only in grasping language as concept and communication, but also in viewing flags, words, actions, and speech alike as resources available

---

emption . . . for disposal of 'worn or soiled' flags protects certain acts traditionally associ-ated with patriotic respect for the flag" (2409).

[31] Kmiec, "Aftermath," 616, uses this phrase.

[32] Linda Ross Meyer, "Is Practical Reason Mindless?" *Georgetown Law Journal* 86 (1998): 670.

for human utilization, law manifests its embeddedness in the worldview of an age of technique.

The Calling of Words

After the *Eichman* ruling, supporters of an amendment claimed that the public was "overwhelmingly on their side," although poll takers had begun suggesting that "voters' emotions are 'not nearly as intense' as they were last summer when the first ruling on the issue came down."[33] An editorial notebook in the *New York Times* pointed to the "relative calm" that accompanied the public's now "flagging interest" in the issue. "Passions have cooled," the *Times* indicated; "lawmakers and political strategists said mail and telephone calls in favor of the measure were nowhere near as heavy as last year."[34] In June, the House rejected a proposed constitutional amendment, ending the possibility of any such amendment for that session of Congress. The Senate nevertheless insisted on a roll-call vote, in which the measure also failed. Public calm, or at least media silence, followed, although, since *Eichman*, unsuccessful bills to protect the flag have been introduced in Congress (sometimes as riders) almost every year. As the twenty-first-century fortunes of "America" and its flag fluctuate, what will happen?

News media continue to grasp the rise and fall of the flag-protection controversy as the effect or outcome of a "politics" that seems continually to evade any issue. They present events surrounding flag burning—from protesters' actions, to Supreme Court decisions, to critics' responses—as attempts to manipulate public attitudes and emotions. While describing public opinion as a political "tide," as a shifting "mood" or "momentum" that can never be completely mastered but must instead be followed, media attribute the unfortunate, yet necessary, manipulation of public opinion to the interests and motives of elected officials.

"Politics" thus simultaneously names strategic rationality, an overwhelming emotivism, the confrontation and the impossibility of confrontation between the two. As discussion focuses on how various parties got, or failed to get, others to drop particular claims or to cede advantage or control of positions to the opposition, the issue of flag burning itself remains unaddressed in discussions of the politics that are said to have caused it to become an issue. Focusing on who-is-saying-what-to-manipulate-whom-to-what-end-and-with-what-success loses sight of what at least the Supreme Court said was at stake in flag burning: speech.

[33] *New York Times*, June 17, 1990, I–22, col. 1.
[34] *New York Times*, June 20, 1990, A24, col. 1.

Of course, the Supreme Court itself, in its analysis of speech, drew on models of expression that take language, like the flag, to be an instrument of communication. To the majority in *Texas v. Johnson*, flag burning is protected speech because the flag, like a word, functions as a symbol that communicates and signifies. Even the dissents agreed that a flag is the deployable resource, if not the linguistic instrument, of a subject who utilizes objects. The majorities in the *Johnson* and *Eichman* cases aim to maintain access to that resource. The dissents fear that open access will deplete or diminish the value of the resource to such a degree that it will not be utilizable at all.

Analysis in terms of utility comes to a head in Stevens's dissent in *Eichman*. Stevens writes that "the Court's opinion ends where proper analysis of the issue should begin" (2410). For Stevens, "proper analysis" would entail balancing a speaker's interest in freely choosing an effective method of expressing ideas, the point at which the Court leaves off, against societal interests that are independent of expression. At first it seems that Stevens will seek to balance the communicative or "expressive interests" by which "speech" has come to be known, against the "nonexpressive interests" in "property" that proponents of the Flag Protection Act sought (and some still seek) to articulate. Stevens ultimately turns the issue into the balancing of two linguistic interests, however:

> Does the admittedly important interest in allowing every speaker to choose the method of expressing his or her ideas that he or she deems most effective and appropriate outweigh the societal interest in preserving the symbolic value of the flag? (2411)

The economically inspired notion of a balancing test replicates, in law, the instrumentalism of approaches to politics and speech described above. Regulating the flag—a resource that "subsidizes private speech"[35]—becomes the outcome of balancing that is concerned with maximizing the utility of the flag as a resource to be marshaled in the interests of free speech. The individual interest in the balance is even buttressed for Stevens "by the societal interest in being alerted to the need for thoughtful response to voices that might otherwise go unheard" (2412). Law here becomes a matter of the strategic maximization of speech interests of individuals in society.

But if flag-burning discussions show the pervasiveness of instrumental conceptions of politics, speech, and law, they also suggest the possibility of other ways of thinking. The section "Politics, Speech, or Property?" above, suggested that flag protection advocates' responses to *Texas v. Johnson* may not be simple strategic attempts to circumvent law. Some

[35] In the words of Kmiec, "Aftermath," 627–29, and text accompanying notes 207–52.

advocates seem equally concerned with law—its silences and speech. Flag protection advocates responded to the Court's decision in *Texas v. Johnson* with claims about law. Their claims of law at once constituted responses to the law—the words and silences of the Supreme Court—and initiated law—legislation. The Supreme Court's many opinions constituted responses to parties' legal claims while themselves claiming to be law.[36] As all concerned—parties, Court, critics—appeal to and initiate law, their claims invite further responses.

In this chain of claim and response, what is said—and what is heard—as law and at law becomes key. As in the sociolegal studies and other works discussed in chapter 2, the word *justice* seldom appears. And yet the claims and responses, appeals and declarations, of law, again like calls for voice, only have valence as something other than instrumental deployments of power when they are made in the name—however silent—of justice.

"Positive law" is the form that claims and responses of law take today. In positive law, declarations of law are made through the language and conduct of legal officials. The "professions" of law in flag-burning discussions come largely from legally elected or appointed officials and legally recognized subjects. But the "profession of words" that is law is grammatically ambiguous.[37] Not only does "profession" carry with it three different meanings, but "words" may be the object or subject of the genitive "of." In the First Amendment flag-burning cases, words and speech are the object of declarations or professions of law at the same time as law names an avowal belonging to the words that would challenge official declarations.

Even as the chain of claims and responses of law in flag-burning discussions seems to appeal to an unspoken justice, however, these calls manifest themselves in modern law as instrumental tactics of strategic rationality. Positive law neither appeals explicitly to justice nor acknowledges justice as that out of which its declarations come. Can it be otherwise in modern law? Can critics or advocates of law today translate claims to justice into words without falling back into the strategic communicative rationality of a technical age?

---

[36] Again, Eugen Rosenstock-Huessy, "Articulated Speech" (1937), in *Speech and Reality*, 48: "for human speech, two things are essential: names and answers," explaining the difference between yelling "ooooh" to someone who duplicates the yell and calling an other by name to which the other responds.

[37] The genitive case is ambiguous as to which of its two nouns is "subject" or "object." "Knowledge of God," for instance, may mean either "knowledge belonging to God [that God possesses]" or "knowledge [one possesses] about God." The "problem of Socrates" may belong to Socrates, or Socrates may constitute the problem.

Chapter 5 _____

Behind the Rules

Poets don't invent poems
The poem is somewhere behind
It's been there for a long long time
The poet merely discovers it.
  —Jan Skacel

Law does not just stand there to be watched.
  —Frederick Schauer, *Playing by the Rules*

WHAT HAPPENS TO THE AVOWALS of law—the chain of claims and responses that call to and for justice—when words become the resources of a technical age? This chapter and the next turn to the rules and institutions of modern law to take up the issue of what becomes of law and justice in a technical age. This chapter supplements the brief discussion of the rulelike character of legislation from chapter 3 with a more sustained look at rules and what they can tell us about modern law and its possibilities of justice. It is worth noting that the sociology of law discussed in chapter 2 often distinguishes itself from a philosophy of law that conceives of law as a system of rules. This chapter suggests that rule systems remind us of something that is ultimately not so different from what one finds in the sociology of chapter 2, the legislation of chapter 3, and legal opinions of chapter 4: that the justice of modern law lies in silence.

In the editor's introduction to *The Law and Society Reader*, Richard Abel writes:

> When asked what I study, I usually respond gnomically: everything about law except the rules. This may be oxymoronic, but it is also accurate. Lawyers seek to understand rules—ascertain, criticize, change, organize, apply, and manipulate them. Social scientists examine everything else: institutional structures, processes, behavior, personnel and culture.[1]

This chapter agrees that there is more to law than the rules that lawyers deal with. The justice of law lies somewhere behind the rules. It comes

---

[1] Richard L. Abel, "What We Talk About When We Talk About Law," in *Law and Society Reader*, ed. Richard L. Abel (New York: New York University Press, 1995).

from a place that is grasped neither by rules nor even by the addition of "everything else" that social scientists examine, however. That legal theory today often fails to acknowledge this place as anything other than an amorphous "social" differentiates legal theory from a sociology that examines in detail the existent social dynamics of law. But as we shall see, legal theory, like sociology, threatens to forget—or neglect—law's relation to justice.

The chapter takes as its focus Frederick Schauer's *Playing by the Rules: A Philosophical Examination of Rule-Based Decision-Making in Law and Life.*[2] If Hart's system of rules, like Austin's sovereign, marked the (fourth) Nietzschean moment in which law comes down to earth, Schauer's rule-based system moves into a Nietzschean fifth moment that declares former ideals of justice no longer of any "use." Brian Tamanaha quite rightly criticizes the emptiness of the "social" in contemporary accounts of legal positivism. But the social realism with which he and others, including Robert Cover (discussed in chapter 6), would replace a metaphysical legal positivism of rules sounds the death knell of "justice."

In his work, Schauer argues that law tells us what to do at least in part through rules. Rules, as nonabsolute reasons for action, Schauer claims, establish presumptions that certain factors will be taken into account and that others will not. The "silent virtues" of rules involve what Schauer calls their "agenda-setting" function (233). Schauer calls the systemic analogue of a rule "presumptive positivism." Presumptive positivism names "the interplay between" recognized rules and possibly overriding considerations from the normative universe. A recognized or pedigreed set of rules or norms, which can be distinguished from a fuller and nonpedigreeable normative universe, presumptively controls decision makers. Presumptive positivism, Schauer suggests, "may be the most accurate picture of the place of rules within many modern legal systems" (206).

This chapter explores presumptive positivism as an account of law, while attending to its silences and the silences surrounding statements of rules. Schauer locates both rules and the factors that override them in the social realm. "Whether we call [the] array of overriding factors [in presumptive positivism] 'law' or not," he writes, "is a dispute that is to some extent terminological," although it also "goes to the rhetoric of legality" (205–6). This chapter attends to the rhetoric of legality in Schauer's text to see how rules tell decision makers what to do and how this telling corresponds to law.

The first section, "Playing by the Rules," describes and explores the process of rule-based decision-making that Schauer presents. It shows how, in presumptive positivism as in rule-based decision-making more

[2] Frederick Schauer, *Playing by the Rules: A Philosophical Examination of Rule-Based Decision-Making in Law and in Life* (Oxford: Clarendon Press, 1991).

generally, "social" considerations mark the decision-making process from outset to result. The second section, "Laying Down the Law," then investigates how rule-based decision-making relates to law. It suggests that while modern legal systems may indeed be describable as presumptively positivist systems, law involves something more or other than what presumptive positivism provides. In claiming that *law* involves something more or other than *rules*, the section does not depart from what Schauer himself in effect argues. But it goes further, showing how a presumptively positivist account that places legal decision-making in the context of social norms, accurate as it may be in describing aspects of particular modern legal systems, fails to address how rules bring law's addressees to judge and to act. Insofar as accounts of rules leave out or reconstrue as social pressure what makes rules binding, accounts of rule systems fail to present anything particularly lawlike about law. The third section, "To Judge and to Act," points out that this limitation of rule systems as an account of law can remind us that law lies not so much in rules themselves, their linear temporality, or their social surroundings, as in judgments that lie "somewhere behind," as Milan Kundera so poetically puts it in his commentary on Kafka. Behind rules lie silences, out of which comes not only the need for action, but the necessity of responding to such need. In the correspondence (about which rule systems do not speak) of calls to action to the human need to act, lie the judgments that establish the possibilities of just action offered by law.

Playing by the Rules

What is a rule? Rules, for Schauer, lie in entrenched semantic meaning. One can distinguish the "meaning of a rule-formulation" from its background justifications, canonical formulation, or inscription. A sign at the front of a church saying, "No hats may be worn inside" might serve as a mandatory rule, writes Schauer, such that a result unfaithful to the rule's justifications might follow. The same sort of constraint on hat wearing might follow, Schauer continues, even absent the sign, because "a community of putative rule-followers, even without a sign, could still have in mind the same meaning, and all treat it as entrenched." This could happen, Schauer suggests, through the convergence of a series of linguistic but noncanonical formulations, as when parents instruct their children, or even through an inductive process in which community members sharing common patterns of perception generate similar semantic content about a series of instances of behavior.

> [I]f at some point each member of the community were asked to write down the rule about hats in church, they might write down pretty much the same

thing, or at least write down sentences with approximately the same meaning. As long as we can suppose that many rule-subjects and many rule-enforcers could if asked articulate the same rule, there is no reason to believe that the fact they have not yet done so, or that no one has written down an authoritative version, eliminates the existence of the common understanding of meaning upon which any rule rests. (69–70)

This "common understanding of meaning," insofar as it is semantic, becomes entrenched and as such constitutes the rule for Schauer:

> The rule against wearing hats in church, therefore, exists (provides a reason for action, independent of its background justifications, for some set of putative rule-followers) insofar as "hat in church (forbidden)" is treated *as if* it were canonically formulated, and this treatment does not require that the formulation appear as marks on a sign . . . or anywhere else. (71)

Like the imperative to be quiet in a library, rules do not require signs. For Schauer, rules do not definitively answer the question of what to do. Rather, they "elevate the burden of justification necessary to take an action inconsistent with its indications" (231). They provide a presumption that what they indicate is to be done or establish that (as Joseph Raz puts it)[3] there is reason to believe that what they indicate is to be done. To be guided by a rule is to take the rule as a not necessarily absolute reason for action; to follow a rule is to be guided by it and, further, to comply with its indications (113).

The value of rules, for Schauer, lies in the way they constrain power and allocate responsibility in a "complex and multi-jurisdictional world" (232). In the context of decision making, the ability of rules "to take things off the agenda as well as to put them on" explains their value (232–33). "As devices for the allocation of power, rules are most effective not in determining the result in the cases on some decision-maker's agenda, but *in determining at the outset what is on the agenda at all*" (xvii; emphasis added). The ability of rules to determine the agenda

> frees [a rule's] addressees from determining whether this is the one case in which the results would have been different [had the general rule not been used]. Only because of the rule is the addressee freed from looking behind the rule *in every case*, and thus the rule, extensionally divergent [from its background justification] in one case out of a thousand, influences the nature of the decision-making process in the other 999 as well. (230)

---

[3] On the logical equivalence of "ought" statements and their corresponding "there is reason" statements, see Raz, *Practical Reason and Norms*, 32.

Rule-based decision-makers need not look "behind" rules to their background justifications. "[T]he essence of rule-based decision-making," for Schauer, thus "lies in the concept of jurisdiction, for rules, which narrow the range of factors to be considered by particular decision-makers, establish and constrain the jurisdiction of those decision-makers" (231–32).[4]

Schauer's depiction of rules, which are nonabsolute reasons for action, as nevertheless determining a decision maker's agenda from the outset and freeing decision makers from looking behind rules raises questions about "decision making." First, what is the outset of decision making? Second, if rules determine agendas from the outset, when and how is new business recognized and introduced—or can it be? Third, who is the decision maker for whom rules at the outset determine an agenda? Schauer's work clearly and unself-consciously locates the answers to these questions outside of or beyond rules in an empirically knowable social world in which rules are "social facts" and decision makers are social agents.

Schauer makes clear, in addressing the question of the outset of decision making, that although rules in some sense govern "at the outset," they do not and cannot completely determine themselves. A rule's "initial applicability"—the likelihood, extent to which, and way in which a rule is treated by an agent as a reason for action in a particular situation—depends in part on the rule's designation of its scope and its internal validity, but also on individual decision-makers' non-rule-based reasons for accepting, or rather "internalizing," the rule's status as a rule and on the decision-making environment. The decision maker's internalization of rules is a social and individual (psychological) process, somewhat like that of Tyler's people who obey the law (in chapter 1). Questions as to the internalization of a rule by an individual decision-maker, like questions as to the relevance and weight of a rule in the broader decision-making environment, depend on something external to the rule being imported into the rule to make it operational and to give it weight (118–28). "Something *about* a rule and not the rule itself determines not only what weight the rule will have, but whether it is even a rule at all" (128).

This "something" turns out to be a "social" something, in particular social "judgments" or "decisions," and in the decision-making situations Schauer is most concerned with, decisions about power. "Now that we have seen that rules serve primarily as vehicles for the allocation of power," Schauer writes, "we can appreciate that the extent to which decision-makers adopt (or are compelled to adopt) rule-based decision-making modes is likely to embody social judgments about the distribution of

[4] See Jeremy Elkins, "The Force of Rules," in *Rules and Reasoning: Essays in Honor of Frederick Schauer*, ed. Linda Meyer (Oxford: Hart, 1999), 79–108.

jurisdiction" (173). Rules reflect "a society's decisions" about such matters as who decides what, who is to be trusted or not, who is to be empowered or not, and so forth (173).

In response to the second question about the introduction of new business, Schauer suggests that rule-based decision-making stands in a particular relation to the "new." He contrasts an "entrenchment" model of decision making through generalizations to a "conversational" or particularistic model of decision making. The latter allows for response, qualification, and adjustment of general statements. The former, which describes rule-based decision-making, "entrenches" what already exists. In part through psychological and social processes in which "minds" using generalizations "project" expected similarities onto the future (43), in part because of the inevitable over- or underinclusiveness that characterizes linguistic or semantic classification, entrenched generalizations or rules favor the past over the present, the present over the future, the status quo over the new (160). Rules and rule-based decision-making limit the possibilities of judgment:

> rules can never allow a decision that could not otherwise be made, but can preclude otherwise eligible and indeed optimal decisions. . . . Entrenching the past may provide the purchase from which political agents can now do what would otherwise be politically or psychologically impossible, but when the circumstances require a departure from the past rather than obeisance to it, a decision-making apparatus operating in rule-based mode will find itself impeded and not empowered. (173–74)

Rules thus serve the goal of stability for stability's sake (158).

Whether the favoring of the status quo over the new and stability for stability's sake is judged worthwhile is again not a matter of rules. It depends instead on "a substantive conception of where we are, and where we want to be" (158), in effect a matter of "social and political context" (157). And the extent to which rules *actually* limit potential and possibly optimal departures from the past is—again—an empirical question, Schauer writes. The answer depends on the extent to which elements of particularistic decision-making temper the rule-based decision-making processes of a decision maker and a decision-making environment.

Schauer's answers to both the first and second questions about how rules determine decision makers' agendas indicate that non-rule-based decisions and judgments of empirically knowable *societies* lie behind deployments of rules in particular situations. "Social" judgments and "societal" decisions constitute an empirical background of social facts that exists prior to, and as the context for, the deployment of particular rules at the outsets of particular decision-making situations.

The third question concerns the character of the decision maker for whom the rules determined by society set limits and determine agendas. On the surface, the decision maker who emerges from Schauer's text is, frankly, not an attractive character. "She" (99, e.g.) is, perhaps not accidentally, an "agent" operating in a world of causation and cognition, rather than, for instance, a person acting in a world of freedom and reason. (Recall the distinction between Kant's person who wills to act in accord with reason for the sake of duty and the utilitarian agent who rationally calculates the behavior that will produce the most desirable consequences.) Her concern, like Schauer's, is "rational decision-making" of the sort Heidegger identifies in "The Question concerning Technology" (see chapters 3 and 4). Her knowledge is one of cognition and her aim is that of technique. In the name of decision making, she "alienate[s] some of [her] freedom" and "relinquish[es] some of [her] ability to make choices she might otherwise have been able to make" (231). She does so "in the service of the psychological impossibility of treating [her] life as a series of constant and unbounded choices" (231).[5] In this respect, and in the ease with which she is satisfied by rules, she is like the rest of "us," according to Schauer:

> [F]ew of us can deploy our rational faculties fully with respect to every decision we make. Consequently we take certain families of decisions to be less important, and are satisfied simply to follow the rules without inquiring whether they accurately serve their background justifications in this instance. (124)

Even the "moral considerations" that Schauer claims guide this decision maker sound suspiciously instrumental:

> [F]rom the agent's point of view, the arguments for taking a rule to be a reason for action might stem from agreement with and willingness to co-operate in the system from which the rule emanates. By simplifying the decision process and by making certain results salient even if suboptimal, rules may assist in the solution of Prisoner's Dilemma or co-ordination problems, or assist in other dimensions of co-operative enterprises, and thus an agent with a reason to participate in and assist in the effectiveness of some co-operative enterprise would have a reason for following rules emanating from that enterprise. (125)

The "enterprises" in which the agent may have reason to participate or in whose effectiveness the agent may have reason to assist stand in sharp contrast to any moral community or former Kantian "kingdom of ends."[6]

---

[5] The impossibility of treating one's life as a series of constant and unbounded choices could lead to habits that are second nature or to routine. Schauer implies that it leads to routine.

[6] Kant, *Groundwork*, 100–102.

The autonomous persons who, thinking of—and of themselves in—an intelligible or noumenal world, act for the sake of duty, give way to "enterprises" that exist in a—clearly social—world populated by decision-making agents who "serve different functions, have different abilities, live in different places." Differences among agents make the "allocation of authority among people, groups, and institutions" not only "necessary" (232) but also "frequently desirable" (233).

Schauer's agents lack the "mental capacity incessantly to consider all of the things that an 'all things considered' decision-making model requires of us" (229). Because all people have "too little time to consider too much" (229), rules simplify people's lives by making decisions more manageable. They do so by constituting for decision makers the "outset" of otherwise seemingly endless decision-making processes.

Rules—nonabsolute reasons for action—thus function for Schauer as potentially powerful and effective time-saving devices insofar as they do not require that every factor be considered in every case. Their desirability stems from human incapacity and finitude at the same time as they are human productions. Operating in the background of decision making, non-rule-based decisions, judgments, and values of "society" produce rules "behind" which a decision maker need not go. The details of "society"—the "everything else" of institutional structures, processes, behavior, personnel, and culture of Abel's social scientists—remain vague in Schauer's account, although they play a crucial rule. Background social processes existing prior to the rule and more or less taken for granted by the decision maker, shape rule-based decision-making from behind and thereby establish at the decision-making outset the suppression of the decision maker's consideration of background justifications.

If, according to Schauer, social processes lie behind the rules, then the possible overriding of their presumptions lies ahead. The nonabsoluteness of a rule means that *between* the determination of the agenda by the rule and the decision-making result lies the possibility of overriding the presumption provided by the rule that what it indicates is to be done. Distinguishing between "a careful look" and "merely a perfunctory glimpse" (91), Schauer maintains that through the latter, the rule-based decision-maker governed by a particular rule admits certain factors excluded by the rule "when and only when they are particularly compelling" (90). The nonabsoluteness of rules means that decision makers have "recourse to the very kinds of facts the consideration of which the rule appears to exclude" (90). Override occurs when a "merely . . . perfunctory glimpse" reveals circumstances so "obvious" or "dramatic" as to warrant that the decision maker "pierce the [rule's] pre-emptive exclusion" of particular factors (89–90).

Just as rules provide "nonabsolute" reasons for action, so too does the pedigreed set of rules or norms in presumptive positivism provide nonabsolute reasons for decision. Just as a rule-based decision-maker "retains the ability to glimpse at the full array of available factors to determine if this is a case in which those factors might provide a reason of such exceptional strength as to provide a stronger reason for overcoming the exclusion of those factors than the rule provides for the exclusion itself" (195–96), so too a legal decision-maker may glimpse at the broader social considerations that may override a pedigreed set of rules. Legal decision-makers override a rule "not when they believe that the rule has produced an erroneous or suboptimal result in this case, no matter how well grounded that belief, but instead when, and only when, the reasons for overriding are perceived by the decision-maker to be particularly strong" (204).

The perceptions of reasons for overriding come about through what Schauer calls the decision maker's glimpse or " 'peek' behind the curtain that is the presumptive rule" (205). This "curtain" or presumptive rule distinguishes rule-based decision-making from what Schauer calls "rule-sensitive particularism," in which the "transparency" of rules of thumb "allows their very existence and effect *as* rules of thumb to become a factor in determining whether rules should be set aside" (97). Decision makers, Schauer writes, can tell the difference between factors "that would control were the decision process particularized" and those "that [do] not control because of the presumption or burden of persuasion that [is present by virtue of the existence of a rule and] prevails in a particular decisional environment" (205).

As in his account of rule-based decision-making, so too in Schauer's account of presumptive positivism, "society" is a significant subject or agent. The overriding factors against which pedigreed rules are "tested" (205) *after* the outset of decision making, *between* the outset and the result, are "social norms" that come into play in the limited time or space between the presumption of the rule and the decision. Schauer refers in various ways to these overriding factors, which comprise the "larger and unpedigreeable set of considerations" that are glimpsed, in presumptive positivism, in the lifting of the curtain that is the presumptive rule. He refers to these considerations as a "larger and more morally acceptable set of values" than those indicated by the "locally applicable and pedigreed rule" (205); as "non-epistemic" (204); as the potentially "conflicting norms" of "a normative universe" (204); as "all morally, socially, and politically relevant considerations" (202). To Schauer, as was mentioned in the introduction to this chapter,

Whether we call this array of overriding factors "law" or not is a dispute that is to some extent terminological. It is also a dispute, however, that goes to the rhetoric of legality, to the extent to which legal decision-makers relying on a *non-pedigreeable universe of social norms* shall when doing so be buttressed by the connotations of deduction, constraint, and limited domain suggested by the word "law." (204–5; emphasis added)

Whatever their status as law, these "social norms" or non-pedigreed-rule considerations, which may include "moral, political, economic, or other factors," establish the possibility of overriding a rule's indications. The social factors overriding rules that are supplemented by the accoutrements of a particular kind of reason and logic—that of "deduction," "constraint," "limited domain" (recall the rationality described by White in chapter 3)—may (or may not) be (called) "law." At the stage of decision making between outset and result, society—its decisions, judgments, values, context, processes, pressures, and norms—plays, for Schauer, a determinative if somewhat indeterminate role. (Schauer is not alone here. Recall that Rawls introduces his topic in *A Theory of Justice* by using *social* or *society* fifteen times in the same paragraph.[7] Though Schauer's and Rawls's "social" are not the same as that of sociolegal study, they are in some sense the "everything else" that undergirds rules or principles.)

"Society," in Schauer's account, ultimately determines what lies both before and after the outset of rule-based decision-making. The pasts and futures of rules in decision making, like rules themselves, are matters of empirical investigation, "social fact" for Schauer, observable in and of a society. The ubiquity of "society" and of "social" or sociological terminology provides Schauer great argumentative opportunity. It allows Schauer's presumptive positivism, as a "descriptive claim" about decision making in modern legal systems, to reconcile differences between Dworkin and legal positivism—and, as an account of law, to exemplify the sociolegal positivism of the Nietzschean fifth moment in the history of jurisprudence.

The beautiful ambiguity of "social norms," in particular, allows presumptive positivism to reconcile what Schauer calls the "opposing observations" of Dworkin and the positivists (205). Recall that *norm* refers both to an observable average or regularity (what is "normal") and to a standard or prescriptive measure or test ("normative").[8] The significance

---

[7] The passage begins, "Our topic . . . is that of social justice. For us the primary subject of justice is the basic structure of society, or more exactly, the way in which the major social institutions distribute fundamental rights and duties and determine the division of advantages from social cooperation. By major institutions I understand the political constitution and the principal economic and social arrangements." Rawls, *A Theory of Justice*, 7.

[8] Georges Canguilhem writes, in the context of discussion of Lalande's medical dictionary, of the way an observed convergence, an average, the "normal," is taken as "normative." *The Normal and the Pathological* (1966; reprint, New York: Zone, 1989), 125. Canguil-

of this double meaning of *norm* for understanding law today cannot be underestimated. It allows one to understand how legal scholarship, "in deference to its normative interests . . . has embraced a diversity of social sciences to assist in the discovery of the best laws" (as Roger Berkowitz puts it), at the same time as law, in deference to objectivity, has embraced social scientific accounts of reality. Both relations are "rooted in the assumption that law serves social and political ends."[9]

Schauer puts the double meaning of *norm* to work:

> On the one hand, positivists observe [noting regularity] that most of the *things* people call laws exist in a moderately limited collection of books, that lawyers refer to a moderately limited *collection of sources* with remarkable frequency, and that it does not seem all that difficult in most easy cases to figure out *what the law requires*. But in other cases, Dworkin and others observe, norms [as standards] that in no way constitute such a closed set seem to control, even when a norm that is legal in the narrow sense goes in the opposite direction. (205; emphasis added)

Presumptive positivism shows how both the positivists and Dworkin can be correct. It transforms the regular "things," "sources," and "requirements of the law" of positivist observation of regularity into a narrow set of "rules" or normative standards and converts the "control" of broader Dworkinian standards into regularities:

> In most cases [regularity], the result generated by the most locally applicable and pedigreed rule [standard] controls. But in every case [regularity] that rule will be tested against [the standards of] a larger and unpedigreeable set of considerations, and the rule will be set aside when the result it indicates is egregiously at odds with the result that is indicated by this larger and more morally acceptable set of values. (205)

Schauer thus locates the differences between Dworkin and the positivists in a common "social" space that allows both to be correct. Positivists are correct that, in most cases, a pedigreed presumptive rule that is a social norm generates the result. Dworkin is correct that, in some cases, a backward-looking judge reaches behind the rule to the social norms constituted by the rule's background justifications and other social values to fill the space between presumptive rule and resulting judgment.

Presumptive positivism, then, as we have seen, situates the rule-based decision-making of legal systems in "social" context. Its focus grows out

---

hem's student, Michel Foucault, has a heyday with this in the context of law in *Discipline and Punish.*

[9] Roger Berkowitz, "Friedrich Nietzsche, the Code of Manu, and the Art of Legislation," *Cardozo Law Review* 24 (2003): 1132.

from the positive law of a Nietzschean fourth moment, which could be used to improve society, to the social policy that designs "decisional environments." In these decisional environments, rules allocate power by constraining decision makers' options. "There is nothing inherently *just* about rule-based decision-making," writes Schauer, in his only use of the term (137). Rule-based decision-makers, he writes, shed a specifically "perfunctory" glimpse at both social values (including background justifications) and other possible social considerations. Operating in the presence of rules, a decision-making agent lifts the sticky curtain of entrenched generalizations, then finds it "not psychologically impossible," in Schauer's words, "to ignore what [she] already knows" (205). Her decisions, Schauer admits, are not all "optimal"; the costs of errors built into the rules may even "be potentially greater than the costs of allowing decision-makers to use their best judgement" (154).

Even as Schauer acknowledges that rules do not necessarily bring about optimal results and that justice is irrelevant in the decisional environments of concern to him, he declares that rules' "jurisdiction-allocating determinations need not be considered morally sterile" (232–33). Their "morality" is that of an environment in which decision making relies on communication of semantic meaning among agents who differ in interests, concerns, and ability; where time is a scarce resource, efficiency is of the essence, and allocation of power the issue.[10] Even as presumptive positivism describes a social system of rules, one asks to what extent it corresponds to law.

Laying Down the Law

Prescriptive positivism describes the social and systemic use of the time-saving devices that are rules, to set out the agendas of rational decision-makers who, perfunctorily taking social considerations into account, on occasion disregard those agendas or otherwise ignore what they know. This section considers how this social systemic account of rule-based decision-making relates to law.

Schauer asks:

> Is there a connection between rule-based decision-making and decision-making within that institution we conventionally refer to as "law"? What is the place of rules within a "legal system"? (167)

---

[10] Linda Meyer, " 'Nothing We Say Matters': *Teague* and the New Rules," *University of Chicago Law Review* 61:2 (1994): 480 n. 232. Meyer points out that for Schauer, rule-based decision-making is useful for decision makers "who (1) have little time to take into account all the relevant factors, (2) are not capable of making an accurate decision using all

Schauer's answer to the first question is a qualified yes. There is a connection between rule-based decision-making and law, he claims. As to the second question, the extensiveness and significance of rules within a given legal system depends, he argues, on the social values informing the system. Insofar as a legal system aims to serve particular values—the values of "stability for stability's sake, unwillingness to trust decision-makers to depart too drastically from the past, and a conservatism committed to the view that changes from the past are more likely to be for the worse than for the better"—the "inculcation of rule-based decision-making is likely to be the implement of that aim" (174). The extent and desirability of rules in a legal system thus depends on the character of the legal system and the norms of the society in which it exists.

That character and those norms are empirical and normative issues that Schauer does not go into. Conceptual analysis such as Schauer's "can explain what happens when decision-makers take rules seriously. It cannot explain if and when they do so" (196). Establishing that decision makers indeed act according to rules or nonabsolute reasons for action would require establishing that decision makers do put rules into practice or transform reasons for action into action, which Schauer's analysis of rules does not do.

Instead he shows the resemblance of modern legal systems to rule-based decision-making environments and argues that actual common-law systems contain elements of rule-based decision-making and thus appear to be legal systems (Schauer argues explicitly that rule-based decision-making is important to the common law. The common law, as Schauer first describes it, is not especially rule-based. As in his initial account of particularistic decision-making, Schauer's preliminary discussion of the common law seems to acknowledge that rules are not in fact necessary to decision making. Yet as Schauer continues, even particularistic decision-making turns out to involve rulelike prescriptive generalizations, subject to over- and underinclusiveness and differing from rules only in their revisability [78]. Likewise, the common law turns out to reveal an affinity between rule-based decision-making and precedent that suggests to Schauer that actual common-law systems contain elements of rule-based decision-making and, as such, appear to be legal systems [174–87].) He argues that even a minimal system of rules may be a legal system. A system "comprised largely of naked jurisdictional rules with little substantive regulative content," writes Schauer, "is both possible and still plausibly considered a legal system" (172). Once this is granted, he continues, "we"

---

relevant factors, (3) are untrustworthy or likely to be systematically biased, or (4) need to coordinate their actions with others without the opportunity for communication" (439–80, referring to Schauer, *Playing by the Rules*, 137–66).

are free to focus on factors of potential concern to designers of decisional environments (172).

Schauer's rule-based social systems do indeed capture aspects of modern law. They resemble the workings of actual large-scale bureaucratic regulatory organizations that Max Weber and others have described so well. Weber describes the ideal type of bureaucracy; Foucault, the way in which power circulates within it; Kafka the experience of one who is thrown into it. Presumptive positivism is also compatible with aspects of contemporary law: with systems of diference and review in administrative law; with the incapacitation of the dangerous in penal law; and with the strict liability that accompanies parking and speeding violations in a context of routine noncompliance, for instance.

The resemblance of Schauerian decisional environments to modern bureaucracies, like the common law's "sticky" (180) use of "encrusted" (180) or "ossified" (175) rulelike generalizations, fails to establish the centrality or necessity of rules to "law" as such, however, as Schauer admits. And neither does Schauer's analysis show what if anything is distinctively lawlike about law.

Presumptive positivism indeed implies that there is nothing distinctive about law beyond the social convention of calling it so. Schauer maintains that the rules of a golf game may constitute a legal system just as well as do the rules of what are conventionally taken to be law.[11] Seeking to avoid the limitations of perspectives that Schauer thinks have overemphasized the standpoint of the moral agent (232), presumptive positivism avoids the standpoint of the moral agent and leaves out the lawfulness of law.

Presumptive positivism thus goes further than Hartian legal positivism. Hart's positivism itself qualified Austin's by arguing that the command of a sovereign does not account enough for obligation. Yet recall (from "Sociolegal Positivism" in chapter 1) that Hart's positivist account of law, like Tyler's socio-psychological one, explains obligation as social pressure and thereby asserts that there is no necessary connection between law and morality. Hart's very claim of a possible absence (a "lack of necessary connection" between law and morality) in the context of commitment to social betterment engages his positivism in a particular relation between law and justice. Presumptive positivism, in its discussion of social systems of rules in decision-making environments in which justice and morality simply drop out, forgoes even such a relation.

In presumptive positivism, the subject, the telling, and the doing of "law" all take on a particular cast. The subject of this law, as has been seen, is a decision maker, a psychologically and politically constrained

---

[11] Schauer, comments at Legal Reasoning Conference in Honor of Frederick Schauer, Quinnipiac Law School, October 1997.

rational agent, who looks to the rules to set the agenda. A "putative rule-follower," this ostensible agent need not act, at least in the sense of action as involving initiation and judgment on the part of an actor. Rather than instantiating action, Schauerian decision represents the culmination or endpoint of a social process. The particular social process with which Schauer himself is concerned is the "design" of decisional environments for such an agent. In the engineering of these environments, human beings themselves become included within the resources and personnel of a technical world in which all is viewed as a matter of cause and effect, means and ends.

In presumptive positivism, the "doing" of what law calls for, like the subject of law, also takes a particular form. Schauer's decision making involves a determination via the rules of which factors to take into account. But *before* the invocation of any rule, a question of action or of what to do in a particular case must already have arisen. Just as presumptive positivism does not explain how a rule tells an addressee *to do*, neither does it account for this *need* to act or to do. Schauer's account of what lies prior to a rule in decision making takes no notice of—or at best takes for granted as social—any preexisting human need to act or any call or demand for decision or judgment. Schauer instead shows that a multitude of social considerations lie prior to a rule: background justifications; social processes, decisions, and judgments; social or psychological factors; moral and political factors; and so forth. As the interplay among norms (or between rules and norms) that occurs between the outset and result of rule-based decision-making, presumptive positivism explains decision making as resultant behavior, rather than as initiated and responsive action.

In presumptive positivism, the telling of law, like its subject and doing, also takes a particular form. In "controlling" decision-making behavior from the outset, Schauer's rules constrain behavior and limit options or choice. Yet they provide reasons for action, without giving reason *to* act. Rules may explain what results from decision making, but they do not adequately account for how decision making "results." The constraint of rules in Schauer's account differs from the various forms of binding which law has traditionally taken and about which it variously tells. Giving reason *to act*, or transforming reasons for action into action, is precisely what law has done throughout the Western tradition. Whether as ultimate threat or as authoritative command or as constitutive claim or as obligation, law has named the ultimate appeal to a "must" or necessity in which an addressee is told what "must" be done. When one asks, "Why must I?" the answer has been law and the subject's responsibility to it. "Must" lies behind the telling of rules, just as the need to act lies behind a subject's doing or decision making.

Consider a variation on H.L.A. Hart's much belabored hats-off-in-church example of a rule. A young child wants to wear something on his head into church. His parents provide some version of the rule. The child asks why. The patient parent offers some justification of the rule. The child again asks why. The parent offers a justification for the justification of the rule. The child again asks why. This continues for some time. Finally, the parent exclaims, "Because I said so!" or "Because that's the way it is!" or "That's how we do it around here!" or "That's just who we are!" The parent's final words mark the moment, *beyond rules*, where law—or what traditional jurisprudence has considered law—comes into play. The parent's final words—whether threat or authoritative command or claim as to the constitution of "who we are" as "persons who do it this way"—give the child (instantiated in this moment as a second person to be included in a first-person plural)[12] an imperative or reason *to* act in the particular way that the rules have only given reasons for.

In its answers to "Why must I?" law's appeal to the "we in this world" transforms the "to whom it may concern" of rules into an address to "you." Schauer, in his conceptual analysis of rule-based decision-making, provides no account of this moment. Presumptive positivism provides no account, other than vague references to social processes, of the telling of the "must" in what is to be done or of how rules address those whom they do. Recall that at the ultimate level of "bedrock justification," there is no further generating justification for which the bedrock justification can serve as instantiation or rule. At this layer, Schauer implies, rules run out. Presumptive positivism provides no account of how the telling of rules activates its addressees and engages them in producing the rules' results.

Hart's positivism had already constituted the "force" of rules as social and normative pressures that individuals internalize (see "Sociolegal Positivism" in chapter 1). But Schauer's psychological "internalization" is even weaker than the "acceptance" of secondary rules of H.L.A. Hart's officials, as Schauer acknowledges (121–22). It is different too from Hart's initial formulations of the "internal" aspect of rules. The internal "point of view" refers, for Hart, to the standpoint of members within the community that accepts a rule as a general standard or guide to conduct. The rules manifest themselves for those who accept them in statements of "obligation" that bespeak the internal aspect of rules. "External" points of view refer to the variety of vantage points from which observers who do not accept a rule as a standard for themselves may refer to it. Obligation, at least initially for Hart, is distinguished from "being obliged" or feeling coerced, whether

---

[12] *We* can include multitudes, but does not necessarily include "you." Here it comes to include "you." See Rosenstock-Huessy, *Speech and Reality*, and text accompanying chapter 2, n. 52.

by social or other pressure.[13] The psychological internalization, prudential reasoning, and socialization that Schauer describes as "the roots of normative force" (118) constitute a way of "being obliged" rather than "having an obligation." In Hart's terminology then (and to a degree that surpasses Hart), Schauer's account of a system of rules in effect turns obligation into being obliged. For Schauer, rules have no force independent of social pressures. Thus rules provide no more than in Schauer's words "reasons for action" (or reasons *to believe that* something is to be decided), and provide no reason *to act* (except through psychological internalization, rationalization, or socialization). Like social science, Schauer takes an external standpoint toward rules.

If Schauer's rules, as psychologically internalized prescriptive generalizations that result from socialization, do not give reason to act, Schauer's presumptive positivism, as descriptive claim, taking an external and sociological approach to systemic rule-based decision-making, provides no account of responsiveness to anything other than rules and social norms. It precludes responsibility at law. In locating the "force" of rules in social pressure, Schauer nullifies the responsibility of rule-based decision-makers for their own decisions. Insofar as Schauer maintains that social conditions oblige rule-based decision-makers to make the decisions they do—whether in following or overriding rules—he suspends their capacity *to* act and be held responsible for what they do. Corresponding to presumptive positivism's limited conception of human agency is a restricted view of the legal subject's freedom to initiate or be responsible for action.

This issue is again tied to the temporality of Schauer's account. Schauer attempts to fix the interval of outset to decision as a linear period within which rule-bound decision-making occurs. Schauer does not discuss the need or call to act or judge at all, a condition that lies prior, in the sense that it must arise before the application of decision-making rules. In responding to what has been already called for (before Schauer's "outset" of decision making) lies responsibility. In Schauer's account, rules provide nonabsolute reasons for action and allow one not to have to start over every time that decision making is called for. The agent's not starting over means that the initiation of action no longer responds to a prior call to action. Rather, action or doing in presumptive positivism is the rule-following that is the result of the decision-making process. The paradoxical beginning every time (or natality of which Hannah Arendt writes)[14] and responsibility that accompanies human action is lost in the decision makers' mere compliance to the rule.

[13] Hart, *The Concept of Law*, 86–89.
[14] Hannah Arendt, *The Human Condition*, 2nd ed. (Chicago: University of Chicago Press, 1989), 8–9, 247.

Presumptive positivism's account of playing by the rules, or *Playing by the Rules'* account of presumptive positivism, thus lays aside law, or at least issues of action, obligation, and responsibility that have so far been the distinctive subject matter of law in Western jurisprudence. Schauer's depiction of rule-based decision-making indeed captures something of modern law. It captures the rationality and the tenor—the constraints, the limited domain, the boredom—of what Milan Kundera calls, in an essay on Franz Kafka, "the bureaucratic world of the functionary." In this world, Kundera writes, "there is no initiative, no invention, no freedom of action; there are only order and rules: *it is the world of obedience.*"[15] That Schauer's depiction of a rule-based decision-making environment appears as such should give Schauer's readers pause. For reliance on Schauer's presumptive positivism as law, coupled with its neglect of the claims of the tradition as to the character of law, gestures toward the disappearance of what the West has known as "law" in favor of rule-based social systems where outcomes are determined from the outset of a decision-making situation by social considerations and normative pressures.

To Judge and to Act

"Law does not just stand there to be watched," Schauer writes (202). (He has just glossed the distinction between Dworkin and the legal positivists as the difference between Dworkin's standard of law as "seeing law largely through the eyes of the judge" and positivism's concern for regularity or "the normal operation of legal rules in everyday life" [200–201 n. 45].) But even as Schauer explicitly rejects the possibility of watching law, law enters quietly via the "glimpse" that lifts the curtain of a presumptive rule.

In presumptive positivism, a particular sort of "responsibility" attaches to the "maker of rules or designer of a decision-making environment" (124) with whom Schauer identifies. This rule maker or social engineer structures the decision making of others according to a given society's values and norms. Schauer suggests that when this rule-based decision-making agent says, "This is not my job," she is not necessarily abdicating "responsibility." Even as she abdicates responsibility for a result, he claims, she may be taking responsibility for leaving responsibility to others.

The designer of decision-making environments, herself participating in ostensibly rule-based decision-making, like others to whom she would

---

[15] Milan Kundera, "Somewhere Behind," in *The Art of the Novel*, trans. Linda Asher (New York: Perennial Library, 1988), 112.

leave responsibility, takes responsibility, one must add—although Schauer does not—if behind the rules effectively allocating power, she *glimpses* and finds—not simply social considerations and normative pressures that may or may not be too compelling to ignore—but reason *to* act, to responsibly abdicate to others. Reason to act is found in her situation and in her recognition of her situation in the rules.

The "glimpse" that lifts the curtain of a presumptive rule, that is, involves something other than what Schauer describes as the psychological possibility that a decision maker may look behind the rules, then ignore what she knows, so as to override rules only in the most compelling cases. It involves another sort of possibility, which comes out of the situation in which the decision maker is called to act. The possibility that a decision maker glimpse or not behind the curtain that is the rule, ignore or not what lies behind the curtain, override or not the rule—that, in other words, the decision maker judge or act responsibly—is not simply social and psychological. It is the possibility of response given by the situation. Glimpsing behind the curtain of a rule, the responsible designer must not only succumb to and take part in social processes, but must also do what is called for. In doing what she must, she acts responsibly. Action is responsively doing what one must or what law, in its response to a prior call or demand to act, itself now calls for.

Some would call the initiation of action here freedom. Dorothy Lee writes, "Freedom lies where *be* becomes *to be*; where the vague, the timeless, the not phenomenal, the unasserted, is transformed into an assertion, at the point where the individual *chooses* to be, to walk, to think, to suffer, to see."[16] This freedom is neither that of individual control—the stereotypical autonomy of free will or of moral agency that Schauer thinks has been overemphasized—nor that of absolute undecidability. For Schauer, between the outset and result of rule-based decision-making lies an interplay of social norms. But between the need for action, with the arising of a call or demand to act or to judge, and action, as responsible judgment, lies the freedom to act responsively. The freedom or initiation of action that lies between the need or call to act and action is not the same as the interplay of social norms; it does not consist of sociologically determinable decision-making processes that control agents who alienate freedom and relinquish choice from the outset. The possibility of acting is not exhausted by reference to the social world. *Action* is grounded rather in a world that is already there, giving rise to the human recognition of the need and corresponding responsibility *to act.*

[16] Dorothy Lee, *Valuing the Self: What We Can Learn from Other Cultures* (Englewood Cliffs, NJ: Prentice-Hall, Spectrum, 1976), 68. See also Dorothy Lee, *Freedom and Culture* (Englewood Cliffs, NJ: Prentice-Hall, Spectrum, 1959).

Freedom is, if anything, akin to what Milan Kundera counterposes to the obedience of the bureaucratic functionary in an essay on a text very different from Schauer's. Franz Kafka's novel *The Castle* displays what Milan Kundera calls "a kind of beauty never before seen." Kafka, an employee in one of the first worker's compensation insurance offices, turns "a very ordinary story of a man who cannot obtain a promised job"—a story of bureaucracy, of red tape, of lost files, of incompetent and lazy officials, of misdirected phone calls—into an amazing epic that gives rise to the word *Kafkaesque*. Kafka, according to Kundera, "unwittingly succeeded in creating an image that fascinates us by its resemblance to a society [Kafka] never knew, that of today's Prague." And yet, writes Kundera, citing Skacel's poem used in the epigraph to this chapter, "Kafka made no prophecies. All he did was see what was 'behind.' " Kafka " 'only discovers' a human possibility (. . . that has been there 'a long long time') that History will in its turn discover one day."[17] In other words, "Kafka did not intend to unmask a social system. He shed light on the mechanisms he knew from private and microsocial human practice, not suspecting that later developments would put those mechanisms into action on the great stage of history" (116). Kundera writes

> [I]f instead of seeking "the poem" hidden "somewhere behind" the poet "engages" himself in a truth known from the outset (which comes forward on its own and is "out in front"), he has renounced the mission of poetry. . . . If I hold so ardently to the legacy of Kafka, if I defend it as my personal heritage, it is not because I think it worthwhile to imitate the inimitable (and rediscover the *Kafkan*) but because it is such a tremendous example of the *radical autonomy* of the novel (of the poetry that is the novel). This autonomy allowed Franz Kafka to say things about our human condition (as it reveals itself in our century) that no social or political thought could ever tell us. (116–17)

The decision maker in the rule-based environment of presumptive positivism is no poet. The presumptively positivist decision-maker engages herself in rules known at the outset, refusing what is hidden "somewhere behind" the rules and renouncing the mission of law . . .

Schauer of course is not concerned with the mission of law or of poetry, nor with autonomy and freedom, radical or otherwise, but with designing decisional environments. He does not deny justice; he barely asserts its irrelevance. In Schauer's account of rule systems, as in much contemporary philosophy of law and legal theory, as in many texts of modern law, "justice" lies in silence. The silence of Schauer's text as to justice does not establish—nor even attempt to say—that justice exists or that it does not.

---

[17] Kundera, "Somewhere Behind," 99, begins with the verse from Jan Skacel cited at the beginning of this chapter.

But silence as to justice, in a work on rules that suggests it provides an account of "law" as we conventionally call it, does say something. It suggests, to those who recognize their legal systems in the work, that those systems are in danger of forgetting a tradition in which justice was a possibility of law. Such silence also suggests the danger of forgetting oneself, insofar as one's own jurisprudential traditions are an aspect of who one is. The silence as to justice of Schauer's text on rules suggests that law, insofar as it relates to justice, is not to be found in the entrenched semantic meanings of rule formulations. In modern legal systems, justice takes place not in rules understood as social phenomena nor even in the social factors that may override the rules. Possibilities of justice lie "behind" the rules—in the law that establishes what must be done when one needs to act. Behind the rules lies not only "everything else" that socio-legal scholars examine, but silences surrounding the calls to judge and act that correspond to human beings' needs and responsibilities to do so.

Chapter 6 _____

The "Field of Pain and Death"

> [W]ould thinkers or activists, even radical or
> critical ones, seriously consider putting the
> *possibility* of justice into question? Certainly
> some questions about its existence, its realiza-
> tion, have been raised—especially in the contem-
> porary United States, where every day and
> every night more and more women, people of
> color, gays and lesbians, prisoners, people
> without housing, and poor people are singled
> out for discrimination and death, in a continu-
> ing wave of violent economic, psychic, social,
> political, medical and juridical assaults. But
> these critical questions have, at least to my
> knowledge, generally operated well within the
> horizon of justice's possibility. Indeed, it is on the
> basis of the presumed possibility of justice that
> the critiques would have their meaning and perti-
> nence: because justice is possible, but not ac-
> tual, action is called for to bring it out of the
> taunting ideality of the potential and into real-
> ity. But this phrase ["possibility of justice"],
> without abandoning any of the critical force
> associated recently with the more daring wings
> of literary and political and legal studies, hints
> at a more unsettling thought: the possibility that
> justice might simply not be possible.
> —Thomas Keenan, *Fables of Responsibility*

CHAPTER 5 LOOKED AT SCHAUER'S positivist account of law as a social
system of rules to show that possibilities of law and justice are not what
they used to be. Justice, if any, lies in an ambiguous silence behind the
statements of rules of modern legal systems. Robert Cover offers an even
bleaker view. He argues in "Violence and the Word" that behind modern

law lies a social organization of violence that denies its own violence.[1] "Legal interpretation," he writes, "takes place in a field of pain and death" (203).

Like Schauer's account of rule-bound decision-making, Cover's account of a violent law that plays on a field of pain and death provides a possibly accurate understanding of modern law. Both accounts share in the predominant legal positivism of an age in which subjects of law, whether citizens or officials, use rules as templates to project imagined futures upon reality; in which social cues trigger the direction and management of social organizations by institutional role players; in which social agents deploy interpretations to claim, resist, or declare significance, no matter how incoherent; in which law manifests itself ultimately and predominantly as social control; and in which there seems no necessary connection between law and justice.

But there are differences between the two, just as there are different silences. First, if Schauer, like Hart and Tyler, grounds systems of rules in social pressure (only more so), Cover claims that the power of positive law grounds itself in a violence that diffuses itself through the institutions of law. The will of the Austinian sovereign who dominated his subjects gives way in Hart, Schauer, and now Cover to a new form of social power. The institutional problem Cover describes involves not simply a Schauerian structuring of decisional environments to constrain rational agents, but the organization of cues that trigger behavior in which the responsibility of the agent—and hence the correspondence of law with any (or even) "normative" value—is foreclosed.

Second, silence as to justice in Schauer's text about rules seemed to signal the disappearance of law—or at least of the law that the tradition of Western jurisprudence has associated in various ways with justice. But silence as to justice in a text about law may also remind us—as does Cover's essay—of the inadequacy of conceptions of law without justice.

Cover describes contemporary U.S. law in several ways. Law, to him, involves "the projection of an imagined future upon reality" (206); it is a practice (210, 216), a meaning-giving system (215), a set of resources for claiming significance (204, citing White). Above all, however, "it is those things in the context of the organized social practice of violence" (204 n. 2). Cover criticizes scholars of the 1980s for concentrating too single-mindedly on the interpretive aspects of judging and for systematically ignoring or underplaying "the violent side of law and its connection to interpretation and rhetoric" (204 n. 2). He himself distinguishes be-

---

[1] Robert Cover, "Violence and the Word," in *Narrative, Violence, and the Law: The Essays of Robert Cover,* ed. Martha Minow, Michael Ryan, and Austin Sarat (Ann Arbor: University of Michigan Press, 1993), 203.

tween the word, or "interpretation," with its suggestion of "social construction of an interpersonal reality through language" (205), and "violence," as "pain and death," with its language- and "world-destroying" capacity (205). At the same time, he argues that "the 'interpretations' or 'conversations' that are the preconditions for violent incarceration are themselves implements of violence" (211) and key to law. "Legal interpretation is either played out on the field of pain and death or it is something less (or more) than law," he writes (210).

At one level, Cover's argument appears unexceptional. There seems little here with which to disagree and there are few who seem to do so: yes, legal interpretation is different from literary interpretation; yes, judicial decisions may trigger institutional responses of violence; yes, a defendant experiences the violence of the system differently than a judge does. Why then was—or is—the essay important? It is doubtful that law professors twenty years ago were in need of another legal realist reminder; despite their ostensible focus on doctrine, interpretation and application, law professors then as now seem all too aware of what they take to be the social and economic realities governing life and constraining possibilities of law (whether or not they agree with their sociologist and economist colleagues about what precisely those "realities" are!). Certainly many of the scholars Cover mentions—as he acknowledges in his footnotes—do locate law in a context of social control and state coercion, and many go so far as to make coercion central to law. Dworkin acknowledges that legal interpretation occurs in the context of a state monopoly of legitimate violence.[2] Hart argues that legal rules characterize what is fundamentally a coercive legal system.[3] Sociologists of law have long been fixated on law as social control.[4] Even sociolegal scholars of language, as chapter 2 showed, treat law primarily as a matter of power.

This chapter suggests that the significance of "Violence and the Word" lies not so much in the newness of its description of law as in the questions it raises for those who would think about law further. The first section, "Cover's Loss of Self," summarizes the account of law in "Violence and the Word" and shows how Cover—unlike Foucault and Freud—colludes in the loss of self and collective meaning that his essay attributes to a

[2] Ronald Dworkin, *Law's Empire* (Cambridge: Harvard University Press, 1986), 93.

[3] Hart, *The Concept of Law*, 193.

[4] Studies of crime, deviance, and punishment provide obvious examples of sociological scholarship that treats law as social control. But conceiving of law as social control is widespread and is apparent early in the twentieth century in the writings of such great sociologists of law as Ehrlich, Pound, and Weber. See, too, the essays reprinted in Ronald L. Ahers and Richard Hawkins, eds., *Law and Control in Society* (Englewood Cliffs, NJ: Prentice-Hall, 1975), especially F. James Davis, "Law as a Type of Social Control," 17–32, and works cited therein.

violent law. The second section, "Modern Law," asks how Cover's conception of law as mediated violence has grown from a tradition that long has associated law—and language—with justice. Cover not only associates law with violence, but argues further that violence in law "is so intrinsic . . . that it need not be mentioned" (224). When Cover aligns the violence of law with both silence and the word, there indeed seems little justice in the modern law on which he focuses. The law of "Violence and the Word" that plays exclusively on a "field of pain and death" precludes the aspirations of justice in law to which Cover gestures in other essays that turn to narrative, myth, and folktales.[5] One need not understand the "field of pain and death" as exclusively violent, however, as the third section, "The Issue of Justice," points out. Cover's "field of pain and death" is a site not only of violence but also of human vulnerability and finitude that calls precisely for what Cover terms a "normative world." Law, as the necessity of and the response to such a call, establishes a world disclosed through language. The correspondence of the words and world of law to human finitude or need is the issue of justice. From this issue arises the particular justice and injustices in and of this world. If, in declaring the violence of modern law, Cover is silent about justice, it is to Cover's silence and to the silences of modern law that one must turn to recall the issue of justice from out of which Cover's claims matter at all.

Cover's Loss of Self

In "Violence and the Word," Cover presents modern law as mediated violence. He criticizes those who put interpretation at the center of law.[6] Both Cover and those he would criticize write about a modern positive or state law in which judges command or rather, in Cover's terms, trigger particular responses. To Cover, the response to such a trigger is an expression of institutional mechanisms. Judges are not sovereign, and Cover refuses to call the activation of mechanisms "a matter of will" (217): the "act of legal interpretation" is less "a single mind placed in the admittedly hypothetical position of being able to render final judgments sitting

[5] See, for instance, "Nomos and Narrative," "The Folktales of Justice: Tales of Jurisdiction," and "Obligation: A Jewish Jurisprudence of the Social Order," all three reprinted in Cover, Narrative, Violence, and the Law. See also Justice Accused: Antislavery and the Judicial Process (New Haven: Yale University Press, 1975).

[6] In a long footnote, "Violence and the Word," 204 n. 2, Cover points to a "recent explosion of legal scholarship placing interpretation at the crux of the enterprise of law." He refers to "various articles" in two symposium issues, published in Texas Law Review 60 (1983): 373, and Southern California Law Review 58 (1985): 1, and singles out Ronald Dworkin and James Boyd White for their eloquence on the issue.

alone" than "products of judges acting under the constraint of potential group oversight of all decisions that are to be made real through collective violence" (236). Legal interpretation is "the violent activity of an organization of people" (236).

In this activity, according to Cover, "a substantial part of [the judges'] audience loses its capacity to think and act autonomously" (221). Judges speak; from them issue "words," "utterances," "language" (216), but they cannot "act" alone (235). Instead, the social mechanism of which they form part deploys the violence of the law in restraining, rendering helpless, or otherwise hurting defendants.

Cover thus presents a modern penality that involves something other than the direct laying of hands on a body by the representative of a sovereign. Cover argues, in a way like Michel Foucault, that traditional concepts of sovereignty no longer serve as privileged descriptions of power insofar as many others necessarily accompany a judge in the deployment of law. (Foucault, as is now well known, shows how punishment changes from the spectacle of torture, which was both public and involved laying direct hold on physical bodies, to the prison, in which punishment is concealed or hidden from the public and involves only an indirect use of force on the body. Foucault argues that such a shift corresponds to the emergence of a network of social professionals whose evaluations replace the formerly clear juridical powers exercised by judges. He thereby suggests that power is no longer exercised outwards from a determinate center [or sovereign] but rather involves a complex of power-knowledge relations of which discipline is but one form.)[7]

Foucault's critique of the Enlightenment subject who wills is in the service of a critique of certain metaphysical distinctions—between ideal truth and real power, discourse and practice, mind and matter. In his appeal to the circulation of what he calls power-knowledge, Foucault refuses to allocate agency to any determinate site.[8] Instead, he explores what might be considered, in the parlance of contemporary philosophy of language, the "performative" aspect of speech that has been stripped of a single controlling or sovereign subject.[9] For Foucault, it makes little

---

[7] Foucault, *Discipline and Punish*.

[8] See Michel Foucault, *Power/Knowledge: Selected Interviews and Other Writings, 1972–1977*, ed. Colin Gorden (New York: Pantheon, 1980), especially "Two Lectures," 78–108, and "Truth and Power," 109–34. See also Marianne Constable, "Foucault and Walzer: Sovereignty, Strategy, and the State," *Polity* 24 (1991): 269–93.

[9] Some scholars analyze and evaluate speech for the way that it succeeds in persuading an audience of the claims a speaker intends to make. Like the rhetorician of chapter 1 above, Foucault would reject this traditional communications approach to discourse. Like J. L. Austin in *How to Do Things with Words*, discussed further in chapter 7, Foucault recognizes a "performative" aspect of speech: speech not only says, but also does. He goes further,

sense to speak of a "gap," as Cover calls it (217), between word and deed; the problem is to grasp how particular sorts of discourse lend credence to, reinforce, or produce particular practices and, conversely, how particular practices structure, reinforce, or produce particular sorts of discourse.[10]

By contrast, Cover displaces agency or will from judge to grander "social" entity in an argument that reiterates the very dualities between mind and deed, thought and action, speech and behavior, that Foucault aims to disrupt.

> Bridging the chasm between thought and action in the legal system is never simply a matter of will. The gap between understanding and actions roughly corresponds to differences in institutional roles and to the division of labor and of responsibility that these roles represent. Thus, what may be described as a problem of will with respect to the individual becomes, in an institutional context, primarily a problem in social organization. (217–18)

For Cover, the sociological relocation of agency from willing actor to institutional role-player fills a "gap": it explains the transformation of legal interpretation or of the judicial word into such violent deeds as incarceration and capital punishment.[11] Cover tries in some sense, then, to account for what Schauer's presumptive positivism leaves out: the transformation of reasons for action into action or doing, or what in Schauer is called responsibility. In Cover's account, though, the power of law grounds itself in violent institutional conduct in which subjects are stripped precisely of responsible agency. Legal interpretation, he writes,

> must be capable of transforming itself into action; it must be capable of overcoming inhibitions against violence in order to generate its requisite deeds; it must be capable of massing a sufficient degree of violence to deter reprisal and revenge. (223)

---

however, and, in parallel with his critique of the sovereignty of the subject (see nn. 7 and 8 above), challenges the authoritativeness attributed to the speaker and the meaningfulness of intention and will. See also *History of Sexuality*, vol. 1, trans. Robert Hurley (New York: Vintage, 1978); "What Is an Author?" in *Language, Counter-Memory, and Practice*, trans. Donald F. Bouchard and Sherry Simon (Ithaca, NY: Cornell University Press, 1977), 113–34; and the appendix to *The Archaeology of Knowledge* (the best translation of this appendix is by Ian McLeod and appears in *Language and Politics*, ed. Michael Shapiro [New York: New York University Press, 1984], 108–38 ["The Order of Discourse"]).

[10] In addition to "The Order of Discourse," see the great case studies: *Madness and Civilization, Birth of the Clinic, Discipline and Punish, History of Sexuality*. Note that discourse is not same as practice, power not the same as knowledge.

[11] Austin Sarat also points out—in another spirit—the sociological character of Cover's analysis in "Robert Cover on Law and Violence," in *Narrative, Violence and the Law*, 255–65.

Citing Milgram's experiments, Cover explains that in the organized hierarchies of an "agentic state," institutional systems of authority provide
the cues needed to cause a "shift from autonomous behavior to the
agentic behavior cybernetically required to make hierarchies work"
(220). Law operates "as a system of cues and signals to many actors who
would otherwise be unwilling, incapable or irresponsible in their violent
acts" (220).

Taking law as "cue" and "signal," then, Cover argues that law in effect
transforms otherwise "*un*willing" "actors" into *non*willing "agents."
This "shift" involves a loss of self, he argues, which lost "self" he distinguishes from the "institutional roles" produced by the system of legal
interpretations that call for violence.

For Cover, adopting agentic and institutional roles threatens and destroys the autonomous self. It destroys the self of all participants.
Not only do interpretive agents lose autonomy and judges lose the ability
to act, but defendants too lose themselves. The defendant's "civil facade"
is a role, according to Cover; it is "grotesque" to think it is "voluntary,"
except insofar as it represents the defendant's so-called "autonomous
recognition of the overwhelming array of violence ranged against
him" (211).

Furthermore, Cover argues, loss of self is accompanied by betrayal
of a normative world. The defendant's experience of pain reveals this
most explicitly, he writes, drawing on Elaine Scarry's work on torture.
But loss of a normative world is not limited to the defendant. Everyone
loses a normative world in the deployment of violent law, Cover explains,
since such deployment limits the commonality and coherence of meaning
two ways.

First, according to Cover, the absence of a singular sovereign or will
makes unified or coherent meaning improbable. This "practical" limit, as
Cover puts it, "follows from the social organization of legal violence [in
which no] single individual . . . renders any interpretation operative as
law—as authority for the violent act" (236–37). The legal system requires
the interpretations of many individuals, but convergence of meaning by
various individuals is "unlikely." Identifying, in effect, commonality with
aggregation of differences and coherence with identity or unity, Cover
writes that meaning is unlikely to be coherent if it is common; it is not
common if it is coherent (237).

The second—"tragic"—limit to common meaning for Cover is due to
the unbridgeable gap between the experiences of violence of the victim/
defendant and the perpetrator/legal agent. The "pain and fear" of the
victim is to the perpetrator "remote, unreal and largely unshared. [Pain
and fear] are, therefore, almost never made a part of the interpretive arti-
fact, such as the judicial opinion." The violence experienced by the victim

contrasts with the perpetrator's concern with interpretation: "for those who impose the violence the justification is important, real and carefully cultivated. Conversely, for the victim, the justification for the violence recedes in reality and significance in proportion to the overwhelming reality of the pain and fear that is suffered" (238).

The limits to coherence and commonality of meaning that Cover describes hold no hope for recovery of what he calls a "normative world," the shared world that is betrayed with the loss of self required by a violent law. In some sense like Foucault's Benthamite Panopticon, Cover's legal system involves an incorporation or loss of self in the service of judicial interpretation as societal command. Foucault uses the figure of the Benthamite design for a prison named the Panopticon as a model for disciplinary power in which the normalization of subjects occurs through their own participation in strategies of surveillance.[12] Yet if Foucault's Panopticon is an external projection of a Freudian superego in which a subject/ego internalizes the demands of authority, Foucault—and Freud—unlike Cover, does hold out possibilities other than loss.[13] Cover, however, precludes recovery of autonomy or production of common worlds.

Ironically, then, Cover's account, which least disrupts the traditional metaphysics of will challenged by Nietzsche, Heidegger, and Foucault, among others, also holds out least hope for recovery of self or world.[14] Cover's account relies on a strong subject-object (or autonomous actor-productive agent) distinction, even as it claims to deny the centrality of the subject or will. Like much of contemporary sociology, it transforms subjects into objects and then refuses to acknowledge the commonality

---

[12] Foucault, *Discipline and Punish*, 195–228. As he puts it,

> [T]he major effect of the Panopticon: to induce in the inmate a state of conscious and permanent visibility that assures the automatic functioning of power. So to arrange things that the surveillance is permanent in its effects, even if it is discontinuous in its action; that the perfection of power should tend to render its actual exercise unnecessary; that this architectural apparatus should be a machine for creating and sustaining a power relation independent of the person who exercises it; in short, that the inmates should be caught up in a power situation of which they are themselves the bearers. (201)

[13] For one account of the superego as internalized external authority, see chapter 3 of *The Ego and the Id* (1923) in Freud, *Standard Edition*, trans. and ed. James Strachey (London: Hogarth Press, 1966–73). For placement in a cultural context, see chapter 2 of *The Future of an Illusion* (1927), in *Standard Edition*. For examples of discussion of how recovery of self or ego development may occur through analysis, see *The Question of Lay Analysis* (New York: Norton, 1950), "Analysis Terminable and Interminable," and other essays in *Therapy and Technique* (New York: Collier, 1963).

[14] This is not to say that their hopes are grounded successfully in their claims. But Nietzsche, Freud, Heidegger, and Foucault explore various ways of confronting a subject who is no longer in control of him- or herself and his or her deeds.

or coherence of the former subjects' normative world. Thus it turns out to be more radical in its foreclosure of possibilities than either Foucault or Freud. Unlike Foucault's appeal to resistance and Freud's to analysis, Cover seems resigned to the loss of what is lost. His resignation reinforces the loss that his essay describes.

In sum, the field of pain and death in which law plays for Cover is, however subjectively experienced, an empirically ascertainable, socially organized violence. Such socially organized violence not only transforms language into "action" (or, rather, behavior and conduct) and turns word into deed, but also limits the possibilities of collective meaning for all parties. It inures judge, staff person, and defendant to any experience other than alienation and violence. The "achingly disparate significant experiences" of victim and perpetrator mean that the two are unable to share a "reality of common meaning" and that both are alienated from "normative worlds." Not only the "victim" of the organized violence of the legal system, but also the "perpetrator" of that violence, undergoes a loss of self through alienation from collective meaning and a common world. Cover's ostensible resignation to a situation of limited possibilities of common and coherent meaning reveals his own alienation from a normative world. Under his account, this inability to share in a normative world is no fault of his own. Such inability—whether his own or that of others—is presumably something that he deplores elsewhere. Yet the acceptance of an inability to share in a normative world in "Violence and the Word" suggests an even more extensive alienation and loss of self than that of the victim and perpetrator described in the essay. It suggests a growing alienation in which not only the essay, but also those who accept the essay's account without deploring it, participate.

Modern Law

Cover's account of law as mediated violence may or may not accurately describe the law of modernity. Yet it is important to note that his account seems acceptable or even pedestrian to many. However much his account is actually borne out, that is, acceptance of his account—or even its inability to shock—says something about the conditions under which we now think about law. Consider, by contrast, the conditions, *unlike* those under which we live, in which an account of law as violence would be shocking.

Whatever the conditions under which one might be shocked at Cover's account of violent law, those conditions are not the conditions in which Cover, his judges and victims, and most of his readers find themselves. The current familiarity and acceptability of Cover's description of law suggests that modern law may indeed be at least somewhat as Cover describes it. The alienation of the modern self spreads beyond that of the institutional rule-follower of chapter 5. The violence of modern law for Cover highlights the problematic of the "commonality and coherence that can be achieved" by the collectivity. If violence is an attribute of modern law, then such violence does indeed seem to distinguish modern law from poetry, as Cover puts it (although alienation from language may characterize literary interpretation today as much as it does legal interpretation).

The issue for our times, then, is not why or how modern law is not poetry. We who have been raised on the legal positivism and sociology of law of the modern West know that modern law is not poetry. The issue for us, for our times—and indeed what it may have been for Cover, before "Violence and the Word," in "Nomos and Narrative" or "The Folktales of Justice"—is how law is not violence. The issue is how, given a tradition that has strived to identify law with aspirations (if not the essence) of justice, we all now seem to identify what is crucial or essential to law with what was traditionally its opposite—violence and the destruction of a shared world.

Of course, the tradition of law in the West is not unmixed. But, as chapter 1 showed, one can certainly read the history of jurisprudence since the Greeks as the story of the unfolding, through reason or the will to truth, of various configurations of justice and law. Recall (from "The Problem of Nietzsche" in chapter 1) that in the early Socratic dialogues, for instance, justice lies in the virtue of the wise citizen of the polis; although not accessible to all, the relatively sensible custom or law of the community is known to and practiced by or enacted in the good man. With Christianity comes the recognition that justice belongs not to the City of Man, but to the City of God. Although the divine and eternal law is temporally unattainable, Christianity holds out to the pious the assurance of participation in a natural law and the promise of future Justice in a world beyond. Following challenges to the foundations of Christianity, Kant replaces the natural law that was grounded in an inaccessible or undemonstrable God, with a moral law that comes from the autonomy (or "self-law") of persons. It falls to the utilitarians to point out that the categorical imperative and the Kantian absolutely good will are as unknown and undemonstrable as Christian justice and to try instead to ground duty and obligation in what can (actually) be known of human beings in an empirical world. The principle of utility, the positive laws of many empiricists and legislators, the social policies of economists, the values of pollsters, and the arguments of political theorists are still thoroughly metaphysical. They all aim for better worlds, for happiness or fairness or distributive justice or other values to be realized, not perhaps in some heavenly world beyond, but in the future of society.

Since Plato, then, the history of jurisprudence has been, at least in part, the history of a metaphysical quest for justice. In this tradition, human beings never completely grasp the just law whose foundations they posit in various ways. A paradox lies in the simultaneous maintenance of a quest for justice with a positing of founding violence in pursuit of this quest.[15] Cover recognizes this originary violence in his description of the martyrs and the founding of the United States (206–10). Yet in "Violence and the Word," the paradox of law—of a future justice that grounds itself in violence, of a present violence that grounds itself in a promise of justice—flattens out in an exploration of socially organized violence *as* law. Despite his writings elsewhere, Cover here neither follows the tradition that would associate law with an aspiration, successful or not, to justice, nor, as the section "Cover's Loss of Self" above showed, engages in the confrontation with that tradition initiated by Nietzsche. Rather, with social contract theorists and other sociologists, Cover follows in the footsteps of the one-sided Thrasymachus and a bastardized Hobbes.[16]

Legal interpretation plays in fields of pain and death where violence is imposed and justified, writes Cover. But so too do wars and cat fights and insurance adjusters and movies and the Red Cross play in fields of pain and death where violence is imposed and justified in one way or another. The question—for those of us who have been raised on or in Weberian states that hold monopolies on legitimate violence—is what, if anything, *distinguishes*—or has distinguished—law from other fields of pain and death where violence is imposed and justified. The question modifies and radicalizes that raised by Schauer's work: What distinguishes law from any other internalized coercive and social phenomenon?

The question of what distinguishes law as law from other social systems indeed arises for all who would take law to be positive law, whether the commands of a sovereign, a system of rules, or a network of social control. Jurisprudence as a tradition answers by pointing to the ways in which an association between law and justice has been named or sought or contested in terms that are not reducible to sociological ones. Cover and the legal positivists, with their denials of a necessary connection between law and morality, give a different answer to the question of what is distinctive about law. Cover suggests that the difference between law and other internalized coercive and social phenomena is sociological: he points to the particularities of the "social organization" of essentially violent law.

[15] See, for instance, Walter Benjamin, "Critique of Violence," in *Reflections*, ed. Peter Demetz, trans. Edmund Jephcott (New York: Schocken, 1978), 277–300. But see also Dworkin (and others) discussed below.

[16] Plato's *Republic*, Book 1; Thrasymachus appears at 336b ff. See Hobbes of the actual texts of *De Cive* and *Leviathan*.

From out of the tradition of jurisprudence briefly sketched above how-ever, comes another possibility: that modern law is essentially violent may be reason to reconsider its claim to be the whole of "law," rather than reason to think, with Cover in "Violence and the Word," that law essen-tially occurs in a context of socially organized violence. Some may claim and indeed be correct—as Cover implies—that there exists no justice-seeking law within the state. But this is no reason to equate all law with violence. It suggests equally well, as Cover seems to recognize elsewhere,[17] that even today the positive law of the state—whether legal interpretation or institutional mechanism—does not exhaust law. As Cover himself writes, when social control or domination produces behavior, both the acting self and its "normative world" are lost. Only where behavior is not controlled or dominated or triggered, whether by social institutional mechanisms of power or by legal entities such as rules, can persons—whether judges or others—initiate and be responsible for action.

Such responsibility can no longer ground itself in the pure freedom of a determining will, whether that of a sovereign-god or of a sovereign man, however. As Nietzsche puts it, "[N]o one *gives* a human being his quali-ties: not God, not society, not his parents or ancestors, not *he himself* (— the nonsensical idea here last rejected was propounded, as 'intelligible freedom,' by Kant, and perhaps also by Plato before him)." If "in reality purpose is *lacking*," where does one find the limits of the control and domination of positive law?[18]

"Violence and the Word" gestures strangely and despite itself toward such limits. Cover writes that the limits of domination lie in language. He finds what little hope exists for "domesticating violence" in speech or what he calls "many voices" (236):

> As long as death and pain are part of our political world, it is essential that they be at the center of the law. The alternative is truly unacceptable—that they be within our polity but outside the discipline of the *collective* decision rules and the individual efforts to achieve outcomes through those rules. The fact that we require many voices is not, then, an accident or peculiarity of our jurisdictional rules. It is intrinsic to whatever achievement is possible in the domesticating of violence. (236)

"Many voices," writes Cover, "domesticat[e] violence." They tame its excesses, making it presentable and (paradoxically) effective. Many voices do violence "safely and effectively" because they allow responsibility for the violence to be shared. The sharing of responsibility occurs in the form of "secondary rules and principles," writes Cover, reminiscent of both

[17] See note 5.
[18] Nietzsche, "The Four Great Errors," *Twilight of the Idols*, section 8.

Hart and Schauer. Such rules "ensure that no single mind and no single will can generate the violent outcomes that follow from interpretive commitments" (237).

Recall that for Cover, however, a multitude of voices also brings with it the probability of incoherence and an absence of unified meaning. Hence the alternatives to the violence of a "single will" are problematic in their own ways: on the one hand lies the incoherence of multiple voices; on the other, silence leads to further undomesticated violence. In silence, that is, Cover finds neglect and denial by law and legal scholarship of its own violence—the violent preconditions, impositions, and projections that he criticizes others for neglecting: "The violent side of law and its connection to interpretation and rhetoric is systematically ignored or underplayed in the work of Dworkin and White" (204 n. 2).

Simple examination of the texts not only of Dworkin and White, however, but of many texts of and about law, especially criminal law, shows *contra* Cover that the problematic of violence besets the best efforts of judges, legal philosophers, and other commentators to justify and interpret law. Indeed, the problem of violence, as Cover at times acknowledges, serves precisely and explicitly to motivate attempts to justify and legitimate a law that is undeniably violent and in *need* of justification and legitimation. The secondary rules Cover refers to, for instance, come from Hart's account of what he acknowledges to be a "coercive system." Dworkin admits to the need to address the problem of force (or violence) when he writes that governments have goals:

> They use the collective force they monopolize to these and other ends. Our discussions about law by and large assume, I suggest, that the most abstract and fundamental point of legal practice is to guide and constrain the power of government in the following way. Law insists that force not be used or withheld, no matter how useful that would be to ends in view, no matter how beneficial or noble these ends, except as licensed or required by individual rights and responsibilities flowing from past political decisions about when collective force is justified.[19]

James Boyd White locates much of his work on interpretation in the context of the "terrible responsibility" of judges and juries who must decide what to do.[20] The lawyer, he writes, "knows that her clients have to be there, in her office or someone else's, for the law is the instrument of official power; in this sense it is central as nothing else is."[21] Indeed, he criticizes what he calls "one great vice of theory in the law"—that "under

[19] Dworkin, *Law's Empire*, 93.
[20] White, *Heracles' Bow*, 197.
[21] White, *Justice as Translation*, 262.

a pretense that the result is compelled by one or another intellectual system," such theory "disguises the true power that the judge actually has, which it is his true task to exercise and to justify."[22]

Cover too claims that the "ideological functions" of law create meanings that "justify" the event of violence to the judge while "hiding" the nature of their order from them (212). "Violence is so intrinsic," Cover writes, "that it need not be mentioned" (214); according to him, violence lies at the limits of language, as the undeniable yet suppressed context of law.

For Cover then, combating the social organization and generation of violent outcomes by a single will involves either multiple voices and incoherence or else silence and further undomesticated violence. Cover thus finds violence both in speech—in the "utterances," "words," "language," "mental activity of individuals," "thoughts," that constitute the legal interpretations that authorize violent deeds or events—and in the silence that lies at the limits of speech. Agreeing with White that law is a "system of constitutive rhetoric: a set of resources for claiming, resisting and declaring significance," and arguing also that the domestication of violence involves secondary rules and principles, Cover maintains that law is all those things only in what is *already* a "context of the organized social practice of violence," (204 n. 2, citing White, *Heracles' Bow*, 205), a context that precedes speech. "I do not wish us to pretend that we talk our prisoners into jail," writes Cover (211), suggesting that we do talk ourselves into just such a pretense. The pretense of legal interpretation only succeeds, Cover points out, so long as law puts prisoners in jail or plays on a field of pain and death.

The Issue of Justice

Cover claims that others systematically ignore or underplay the violent side of law and its connection to interpretation. He asserts that a field of pain and death is prior to the rules and rhetoric that others identify as law. But one can acknowledge that "we do not talk our prisoners into jail," as Cover puts it, and can even accept the priority of a field of pain and death over the rules and "rhetoric" of law, without granting violence absolute primacy at law. Indeed, one could say that Cover underplays a silent side of law and its connection to a field of pain and death that is not simply violent.

The field of pain and death, that is, is not simply violence and its practice. Even granting, as Cover suggests, that pain and death are always experienced "subjectively," violence is not the same as or coextensive with

[22] White, *Heracles' Bow*, 123.

pain and death. All will suffer pain and all will die. But at least some will do so without simultaneously undergoing the world-destroying socially organized violence of Cover's law.

Hence the "field of pain and death" without which there is no law is open to a radically different interpretation from that of Cover. Cover writes that as long as death and pain are part of our political world, they must be at the center of a discursively domesticatable violent law. Yet it is at least equally the case that what Cover calls our subjective experiences of death and pain speak of our need for—and, in speaking, to our already being in—a world in which we find ourselves limited by something that is not of our own making.

Language discloses a world into which we are already thrown and from which we call out our need. "Law" names the *way* we are bound through those calls and that language to this world. Without language and law, we neither "subjectively" experience our own deaths (or lives and pains and pleasures), nor share in the political world with which Cover begins nor in the normative world that he argues law betrays. Language and law make "subjective" experiences and "common" normative arrangements possible.

Unless we are bound to a world by language, common or collective meaning is not simply limited, as Cover would have it, but gone. Cover argues that so long as pain and death are part of our political world, they must be at the center of a violent law. But so long as we are in a given world, language and law (however violent or silent) first allow us to experience that world as we do.

Pain and death, in other words, do not simply point, as Cover would have them do, following literary scholar Scarry on torture, to the betrayal of what Cover calls a "normative world." They point to a prior relating of human and world, in which finite humans need and call for a so-called normative world. Law names the correspondence, in calls to justice, of this world to human need or finitude. Law names the ordering, the assembling, the establishing of commonality that happens when humans take (or interpret) there to be a world that they judge. The correspondence or order of law constitutes the "reality of common meaning" (however deplorable or celebrated) that grounds claims, such as Cover's or those of others, of betrayal, need, or norm. Law binds Cover's otherwise lost selves into the "common," on the basis of which Cover can write, selves be lost, norms betrayed, and worlds destroyed. Without law, without the assembling and gathering into the common through which finite humans beings correspond with their world, neither normative world, nor subjective experience, nor betrayal would be possible.

All "normative activity," as Cover calls it, whether custom or natural law or morality or legislation or judicial opinion-writing or Supreme Court holdings or etiquette or other practices that may or may not hold the status of law, presumes a belonging-together of persons, in a world that appears to them through their language. The gathering, in (and to) a world, of persons-belonging-together is prior to the violent positive law of which Cover speaks. In some sense this priority does not exist; in another, it is in danger of disappearing. It is the priority of the need and call to act that comes before or lies "somewhere behind" the rules of chapter 5. It is the priority of what is already there and yet needed for the recognition of voice of chapter 2. Law names the necessity of this unsayable priority of being bound in and to a world. It is on the basis of this necessity that Cover's law—or any other law, for that matter—is both possible and may yet one day become impossible. The strange nonactual nonchronological temporality of this priority is constantly in question. For if one modern possibility of justice is that it is impossible, one paradoxical possibility of law is that its necessity disappears.

To "agree" in this context that law *ought* to be interpreted now seems laughable: the utterance of a law professor playing god.[23] Law is already interpretation; it is the necessity of language—the calling of words that happens through voice (even when it does not say what it means)—that establishes our world. Law has already bound us; it has produced the very possibility of "ought" as an interpretation of world. In other words, if language is the naming of world, then law is the establishing of world in the naming—the world is already established in the naming that is the interpreting. Interpretability is the "ought" that must be, which law binds us to. As the necessity of our corresponding as finite beings with a world, law requires of us that we have already interpreted the world.

Cover's account of law seeks to right the imbalance he finds in the privileging of legal interpretation over law's violence. Cover puts interpretation in the service of a violence that it can never master and, at best, can only render more effective. Such an account, acceptable as it may be as a characterization of modern law, underplays at least one aspect of law: the issue of its correspondence to justice—a prior issue that one grants is both irreducible to the modern language of law (see chapter 4) and insufficiently addressed in work on interpretation at law.[24]

Cover's essay suggests in so many words that in positive law, justice might be impossible.[25] In the words and silences of law and legal scholarship, Cover finds, in his words, a neglect and denial of law's violence. In the

[23] See Pierre Schlag, *Laying Down the Law: Mysticism, Fetishism, and the American Legal Mind* (New York: New York University Press, 1996) for engaging ways of making the same point about the interpretations of law professors (although not about law).

[24] Although White clearly addresses an aspiration to justice in his work on interpretation, he takes this aspiration to be an aspect of the power of language (*Heracles' Bow*, 242).

[25] See also Coleman, "Negative and Positive Positivism" and "Rules and Social Facts."

modern law he describes emerges the paradox of positive law: the possibilities of justice in positive law include the possibility, as Tom Keenan puts it, that justice might simply not be possible. For Cover, the correspondence of persons and world that was the naming and binding or necessity of law is no longer. In his essay echoes the bleakness of a world without justice. But the silences of Cover's text are unlike those he finds in the statements of rules and of legislation and judicial opinions that are the objects of interpretation and theory. The silences Cover points to speak of the implementation of a violence that masks itself. The silences of Cover's own text warn—in a way that his words do not—of the danger of forgetting justice.

How does one hear calls to justice in the silences of modern law? By listening to what speaks of silence: poetry. Cover writes of literary interpretation what is more properly said of poetry: that it does not take place in an institutional setting of violence. The poet, unlike the agentic state, may still remind persons of their need for justice—a need whose fulfillment the invocation of law used to call for and, who knows? may yet call for again. If, as Cover puts it, legal interpretation is—or has become—the implement of a violence that destroys both self and common meaning, we moderns must look to law as poetry to recall the possibilities of justice. We must find the call for justice where we can—in the language of the poets and in the silences of law and legal scholarship. Justice lies in silence in the violent law of "Violence and the Word," but this *may* be only to say that there is no justice to speak of, not that there is no possibility of justice at all.

Chapter 7

Brave New Words:
The *Miranda* Warning as Speech Act

Miranda: O wonder!
How many goodly creatures are there here.
How beauteous mankind is. O brave new world
That has such people in't!
Prospero: 'Tis new to thee.
—Shakespeare, *The Tempest*, act 5, scene 1

It is worth ... reminding you, how many of the
"acts" which concern the jurist are or include
the utterance of performatives, or at any rate are
or include the performance of some conventional procedures. ... [I]n this way and that,
writers on jurisprudence have constantly
shown themselves aware of the varieties of infelicity and even at times of the peculiarities of
the performative utterance. (Only the still widespread obsession that the utterances of the
law, and utterances used in say, acts in the law,
must somehow be statements true or false, has
prevented many lawyers from getting this whole
matter much straighter than we are likely to).
—J. L. Austin, *How to Do Things with Words*

WELL KNOWN TO A television-watching public as signaling the successful
apprehension of a suspect at the *end* of a show, the often droning recitation
of the *Miranda* warning also marks a *beginning*: the entry of a suspect into
the formal legal process. Warning the accused that he has a right to remain
silent, that any statement he does make may be used in evidence against
him in a court of law, and that he has the right to the presence of an
attorney, either retained or appointed, is, according to the 1966 *Miranda
v. Arizona* U.S. Supreme Court decision, a prerequisite to the admissibility
as evidence at trial of any statement made by an accused while in custody.[1]

---

[1] *Miranda v. Arizona*, 384 U.S. 436, 86 S.Ct. 1602 (1966).

Criticized on all sides—for its reasoning, its use of history and precedent, its constitutional basis, as policy, as rule, for not going far enough,
for going too far—the Warren Court's (five-to-four majority) *Miranda*
opinion at first seems to offer little to an understanding of just silences,
focusing as it does on police practices surrounding confession, rather than
on the silence of any particular defendant or the potential for silence that
Miranda would safeguard. Neither does the *Dickerson v. U.S.* Supreme
Court opinion, which in the year 2000 affirmed the *Miranda* holding by
claiming its status to be that of a constitutional rule, seem to offer much
in the way of explaining how possibilities of justice may lie in silence.[2]

A closer look at the text of the *Miranda* opinion, however, shows how
the contemporary American right to remain silent may indeed open up
possibilities of justice. Paying special attention to the silences of *Miranda*
and drawing on the work of J. L. Austin, this chapter argues that the right
to remain silent or, more precisely, a felicitous "*Miranda* warning" may
help preserve the trial as a space of proper speech.[3] In such a hearing,
judges and juries—charged with speaking the truth of the verdict (or *veredictum*)—may presume that what they hear has been uttered in conditions
proper to speech. The warning helps establish for a trier of fact the conditions needed for hearing something properly: that it be uttered properly.
This chapter shows how the possibility of a just trial relies in part on an
understanding of speech that is itself inextricably joined with silences.

The argument builds on the idea that a warning puts an addressee on
notice about a named danger. A warning is "felicitous" in Austin's terms
or "adequate" in the Court's when it alerts its addressee to the need to
proceed more carefully into the danger, or to not proceed at all. The *Miranda* warning lets its addressee know of the danger that, as of this moment of entry into the legal process, his or her utterances are liable, in the
contexts of both interrogation and trial, to have different import than
they would otherwise have. The chapter suggests that a felicitous *Miranda*
warning allows a decision maker at trial to presume that an accused's
statements made during in-custody interrogation were themselves properly spoken. The accused's statements constitute proper speech in the minimal yet necessary sense that the speaker accepted the terms of speech
that were available—the opportunities and constraints of speech under
in-custody interrogation. The silence of an accused following a felicitous
warning, on the other hand, must be taken as accepting the law's acknowledgment that conditions during in-custody interrogation may not
be conducive to speech.

---

[2] *Dickerson v. U.S,* 530 U.S. 428, 120 S.Ct. 2326 (2000).
[3] J. L. Austin, *How to Do Things with Words,* ed. J. O. Urmson and Marina Sbisa, 2d
ed. (Cambridge: Harvard University Press, 1975).

In the context of this book, the chapter shows how attending to speech and silence offers ways of thinking about law and justice that differ from the usual ways described in the previous chapters. The language of speech and silence is, in some sense, the same as, and yet different from, the language of social power.

The first section, "The Holding," introduces the *Miranda* opinion and its holding. It suggests that attending to the warning as speech act makes sense of the Court's argument in a way that the usual interpretations of *Miranda* do not. The next section, "Neither Logic nor Experience," explores figures of speech and silence in the opinion. Close reading reveals some surprising insights and commitments on the part of the Supreme Court: the Court refers to the efficacious action of silence in history; it acknowledges a danger that words may be empty forms; it insists on the coerciveness of the actual system; and it distances itself from conventional conceptions of truth as either empirical accuracy or a particular sort of reliability. The following section, "Warnings and Waivers," then briefly explains Austin's account of speech acts before arguing that *Miranda*'s concern with the warning and its complement, the waiver, shows the Court to be, in Austin's words, "aware of the varieties of infelicity and even . . . of the peculiarities of the performative utterance" (19). Such awareness extends to seeing that the very possibility of justice at trial relies in part on felicitous—not "free"—speech. As the fourth section, "The Trial as Hearing and Event," points out, the *Miranda* Court's holding grounds itself less in an interest in fairness to the defendant during interrogation or in the need for reliable evidence at trial than in safeguarding the justice of the hearing. A just verdict ensues from an adversarial hearing only when all parties accept and are able to speak the language of, and before, the court. The silence of a defendant need not be read as intransigence or recalcitrance, as noncooperation in the investigation of facts, much less as evidence of guilt or as an indication of "something to hide."[4] It may instead be an appropriate response to a situation in which even the legal system acknowledges that the defendant's truth cannot be stated within the conditions and constraints offered by the system.

The Holding

Chief Justice Warren sets up the issue in the sixty-page *Miranda* opinion as whether statements obtained from a defendant "while in custody or otherwise deprived of his freedom of action in any significant way" are

---

[4] *Miranda*, 454, quoting an interrogation manual, *Criminal Interrogation and Confessions*, by Fred E. Inbau and John E. Reid (Baltimore: Williams and Wilkins, 1962), 111.

admissible as evidence under the Fifth Amendment privilege against self-incrimination. The holding, the introduction concludes,

> briefly stated is this: the prosecution may not use statements, whether exculpatory or inculpatory, stemming from custodial interrogation of the defendant unless it demonstrates the use of procedural safeguards effective to secure the privilege against self-incrimination. By custodial interrogation we mean questioning initiated by law enforcement officers after a person has been taken into custody or otherwise deprived of his freedom of action in any significant way. As for the procedural safeguards to be employed, unless other fully effective means are devised to inform accused persons of their right of silence and to assure a continuous opportunity to exercise it, the following measures are required. Prior to any questioning, the person must be warned that he has a right to remain silent, that any statement he does make may be used as evidence against him, and that he has a right to the presence of an attorney, either retained or appointed. The defendant may waive effectuation of these rights provided the waiver is made voluntarily, knowingly and intelligently. If, however, he indicates in any manner and at any stage of the process that he wishes to consult with an attorney before speaking there can be no questioning. Likewise, if the individual is alone and indicates in any manner that he does not wish to be interrogated, the police may not question him. The mere fact that he may have answered some questions or volunteered some statements on his own does not deprive him of the right to refrain from answering any further inquiries until he has consulted with an attorney and thereafter consents to be questioned. (444–45)

Five parts follow the introduction. In the first, the Court establishes the coerciveness of in-custody interrogation and argues for the need for protective devices "to dispel the compulsion inherent in custodial surroundings" (458). In the second, it presents a history of and precedents relating to the self-incrimination clause. In the third, it explains the warnings in detail, justifying them as procedural safeguards that protect exercise of the privilege against self-incrimination. In the fourth, it responds to the objection that effective law enforcement's " 'need' for interrogation" outweighs the privilege by showing that the FBI already in effect presents such warnings. In the fifth, it brings its attention to bear on the facts of the cases before it.

The opinion, like most of its critics and many of its defenders, seems to focus on police practices surrounding confession rather than on the law of evidence as such. Commentators both for and against the *Miranda* holding struggle over the ostensible tensions between law enforcement agencies' need to gather information from suspects and the conditions required to ensure that a suspect's statements are voluntarily made.[5] Even when they do not explicitly say so, commentators on both sides presume that an accused's silences indicate, if not the concealment of truth, at least refusal to cooperate or resistance to power in the name of one's own interests.[6]

These critics miss what is admittedly something of a commonplace: that particular statements and silences take on different import[7] in different contexts. Although a commonplace, this insight has important implications for understanding the possibilities of justice that lie in the silences of law and in their protection through the *Miranda* warning. Such an insight shifts the focus of discussion away from rights, away from questions about the nature and appropriate extension of the Fifth Amendment privilege against self-incrimination, away from police-versus-defendant arguments for or against particular interrogatory protections or practices. It focuses instead on the speech act of warning.

"A warning is a clearcut fact," writes the Court (469), contrasting the *fact* of warning to the *speculation* that is otherwise required to ascertain whether a defendant knew his or her rights before interrogation and understood what s/he was doing in talking to the police. "More important" than the fact of warning, though, continues the Court, is what the warning *does* (469).

---

[5] Against: Joseph Grano, *Confessions, Truth, and the Law* (Ann Arbor: University of Michigan Press, 1993); the many law review articles of Paul G. Cassell; Fred E. Inbau, "The Mischief of *Miranda v. Arizona,*" *Journal of Criminal Law and Criminology* 73 (1982): 797; Fred E. Inbau and James P. Manak, "*Miranda v. Arizona*—Is It Worth the Cost?" *California Western Law Review* 24 (1988): 185; and others. Defending: Richard A. Leo, "The Impact of Miranda Revisited," *Journal of Criminal Law and Criminology* 86 (1996): 621; and other work cited by Leo. Leo refers to Robert Tucker's estimate that seventy-five law review articles a year are written about *Miranda,* "Protecting the Guilty—True Confessions: The Long Road Back to Miranda," *National Review* October 1985, 28. Much law review literature about *Miranda* attempts to bring the many cases qualifying and elaborating on it into a consistent pattern.

[6] It is not surprising, of course, that discussion focuses on interests when the issue is framed as one of compulsion or coercion. See, however, Daniel J. Seidmann and Alex Stein, who argue that the conventional view that the right to remain silent is in the interest only of the guilty is incorrect. They argue that it is also in the interest of the innocent who speak the truth that the guilty exercise the right (because of the difference this makes to the trier of fact). "The Right to Silence Helps the Innocent: A Game-Theoretic Analysis of the Fifth Amendment Privilege," *Harvard Law Review* 114 (2000): 430.

[7] *Import* is used here and throughout to avoid the difficulties surrounding other words which might have been used, but have developed particular and specialized meanings that are not always apt: "sense," "meaning," "significance," for instance. The "import" of an utterance refers to both locutionary and illocutionary aspects of the utterance, but not to its perlocutionary effect (or "force"). The "meaningfulness" of speech is not limited to constative or propositional "meaning."

What does the *Miranda* warning do? What, according to the Court, does the *Miranda* warning do that the former totality-of-circumstances "rule" or "test"—for the voluntariness of a confession, and hence its admissibility as evidence under the Fourteenth Amendment's due process clause—does not? This is different from simply asking how a warning could qualify the former admissibility rule or even asking how the *Miranda* holding could be read to amend the admissibility rule to require warnings from now on as evidence of the fact of voluntariness and hence admissibility of confessions. The *Miranda* holding suggests that a warning is less important as evidence for retrospective judgments ascertaining the facts around and hence admissibility of confessions, than for what it does in the time and place that it is said.

A properly administered and taken up warning alerts its addressee about a danger in such a way that the addressee normally proceeds more carefully into the danger or does not enter into it at all. The properly administered *Miranda* warning puts the accused on notice that as of the moment that the warning is given—which is now constituted as the moment of formal entry into the interrogatory phase of the legal process—statements or utterances are liable to do something different than they would have before such entrance. The warning that any statements may be used against the accused in a court of law acknowledges that statements made under interrogation, which take on different import than usual, may take on yet other import when presented as evidence against their speaker in the context of the truth-seeking event that is the trial. The warning not only informs or reminds the accused about his or her rights, but puts the accused on notice about the risk in speaking—and the need for caution in doing so—as of this particular moment in the process.

In the language of the Court, "a warning *at the time* of interrogation is indispensable . . . to insure that the individual knows he is free to exercise the privilege *at that point in time*" (469; emphasis added). Even those who presumably know their rights must be warned at the "outset of the interrogation" (457, 465, 467): the warning must be given irrespective of "age, education, intelligence, or prior contact with the authorities . . . whatever the background of the person interrogated" (469) because at the moment when the adversarial criminal proceeding "commences" (477) and the suspect is "first subjected" to deprivation of freedom of action (477), the warning does something other than simply stating rights that may already be known.

The warning also does something other than serve as evidence of a characteristic (such as voluntariness) to be retrospectively attributed to the defendant or to the defendant's statements, the way that it would if *Miranda* simply established a rule requiring the warning's existence for ascertaining such a characteristic. (*Dickerson* asserts as much. And law review discussion since *Dickerson* explicitly takes up the issue of how the *Miranda* "rule" relates to the former totality-of-circumstances voluntariness "test": whether it replaces, transforms, or supplements the test.)[8] In other words, by the time of *Miranda*, even if it was not always the case, the totality-of-circumstances "test" serves as a statement of a rule for retrospectively determining the fact of the voluntariness of a defendant's statements. The warning does something else.

The warning, rather than primarily constituting such a test, responds in the moment to a particular situation—a situation that the Court describes as one in which an accused is "cut off from the outside world." Itself an event of sorts—what J. L. Austin calls a "performative speech act"—the warning points out a danger and advises caution. It calls for a particular response—caution or avoidance—from those to whom it is addressed. The three dissents in *Miranda* shift between understanding the warning as test or rule and as event. On the one hand, they criticize the majority opinion for the new rule or "new code" that it produces (Clark and Harlan). On the other, they also seem to grasp that as speech act or event, the warning has particular implications. The responses that the warning will evoke, they argue, will produce as yet empirically unknown effects; they fear the worst (Harlan and White).

The Court by contrast suggests that even the former totality-of-circumstances "rule" for the admission of evidence is more properly understood as characterizing an event than as characterizing a statement or a state of mind. The rule for the admission of evidence, the majority claims, is confused and arises

> from a misconception of the subject to which proof must address itself. The rule is not that in order to render a statement admissible the proof must be adequate to establish that the particular *communications* contained in a statement were voluntarily made, but it must be sufficient to establish that the *making* of the statement was voluntary. (462, quoting *Bram v. Stoker*; my emphasis)

The Court quotes *Wan v. U.S.* to say, further, that a "confession is voluntary in law if, and only if, it was, in fact, voluntarily made" (462). At stake—even before *Miranda*, claims the Court—are the conditions of the making, or of the event of uttering, a statement. Like other events, an act of utterance necessarily happens in a time and place. The *Miranda* Court introduces the warning to address problematic conditions of time and place of utterance.

---

[8] Akhil Reed Amar, "Foreword: The Document and the Doctrine," *Harvard Law Review* 114 (2000): 205. Also Albert Alschuler, "A Peculiar Privilege in Historical Perspective: The Right to Remain Silent," *Michigan Law Review* 98:4 (1996): 2672 n. 96.

It does so, this chapter argues, not to isolate a space of silence or to tip some balance of interests towards defendants, as is sometimes suggested, but to address and avert possible threats to the conditions (explored further in the third section, "Waivers and Warnings") that make events of uttering (and hence utterances) meaningful. Responding to the extraordinary circumstances in which the accused finds him- or herself, the *Miranda* warning is an invitation or opening to justice. It opens new possibilities of response to problematic speech conditions. The warning initiates a transformation of circumstances that do not seem compatible with the conventions of proper speech. Upon felicitous warning, an accused is given to understand that his or her statements have different import at interrogation and at trial than they otherwise would. Insofar as an accused who has been felicitously warned then chooses to speak, the accused can be taken to have accepted the conditions under which s/he now speaks as continuous with conventions of proper speech and to have accepted the risk of those statements being used "against him" at trial. Insofar as those who are felicitously warned choose not to speak, they reject the compatibility of the conditions in which they find themselves with the conditions needed for speaking at law. An accused's silence may indeed be an appropriate response to the danger pointed out in the warning. The accused may judge him- or herself unable to find the words needed to speak in a way that can be heard properly in the course of the legal process to follow. Of course, neither speaking nor remaining silent following the warning guarantees any particular outcome to the hearing, which ultimately may be unjust for any number of other reasons.

From the perspective of trial, a successful warning transforms the speech situation. Upon warning, conditions of in-custody interrogation become—paradoxical as it sounds—newly continuous with a past in which ordinary conventions of meaningful speech prevailed. The trial court can presume that a felicitously warned defendant who nevertheless speaks during in-custody interrogation, has taken care to avoid the misunderstandings that are particular to the situation and speaks in a way that can be heard properly at law.

The strange temporality of the establishment of a new continuity that accompanies the utterance of a felicitous warning—what one might call, with a gesture toward both Austin and Shakespeare, a "sea change"— corresponds to the peculiar temporality of law (and of voice) that has been encountered in the chapters above. Like the *Miranda* warning, the holding of the *Miranda* opinion initiates something new or opens to justice, even as it establishes continuity with the past, through its response to or judgment about a prior claim as to the injustice of the situation. This weird temporality—like that of any proper speaking—manifests itself not only in the way that warning works, but also in the funny logic articulated in the opinion.

In its introduction, the opinion claims to "start here" with the "premise that our holding is not an innovation in our jurisprudence" (442). This is a peculiar kind of premise in the sense that one would normally expect a holding—as holding—to follow from articulated premises rather than itself being the subject of (or as discussed in chapter 1, "buried within") the starting premise. The holding appears to be both where the Court "starts" (in its own premise) and also where (as in the summary of the holding cited in the long passage at the beginning of this section) the Court ends. The summary of the holding follows a claim that the holding is not new. The "premise" that the holding is not new itself follows the articulation of the Court's aim, which is precisely not to produce anything new, but rather to "explore" and "guide" through what is presumably already there: "to explore some facets of the problems . . . of applying the privilege against self-incrimination to in-custody interrogation, and to give concrete constitutional guidelines for law enforcement agencies and courts to follow" (441–42). Here the issue of the holding, like that of the warning, becomes even more complex. Is the holding the *event* of applying long-standing principles to the cases before the Court, or is it the general *statement* of a rule of application of these principles? In either case, there is both newness and continuity here: either in the event or in the manifestation of the (old) rule in never-before-articulated, concrete constitutional guidelines. Like all law, the *Miranda* holding instantiates what in chapter 5 was called a "must"—the law tells someone what to do as what "must" be done. It does so in a manner that takes place simultaneously as the initiation or innovation that lies in the event of holding and as a settlement of matters already there. The holding appears as the determination or transformation into actuality of what had formerly been future potential.[9]

Neither Logic nor Experience

If the holding of the *Miranda* opinion is not found in a linear argumentative logic, neither is its justification to be found in experience. The justice of *Miranda*, as shall be seen, relies as much on its interpretation of the possibilities and dangers of silences in history and elsewhere as on facts about the empirical world.

[9] Note: both warning and holding straddle time. They view the past from the standpoint of the future at the same time that they project this future from out of the present moment. (In this way, they work like the Idea of Freedom in Kant's *Groundwork*, the thought of which enables the synthetic *a priori* that is the categorical imperative or the moral law.)

The Court turns to history to explain how its holding exemplifies "application of principles long recognized and applied in other settings" (442). This is a peculiar history in that silence plays a role. The Court cites a passage from an earlier U.S. case that explains how early English state trials adopted the maxim *nemo tenetur seipsum accusare* (no one can be held to accuse himself):

> The change [away from the inquisitorial character] of the English criminal procedure in that particular [adoption of the maxim] seems to be founded upon no statute and no judicial opinion, but upon *a general and silent acquiescence of the courts* in a popular demand. (*Brown v. Walker* [1896] in *Miranda*, 443; emphasis added)

Silent acquiescence by the courts in a popular demand, in this account, actively founds or grounds the principle (*nemo* etc.) as rule of evidence in English law. (Interestingly, *Brown v. Walker* in some sense uncannily foreshadows one of the *Dickerson* opinion's justifications of *Miranda*. *Brown* continues: "But however adopted, it has become firmly embedded in English, as well as in American jurisprudence" [*Miranda*, 443, quoting *Brown*].[10] Compare *Dickerson*: "Miranda has become embedded in routine police practice to the point where the warnings have become part of our national culture" [*Dickerson*, 443].)

Legal historians would have difficulty with the Court's formulation of the process of adoption of the maxim as founded upon no statute and no judicial opinion. As Leonard W. Levy put it, "By now we all know the notorious fact: The Supreme Court has flunked history."[11] In the same decade as the cited case, *Brown v. Walker*, John H. Wigmore had contended that "until the sixteenth century the struggle [over the privilege] is only over the limits of jurisdiction of ecclesiastical courts."[12] He claimed that the maxim "is not a common-law rule at all, but is wholly *statutory* in its authority."[13] Mary Hume Maguire would criticize Wigmore in the 1930s, contending that not just jealousy of ecclesiastical

[10] *Brown v. Walker*, 161 U.S. 591, 16 S.Ct. 644 (1896), at 597.

[11] Leonard W. Levy, *Constitutional Opinions: Aspects of the Bill of Rights* (New York: Oxford University Press, 1986), 193.

[12] Mary Hume Maguire, "Attack of the Common Lawyers on the Oath *Ex Officio* as Administered in the Ecclesiastical Courts in England," in *Essays in History and Political Theory in Honor of Charles Howard McIlwain* (Boston: Harvard University Press, 1936), 200, citing Wigmore. Levy, 206–207, also claims that Wigmore was wrong in asserting that the rule against coerced confessions and the right against self-incrimination had no connection. According to Levy, Wigmore assumed that the right against self-incrimination had a single rationale and a static meaning. But see Langbein, below.

[13] John H. Wigmore, "Nemo Tenetur Seipsum Prodere," *Harvard Law Review* 5 (1891–92): 71. See also Wigmore, "The Privilege Against Self-Incrimination: Its History," *Harvard Law Review* 15 (1901–2): 610.

jurisdiction, but claims as to the inappropriateness of the method of oath *ex officio*, were to be found well before the seventeenth century in records of the common law.[14]

The Court disregards any such historical debate. It locates the provenance of the privilege neither in statutory law nor common law, but in an efficaciousness that it associates, continuing its quotation of *Brown v. Walker*, with silent acquiescence. "So deeply did the iniquities of the ancient system impress themselves upon the minds of the American colonists," the passage continues, "that the States, with one accord, made a denial of the right to question an accused person a part of their fundamental law so that a maxim, which in England was a mere rule of evidence, became clothed in this country with the impregnability of a constitutional enactment" (443, quoting *Brown*).

Immediately after this passage, the Court turns to "the obligation of the judiciary" to apply constitutional rights. It makes clear that its own role will not be limited to silence. But neither does the Court limit itself to words. The obligation of the judiciary, it explains, concerns not only "what has been but what may be." The judiciary must *act* to recognize what may be or general principles risk being "converted by precedent into impotent and lifeless formulas." If the Court does not act, "Rights declared in words might be lost in reality" (443, citing *Weems*). Judicial actions, not words alone, maintain the law. The Court understands *Escobedo* to ensure "that what was proclaimed in the Constitution had not become but a 'form of words' in the hands of government officials" (444, citing *Silverthorne Lumber*). Recognition of the danger that proclamations may become only a "form of words," that words may become "impotent and lifeless formulas," without "meaning and vitality" (443–44, citing *Weems*), "hollow" (473) truths, or "empty formalities" (466, citing *Mapp v. Ohio*), informs the Court's understanding of its role.

The figure of silence in history meanwhile recurs in the second part of the *Miranda* opinion. The introduction, as noted, based the founding of the right not to be compelled to testify against oneself at least partially in silence. Part 2 of the opinion confirms the Court's view that while justice is one possibility of silence, it does not necessarily accompany silence. Recall that in the introductory account, "silent acquiescence" founds the right in England and "one accord" makes it fundamental law in America. In the second part of the opinion, "great struggle" is nevertheless required. After Lilburn's "lofty principles . . . gained popular acceptance in England, these sentiments worked their way over to the Colonies and were implanted after great struggle into the Bill of Rights," writes the

[14] Maguire, "Attack," 199–229.

Court (459).[15] This struggle to embed the right in the Bill of Rights is warranted, continues the Court, as "[t]hose who framed our Constitution and Bill of Rights" knew, because "illegitimate and unconstitutional practices get their first footing . . . by silent approaches and slight deviations from legal modes of procedure" (459, citing *Boyd v. U.S* [1886]). Not only empty words then, but also "silent approaches," threaten the reality of constitutional rights. Silence, in the Court's account, may provide a foothold for illegitimacy as well as founding privileges.

Again legal historians will find this account problematic. A lively debate exists as to whether *Miranda* has run together what some commentators consider to be two different legal strands: the privilege against self-incrimination under the oath *ex officio*, in which parties were protected from having to answer questions in fishing expeditions to find out about their beliefs, and the right not to be tortured or compelled to testify because of the unreliability of testimony obtained in this way (White 526–29; Harlan 510). A pair of *Michigan Law Review* articles criticize depictions of the common-law right to remain silent that identify it with the *nemo tenetur* maxim of earlier centuries. John H. Langbein shows that the right (not to testify) could not have come about, as Levy claims, as an early English invention of the accusatorial system to protect against the European inquisitorial system. Langbein argues that the privilege originated in the European system and that throughout the seventeenth century in England, the defendant's statements were important "testimonial resources" in an "accused speaks" trial. The right to remain silent in England, he shows, follows from the late-eighteenth-century development and expansion of the role of defense counsel, which contributed to the placing of a determinate burden of proof on the prosecutor.[16]

Eben Moglen extends Langbein's analysis to the United States. The right was certainly not implanted after great struggle with one accord in the Constitution, according to Moglen. Rather, he argues, the framers defensively articulated a cluster of jury rights or practices that were not

[15] The opinion cites Morgan, "The Privilege Against Self-Incrimination," *Minnesota Law Review* 34 (1949): 9–11; John Henry Wigmore, *Evidence in Trials at Common Law*, vol. 8, revised by McNaughton (Boston: Little, Brown, 1961), 289–95; Lowell, "The Judicial Use of Torture, Parts I and II," *Harvard Law Review* 11 (1897): 290; Pittman, "The Colonial and Constitutional History of the Privilege Against Self-Incrimination in America," *Virginia Law Review* 21 (1935): 763; and *Ullmann v. United States*, 350 U.S. 445–49 (1956) (Douglas, J., dissenting).

[16] John H. Langbein, "The Historical Origins of the Privilege Against Self-Incrimination at Common Law," *Michigan Law Review* 92:5 (1994): 1047. See also R. H. Helmholz, "Origins of the Privilege Against Self-Incrimination: The Role of the European *Ius Commune*," *New York University Law Review* 65 (1990): 962; and Michael R. T. Macnair, "The Early Development of the Privilege against Self-Incrimination," *Oxford Journal of Legal Studies* 10 (1990): 66.

yet guaranteed as rights and that the framers feared could be taken away. Moglen supports his claim that the right (not to be compelled to testify) is not in the Constitution, by showing how—unsuccessful—colonial claims to such a right do not even appeal to Constitutional law, but only to case law.[17]

The point is that whatever the period and character of the long ago event(s) that founded the right to remain silent in the United States, historians, unlike the Court, are far from locating any impetus for the right itself in silence, whether as efficacious action or as threat to constitutional reality. Historians' various accounts all highlight the distance that the Court, in its singular tale of silence and struggle, has taken from conventional norms of historical scholarship and truth.

The Court strays not only from the conventions of historical scholarship, but also from those of social science. In the first part of its opinion, for instance, the Court associates the in-custody interrogation that characterizes all four cases brought before it with what is "incommunicado" and "private." The Court's difficulty in understanding what happens in in-custody interrogations "stems from the fact that in this country they have largely taken place incommunicado" (445), the Court points out. "Privacy results in secrecy and this in turn results in a gap in our knowledge as to what in fact goes on in the interrogation rooms" (448).

Despite the secrecy and silence that surround such private proceedings, the Court manages to fill the "gap" in knowledge that results from the privacy of interrogation rooms. Rather than drawing on evidence of actual proceedings, however, the Court infers what happens from how-to manuals. It reads "factual studies" undertaken thirty years earlier (445), law review articles, reports of legal cases, and "various police manuals and texts which document procedures employed with success in the past, and which recommend various other effective tactics" (448) to argue that the third degree is still a threat and that interrogation is still psychologically if not physically coercive.

The Court's judgment as to the "inherently compelling pressures" (467, cf. 461) of interrogation thus fills the gap in its knowledge. This judgment rests not on actual knowledge of interrogation but on the very factors that the Court acknowledges make empirical knowledge impossible: privacy and secrecy. Privacy is not only the reason for the *absence* of knowledge about interrogation but *also* "the principal psychological factor contributing to a successful interrogation" (449, again citing an interrogation manual). The claim that secrecy and silence around hidden or nonpublic interactions create possibilities of injustice comes not from social scientific

---

[17] Eben Moglen, "Taking the Fifth: Reconsidering the Origins of the Constitutional Privilege Against Self-Incrimination," *Michigan Law Review* 92:5 (1994): 1086.

research or empirical data, but from the Court's interpretations of texts and silences. White points out that the Court's claims are not tenable as empirical investigation of fact (532–33).

So too the Court's concern for the legal truths that it suggests are at stake in a trial can be distinguished from empirical truth. The ostensible *Miranda* justification for excluding involuntarily made statements—fairness of procedures against a defendant—differs from the more traditional justification mentioned in a footnote—the unreliability of statements so obtained. In the traditional view of a defendant's encounter with the legal system, the inadequacy of coercive interrogatory practices lies in the untruth or unreliability vis-à-vis some external standard of truth of a defendant's statements. In *Miranda*, the inadequacy lies in the ostensible illegitimacy of a coercive process that is to produce an outcome that by definition is just. But how does a warning address this inadequacy? The next section, "Warnings and Waivers," turns to this question.

To summarize: so far, the *Miranda* opinion reveals a Court that recognizes a danger that words may be empty formulas and a possibility that silence may be efficacious action; that insists that interrogation in the current legal system is problematically coercive; and that distances itself from conventional—historical, social scientific, and legal—norms or standards of truth. Against this background, the *Miranda* warning emerges as speech act.

Warnings and Waivers

The Court explains the particular statements that are commonly taken to make up "the *Miranda* warning" in the third part of its opinion. J. L. Austin's analysis of speech acts, together with the points raised in the previous section, helps us to understand these statements.

In *How to Do Things with Words*, a series of lectures given almost a half-century ago, Austin distinguishes a particular kind of utterance (such as "I promise I won't be late" or "I declare you man and wife") that he calls "performative," from descriptive or "constative" statements (such as "The cat is on the mat") that are conventionally considered true or false. A performative utterance—a promise or a warning or a confession—is not usually thought of as "just saying something"—as describing or reporting what is true or false. Rather it is, or is a part of, the doing of an action. To utter a warning or a promise (and so forth) "is not to *describe* my doing of what I should be said in so uttering to be doing (still less [to describe] anything that I have already done or have yet to do) or to *state* that I am doing it: it is to *do* it" (5–7, incorporating 6 n. 1; 2d and 3d emphases added).

Austin looks at the particular and overlapping ways in which performative utterances can fail, to ascertain what makes them successful or "happy." He first focuses on the infelicities that he takes to be particular to performative utterances. Among other things, he argues, ritualized conditions or conventions are required for a performative to be felicitous. (E.g., for "I so and so take whomever to be my lawful wedded whatever" to succeed as a marriage vow, I must not already be currently married, I must be with whomever before a licensed official, the ceremony must be carried through correctly and completely, and so forth.)[18] In addition, a kind of sincerity or commitment to the performance and what it inaugurates is required on the part of participants:

> Where, as often, the procedure is designed for use by persons having certain thoughts or feelings, or for the inauguration of certain consequential conduct on the part of any participant, then a person participating in and so invoking the procedure must in fact have those thoughts or feelings, and the participants must intend so to conduct themselves, and further . . . must actually so conduct themselves subsequently (15; footnote omitted).[19]

Austin then notes that performatives are susceptible to additional dimensions of unsatisfactoriness by virtue of the broader categories to which performatives as speech acts belong. As actions, that is, performatives are susceptible to the same difficulties to which all actions are subject—they are liable to be done, for instance, under duress, by mistake, unintentionally (21).[20] As speech, performatives must also be "understood as issued in ordinary circumstances"; they cannot be understood ordinarily when, for instance, introduced on stage or said in a poem (22). Finally, like any action or speech, performatives may be subject to "misunderstanding" (23).

Taking up the grammar of the performative reveals a further area of possible failure. Austin looks first at performatives that appear in the grammatical form of first-person singular, present indicative, active sentences ("I warn you that the bull is about to charge"). He then recognizes that performatives do not necessarily take this form ("The bull is about to

[18] That these are conventions is underscored by the current issue of gay marriage. That one conceives of the conditions of performatives as conventions does not undercut the point that we are thrown into a world provided by language that is not entirely within our (social) control or power.

[19] See Lemony Snicket, *The Bad Beginning* (New York: Scholastic, 1999), 96–97, in which Klaus (correctly and felicitously) accuses Count Olaf of planning to marry Violet not figuratively, but literally—and legally—in the play that Olaf and Violet will perform, because the nuptial laws require no more than "the presence of a judge, a statement of 'I do' by both the bride and the groom, and the signing of an explanatory document in the bride's own hand."

[20] See also Austin, "A Plea for Excuses."

charge" may be a perfectly good warning).[21] He finds then that even per-formative statements in the first-person singular, present indicative, active may be "false" or mistaken, in the way that constative statements are liable to be (the bull, for instance, may not in fact have been about to charge).

Austin then proposes a "fresh start." This time, he distinguishes the act of saying something—issuing a locution, a "locutionary act" (whether "I promise I will be on time" or "The cat is on the mat")—from what hap-pened *in* the saying—the promising, the warning, the vow of marriage, and so forth—which he calls the "illocutionary act." He distinguishes both of these from what happened *by* the saying, or from what he calls "perlocu-tionary" acts (or effects) such as my persuading you to be on time also, or your laughing at the idea that I would be on time, a shoe getting thrown at the cat, or relatives being relieved or upset at the marriage.[22]

Ultimately, the difference between the performative utterance and the constative statement breaks down, according to Austin. Even an ostensi-bly pure constative statement of fact (such as "The cat is on the mat") *does* something in its being said—illocutionarily: it states, it declares, it exemplifies, it illustrates a point, it even warns. Like earlier examples of explicit performative utterances, the ostensibly constative statement *too* is susceptible to the particular sorts of success or failure—felicity or infe-licity—that depend on a total speech situation—rather than being subject simply to ascriptions of truth or falsity.

Commentators on *Miranda*, both for and against, usually treat the *Mi-randa* holding as requiring particular statements. In Austin's terms, com-mentators then focus either on the *constative*—or true/false—aspects of these statements and of the statements that compose the argument for them, or on the *perlocutionary* effects that commentators take the state-ments and the Court's holding to have. They inquire, on the one hand, into the truth of the proposition that a defendant has particular rights

[21] But see Emile Benveniste's "Analytic Philosophy of Language," in *Problems in Gen-eral Linguistics*, trans. Mary Elizabeth Meek (Coral Gables, FL: University of Miami Press, 1971), 231–38, arguing that Austin should have stuck to form as the only useful way of classifying performative utterances *linguistically*. Benveniste argues that "Shut the door" is an order, but it is not linguistically performative the way "I order you to shut the door" is.

[22] Note that the reading here comes directly from *How to Do Things with Words*. It diverges from some contemporary readings of Austin and of performative speech acts that associate both the illocutionary and the perlocutionary with "force." Although there is some evidence for this in Austin's text, Austin emphasizes that the "conventional force" of the illocutionary act is not causal. I am encouraged in my view by Stanley Cavell, *Philosophical Passages: Wittgenstein, Emerson, Austin, Derrida* (Oxford: Blackwell, 1995) and *A Pitch of Philosophy*. See also Timothy Gould, "The Unhappy Performative," in *Performativity and Performance*, ed. Andrew Parker and Eve Kosofsky Sedgwick (New York: Routledge, 1995), 19–44.

and the argument for that proposition, asking whether any given proposition is true to the principles that lie behind the Fifth Amendment or whether the holding extends the Fifth Amendment beyond its true range. They evaluate, on the other hand, the effects of statements and of the holding: does or will making a particular statement constrain police behavior? Does it discourage cooperation with law enforcement officials? How does the holding shift the balance between social need for law enforcement and individual defendants' interests? Commentators minimize or neglect the issue of what goes on *in* what Austin would call the illocutionary act of warning.

The focus on the constative and perlocutionary aspects of the warning and the holding appears not only in the *Miranda* dissents but in a slew of articles about *Miranda*. Few scholars seem to attend, in the way that *Miranda* does, to the illocutionary act of warning as such.[23] Court opinions that succeed *Miranda* could be read as concerned precisely (although not always altogether correctly) with the total speech situation that surrounds the illocutionary act of warning. How does *Miranda* approach the speech situation of warning?

The *Miranda* opinion, like Austin, seems to recognize both that saying something may do something more than simply or constatively stating true/false propositions and also that saying something may do something in its saying that is other than what is perlocutionarily produced by the saying. Like Austin, *Miranda* recognizes the illocutionary force of utterances—and their fragility. The awareness—throughout the opinion—of the danger that particular words—not just warnings, but also confessions, waivers, declarations of rights—may become empty forms, lifeless formulas, or hollow rituals reveals a recognition of the ways in which speech acts can fail. Speech acts fail not only in the ways that actions "fail" and in the ways that propositions fail when they are untrue. Speech acts also fail insofar as they are unsuccessful in ways that Austin calls "infelicitous." An emphasis on infelicities suggests that one can never completely articulate the way in which an utterance (like a practice) succeeds in being what it is.

Infelicities occur when ordinary conventions of speech and of the particular speech act are not met. The Court understands interrogation precisely as an "atmosphere" or "phase" in which the ordinary conventions of speech situations are not and cannot be met. Utterances that take place in extraordinary circumstance are indeterminate or suspect. Outside all conventionality or common practice, utterances are nonsensical. According to the Court, the danger of in-custody interrogation is precisely

---

[23] The closest may be George C. Thomas III, "Separated at Birth, but Siblings Nonetheless: *Miranda* and the Due Process Notice Cases," *Michigan Law Review* 99 (2001): 1081.

that in being "cut off from the outside world" (445), an accused is deprived of all of the familiar conventions that allow utterances of any sort to be happy. "Swept from the familiar" (461), "alone" and "deprived of outside support" (455) or in "isolation and unfamiliar surroundings" (450), the subject of incommunicado interrogation is "thrust into" a "menacing" situation (457) of secrecy and privacy. In-custody interrogation, suggests the Court, is a situation in which everyday norms and ordinary conventions of speech seemingly no longer apply. In-custody interrogation threatens to become a situation of the worst kind of institutional violence about which Cover writes in "Violence and the Word."

In a situation of in-custody interrogation in which almost by definition "conventions" of all sorts may be suspended, the Court argues, any statement—not just confession—is susceptible to infelicity. "No distinction can be drawn between statements which are direct confessions and statements which amount to 'admissions' of part or all of the offense . . . Similarly, for precisely the same reason, no distinction may be drawn between inculpatory statements and statements alleged to be merely 'exculpatory' " (476-7).

Commentators who grasp *Miranda* exclusively as an attempt "to deal with the problem of confession" or even as "the law's semi-conscious struggle to come to terms with the difficult, layered, perplexing notion of the speech-act that follows from the statement 'I confess,' " omit too much.[24] At stake in *Miranda* is not only what follows, but what surrounds, not only the speech act of confession, but any testimonial speech act. The Court does concede that at trial, as distinct from interrogation, confessions serve as "the most compelling possible evidence of guilt" (466, citing *Mapp v. Ohio*). The Court is concerned with broader issues than confession, however. The Court mentions confession in the context of trial *procedure* and "all the careful safeguards erected around the *giving of testimony*, whether by an accused or any other witness" (466, still citing *Mapp v. Ohio*; emphasis added). The Court thus does view confession as one—perhaps the most likely—way of giving testimony that is "compelling possible evidence" of guilt. But the Court looks simultaneously to the speech situation that enables *any* of an accused's statements—not just confession—to be used as testimony. *Miranda* includes within its purview statements "intended to be *exculpatory* by the defendant" because such statements may be used "to impeach his testimony at trial or to demonstrate untruths in the statement given under interrogation and thus to prove guilt by implication" (477; emphasis added).

---

[24] Peter Brooks, *Troubling Confessions: Speaking Guilt in Law and Literature* (Chicago: University of Chicago Press, 2000), 7, 30.

Miranda's broad concern is with the giving of testimony at trial and the law of evidence. Such law—and such testimony—becomes "empty formalities," as the Court puts it, without warnings (and related safeguards) (466, quoting *Mapp v. Ohio*). Beginning the sentence in its own words, the Court writes,

> Without the protections flowing from adequate warnings and the rights of counsel, "all the careful safeguards erected around the giving of testimony, whether by an accused or any other witness, would become empty formalities in a procedure where the most compelling possible evidence of guilt, a confession, would have already been obtained at the unsupervised pleasure of the police." (466, citing *Mapp v. Ohio*)

The focus of *Miranda* then is best understood as something other than "the place and use of confessions in the criminal law."[25] *Miranda*'s broad concern is with the conditions that make trial testimony felicitous; its narrower focus is on the way that the speech act of warning fosters those conditions vis-à-vis any of the accused's statements up through trial. The warning seeks to establish conditions for proper speech during interrogation. These conditions are presumed to be continuous with—although not the same as—those that hold in an ordinary "outside" world. How these conditions enable statements made under interrogation to be heard properly at trial will be explored in the final section, "The Trial as Hearing and Event."

The chapter so far has suggested that the utterance of the warning marks the formal entry of the accused into the legal process: it occurs at "the outset" of interrogation or at a moment when significant deprivation of the subject's "freedom of action" begins (477). The warning tells the accused of the risk that what he is about to say has different import than what he is used to insofar as it will be used "against" him.

The risk to the accused does not disappear in warning of it nor at the moment of warning. The warnings do not "free" an accused in any magical return of the freedom of action of which custody has deprived him. If anything they make him more aware of the seriousness of his situation insofar as they tell him that this particular deprivation of his freedom of action carries with it the additional danger that his speech itself is under presumably unfamiliar constraints. The warnings make their addressee "more acutely aware that he is faced with a phase of the adversarial system—that he is not in the presence of persons acting solely in his interest" (469).

Because the danger of which the statements warn continues throughout the period of in-custody interrogation, the Court encourages Congress

---

[25] Brooks, *Troubling Confessions*, 10.

and the states to find "procedures which are at least as effective" as the warning and related safeguards "in assuring a continuous opportunity to exercise" the right (467). Through presence of counsel, the Court aims "to assure that the individual's right to choose between silence and speech remains unfettered throughout the interrogation process" (469). And the Court reverses one of the *Miranda* petitioner's convictions because, although FBI agents gave Westover warnings at the "outset of their interview," they began their questioning in the same police station where he had been held and interrogated by others for the past fourteen hours. "The impact on him," then, "was that of a continuous period of questioning" in which he was warned only towards the end (496).

The statements *Miranda* requires do many things in their utterance as warnings, then, according to the Court. In addition to making those unaware of the privilege against self-incrimination aware of it and of their other rights (468, 469), they make their addressee aware of the seriousness of the situation and of the consequences of forgoing the exercise of the privilege (469) and of the risk in proceeding into the danger. The rights that the warning mentions either allow an accused to avoid the danger or to be somewhat protected from it. The presence of an attorney, for instance, furthers the primary aim that "the individual's right to choose between silence and speech" continue throughout the process (469). Should the accused choose to proceed into the danger, however, the presence of counsel mentioned in the warning serves "significant subsidiary functions" (466, 469, 470). The attorney may witness the interrogation and ensure the accuracy of the record. Presence of counsel also suggests that the most basic condition for responsible *action*, let alone speech—that it not be coerced—will be met, insofar as a lawyer's presence "reduces the likelihood that the police will practice coercion" (470).

Together then, according to the Court, the warnings and safeguards "overcome the inherent pressures of the interrogation atmosphere" (468) or "dispel the compelling atmosphere" (465) or "dispel the compulsion" (458) inherent in incommunicado in-custody interrogation. They do so not by returning the accused to freedom or even in the sense of reconstituting the accused as a free agent or as the minisovereign of liberal political thought (discussed in chapter 2). They do so, rather, in the sense that an accused who has been properly warned and proceeds to speak can be presumed to have done so not *because* of "pressures" and "compulsion" by the police but, in some sense, despite them and with care: the properly warned accused who proceeds to speak accepts the constraints on speech inherent in the situation of in-custody interrogation as not inappropriate for what s/he has to say.

For this to happen, though, the Court recognizes, the warning itself must be felicitous. It cannot be made in bad faith, for then its inauguration (as Austin might put it) of opportunities for being careful of, or for averting, the dangers of speech becomes meaningless—an empty form of words. By stating the warning at the beginning or outset of interrogation, interrogators show that—while admittedly not acting "solely" in the accused's interest—they are at least prepared to recognize his privilege, the Court claims (468). Further, should the accused take the interrogators up on their statements, interrogators must follow through on their recognition of his rights. The Court's discussion of the "subsequent procedure" to the giving of the warnings (473 ff.) deals with this expressly. If an accused "indicates in any manner" a wish to remain silent "at any time prior to or during questioning" (473–74), the Court writes, interrogation must stop. If a defendant "states" that he wants an attorney, the Court continues, interrogation must stop until an attorney is present.

The Court recognizes that, like the interrogators' warnings and statements of rights, an accused's waiver of rights must also be felicitous. Like the warning, the waiver must not be allowed to become "simply a preliminary ritual" (476) before continuing the current problematic methods of interrogation. Speech acts tread a fine balance between the ritualized conventions that make them successful and the danger that overly repeated or routinized rituals lose their meaning (just as rule-based behavior in chapter 5 threatens to become rote obedience). A waiver, like a warning, is a prerequisite to the admissibility as evidence at trial of a defendant's statements (473). But given the extraordinary conditions of interrogation, the "mere fact" of a waiver does not approach an intelligent (or felicitous speech act or event of) waiver (492), just as the mere fact of a warning does not prove that a felicitous act of warning took place and the mere fact of an utterance does not establish its import or significance. A decision maker may not presume a valid waiver simply from a "silent record" (475, citing *Carnley v. Cochran*).

In the Court's own words, waiver will not be presumed "simply from the silence of the accused after warnings are given or simply from the fact that a confession was (in fact) eventually obtained" (475). The doubling of the word "fact," to talk about the inadequacy of the existence of a statement of confession as proof of the validity of waiver, emphasizes that the issue is neither the constative (true/false) aspect of the assertion that a statement of confession exists, nor a claim as to *de facto* waiver. Rather, *Miranda* concerns itself here, as throughout, with conditions of proper speech.

The chapter so far has suggested that the *Miranda* Court is concerned with the use, in the giving of testimony at trial, of statements made in the unconventional speech situation of in-custody interrogation. The opinion recognizes not only the danger to an accused of speaking in such a situation, but also the difficulty of successfully conveying the risk to the ac-

cused. Yet to fail to do so, to fail to "adequately" or felicitously warn
the accused about the speech situation s/he enters, the Court maintains,
jeopardizes the trial as a place where what was said can be heard properly.
Such failures—and perceived failures—are indeed what cases after *Miranda* could be said to address, in their consideration of actual conditions
of warning and waiver.[26]

Note that the argument of this chapter does not imply that actual Miranda warnings are felicitous. Indeed, empirical literature suggests that
they are not.[27] Furthermore, it is unclear that felicity, despite its conventionality, can ever be a matter of complete or prospective empirical determination.[28] Actions—including speech acts—come from "somewhere behind" the articulations of conventions determined by rules. They initiate.

Austin contrasts situations in which we may regard ourselves as deciding that a convention does not exist or as deciding that the circumstances
are not appropriate for the invocation of a convention that undoubtedly
does exist to situations in which someone is "initiating" procedures (31).
"The man who first picked up the ball and ran" in football provides an
example of the latter.[29] This man opened the possibility of new conventions or rules that have since indeed become the game. But nothing guaranteed that the man would found a new game, rather than be called "out"
or "non-played" (30).

The *Miranda* opinion is like the man who first picked up a football and
ran. It—paradoxically—initiates new conventions from out of its own—

[26] Among the cases that might be reinterpreted in this light are *Harris v. New York*, 401
U.S. 222, 91 S.Ct. 643 (1971); *Michigan v. Tucker*, 417 U.S. 433, 94 S.Ct. 2357 (1974);
Michigan v. Mosely, 423 U.S. 96, 96 S.Ct. 321 (1975); *Doyle v. Ohio*, 426 U.S. 610, 96
S.Ct. 2240 (1976); *Rhode Island v. Innis*, 446 U.S. 291, 100 S.Ct. 1682 (1980); *Edwards
v. Arizona*, 451 U.S. 477, 101 S.Ct. 1880 (1981); *Oregon v. Bradshaw*, 462 U.S. 1039, 103
S.Ct. 2830 (1983); *New York v. Quarles*, 467 U.S. 649, 104 S.Ct. 2626 (1984); *Moran v.
Burbine*, 475 U.S. 412, 106 S.Ct. 1135 (1986); *Duckworth v. Eagan*, 492 U.S. 195, 109
S.Ct. 2875 (1989); *Minnick v. Mississippi*, 498 U.S. 146, 111 S.Ct. 486 (1990); *Withrow v.
Williams*, 507 U.S. 680, 113 S.Ct. 1745 (1993); *Stansbury v. California*, 511 U.S. 318, 114
S.Ct. 1526 (1994).

[27] See Leo, "Impact of Miranda."

[28] This is in effect one of the arguments between Searle and Derrida in their infamous
exchange. On this point (as on some others), Austin seems closer to Derrida than to Searle.

[29] As to the latter, Austin writes:

> It is inherent in the nature of any procedure that the limits of its applicability, and
> therewith, of course, the "precise" definition of the procedure, will remain vague.
> There will always occur difficult or marginal cases where nothing in the previous
> history of a conventional procedure will decide conclusively whether such a proce-
> dure is or is not correctly applied to such a case. (31)

Austin suggests that lawyers will generally prefer to claim that an existing convention does
not apply than to claim that no conventions exist. Hart, *Concept of Law*, chap. 7, discusses
similar issues in terms of the "penumbra" and "open texture" of rules.

retrospectively felicitous—act, in this case, the Court's articulation of the conventions of warning. In laying out the circumstances and conventions of felicitous or adequate warning, the Court did not thereby perlocutionarily ensure that the conditions of felicitous warnings would be met— nor could it have done so. The Court's issue of the *Miranda* opinion was itself the utterance of a speech act, occurring according to the particular conventional procedures that make those utterances authoritative U.S. law. As a speech act, its perlocutionary effect would depend on many factors—and no effect could be guaranteed. Its illocutionary import, however, can be gleaned from what was said. In being said (illocutionarily, that is), the *Miranda* holding opened up the possibility of recognizing as injustice the myriad of ways in which the conditions for adequate warning might not be met.

The Trial as Hearing and Event

In his discussion of the conventionality of illocutionary acts, Austin writes, "A judge should be able to decide, by hearing what was said, what locutionary and illocutionary acts were performed, but not what perlocutionary acts were achieved" (122). To be able to tell upon hearing what locutionary or illocutionary acts have been performed, a listener must be able to presume that the conventions for proper speech were met—or rather, in keeping with the discussion above, at minimum not unmet.

The trial is a hearing. It is an event—or performance[30]—that culminates in a verdict. The verdict in a criminal trial may be thought of as the *veredictum*, the speaking of the truth of the guilt of a defendant based on what has been heard. (Originally a judgment as to what to do, the verdict today is often conceived as a declarative utterance—or even as a constative statement.)[31]

The law of evidence in part governs the use that may be made at trial of statements made outside the trial. (Together with the law of procedure, it also governs the kinds of statements made at trial.) Like all law, the law of evidence tells those whom it addresses what to do. It tells them whether or how to introduce or admit particular words and things into trial.

The law of evidence recognizes that utterances have different import in different circumstances. It recognizes privileges against testifying, for instance, that protect doctor-patient, therapist-client, and lawyer-client

[30] Robert P. Burns, *A Theory of the Trial* (Princeton: Princeton University Press, 1999).
[31] See Constable, *Law of the Other*, 2, 15–16, 46–48.

relations, as well as spousal communications. The justifications commonly given for excluding statements made in these contexts or for protecting parties in confidential relationships are that the privilege protects the dignity of persons and encourages desirable trust-relations. The particularity of statements made in intimate and trusting relationships is precisely their confidentiality. Upon being heard in public, a confidential utterance is liable to do something very different than in its first saying.

Complicated rules of evidence also govern hearsay. The justification usually given for excluding hearsay is that the original speaker cannot be cross-examined. Cross-examination enables a court to ascertain the import of a cross-examined speaker's utterances in context. The objection to allowing hearsay is that the hearsay utterance is doubly yanked out of context, insofar as it is both spoken by another and also spoken at trial. But Austin himself points out that

> in the American law of evidence, a report of what someone else said is admitted as evidence if what he said is an utterance of our performative kind: because this is regarded as a report not so much of something he *said*, as which it would be hear-say and not admissible as evidence, but rather as something he *did*, an action of his. This coincides very well with our initial feelings about performatives. (13)

A speaker ordinarily enters into many conversations and texts. The proper speaker of a language is both opened up to possibilities through the language and constrained, but not determined, by the language. A speaker may choose not to enter into particular conversations, for instance, or not to enter into conversations with particular parties or in particular situations or on particular topics or in any given language. The speaker may deem some conversations and utterances to be appropriate; others not. One is bound to one's language, whether speaking or not—and perhaps never more so than when speaking without conscious reflection on the language one uses.

Just as a speaker is bound to language, so too are persons bound to law, subject to and of the law—opened up to possibilities of acting and judging through law and constrained, but not determined, by its particular possibilities. One is perhaps never more bound to one's law than when one is not consciously reflecting on one's obedience to it. And ordinarily, like a speaker who may choose not to engage at all in particular conversations, a subject of law may choose not to engage in particular encounters, such as property ownership or voting, whose only terms are those offered by or available at law.

An accused who is taken into custody seems to have no such choice. The law's properly administered or felicitous *Miranda* warnings open up such choice, however. They acknowledge that the terms of in-custody police interrogation may not be those that the accused finds proper for the exchange of speech between oneself as legal subject and one's law. The right to remain silent offers the accused an opportunity to take up and endorse the law's acknowledgment—in the form of the warning—that the terms of police interrogation (like those of trial in the right's earlier incarnation) may not be terms that the accused—as lawful subject—deems appropriate to speech of and at law.

Miranda suggests that an accused who makes such a judgment cannot be forced or compelled to participate. Compulsion would threaten the sort of dialogue to which a hearing that is to culminate in a just verdict must aspire. *Miranda* excludes coerced speech, not because the trial is a sacrosanct or official space of distinct and separate speech but, on the contrary, because despite its difference from the everyday, the justice of the hearing depends on the presumption and preservation of ordinary speech conditions. In the absence of these conditions, one cannot judge what is said.

The justice of *Miranda* comes from the opportunity for silence that a felicitously issued warning offers to an accused who finds himself in the extraordinary circumstance of being asked to speak in conditions in which ordinary conditions of speech no longer seem to apply. The opportunity for silence offered by a felicitous warning does not return an accused to an impossible freedom of action or of speech. Nor does it guarantee justice. It opens up new possibilities of justice and of injustice alike, in the way that the warning happens and in what follows from it. In the warning, the legal system acknowledges that the conditions of the process may not be appropriate to the speaking of the truths of the accused and offers the accused an opportunity for silence that is not be used as evidence against him. The accused's acceptance of the system's offer does not assure justice; it disables one particular possibility of injustice, while opening up possibilities of others.

One need not read *Miranda*'s safeguarding of an opportunity for silence in response to the possibility of coerced speech to be grounded simply in fairness to the defendant or in the need for reliable evidence. Rather, the ground may lie elsewhere: *Miranda* seeks to protect the justice of the hearing. The intelligibility of statements that are introduced as evidence at trial requires that they meet minimal conditions for the proper hearing and understanding of utterances, that those statements take place under proper speech conditions. The felicitous "*Miranda* warning" and waiver and so forth would guarantee the continuity of these conditions during interrogation and would help ensure that the statements of an accused who does speak have value as speech and thus as evidence. The successful speech act of warning (like the rest of the law of evidence) preserves conditions of speech and thus of hearing at trial.

Again, this is not to say that any given instance of a *Miranda* warning actually succeeds. That a so-called warning is uttered does not ensure its felicitousness. Indeed, current articulations of the terms of successful or felicitous warnings are precisely what courts continue to negotiate and what social research challenges. But the point is that a warning does something different than allow a decision maker to figure out after the fact whether a defendant's statements were freely or voluntarily given. It may do something in addition to serving the interests of defendants or constraining the behavior of state officials. A felicitous or successful warning alerts its addressee to a danger that the addressee who hears the warning would ordinarily respond to with caution or avoidance. The danger to an accused is that utterances made in the extraordinary conditions of the in-custody interrogatory phase of legal process carry different import than when ordinarily said. The greatest danger is that they will be used against their speaker at trial. In its holding, the *Miranda* Court insists that an accused be properly informed of these dangers through what has come to be known as the *Miranda* warning. The warning and the opportunity to respond to it by calling for an attorney or by remaining silent allow an accused to proceed to speak with some protection or to avoid the danger of speech altogether.

Given a felicitous warning, the silence of an accused may be an appropriate response. Such silence may admittedly be prudent and in the interests of an accused, as law reviews are quick to remind us. But in response to a felicitous warning, an accused's silence may also point to a legal subject's judgment as to the propriety of conditions of speech in the legal system—a legal system whose institutions epitomize the social power of a positive law that sets justice aside and whose language is characterized by adoption of the social scientific discourse of a technical age.

When law is a matter of words and speech, the justice of law refers (at least in part) to the conditions of speech. The *Miranda* warning and the *Miranda* holding acknowledge limits to the justice of the actual system. The silence of an accused constitutes a response to that acknowledgment, a response that speaks in its own way of possibilities of justice and injustice in law and language.

Conclusion

FOUR THEMES EMERGE from the preceding chapters.

First, modern law is a social and sociological phenomenon. It is an object of sociological knowledge that is taken to be a human and social creation (chapters 1 and 2). Modern American law is informed by sociological research, as legislation concerning Native Americans shows (chapter 3). It shares with the social sciences a linguistic and technical understanding of language, manifest in the flag-burning opinions (chapter 4). Its rules (chapters 3 and 5) and institutions (chapters 5 and 6) are considered social in the senses of being and causing social effects and being and being produced by social causes. Modern law manifests itself as humanly created social power, in structures and agencies of positive law in which the classical strong distinction between powerful sovereign and dominated subjects (à la Austin) breaks down. Government agents and community members alike are implicated in the social pressure and institutions (à la Hart, Tyler, Schauer, or Cover) by which conformity is maintained and (social) policy and legal truths produced (chapters 1, 5, 6, and 7).

Second, the instrumental (chapter 4), power-oriented (chapters 2 and 5), sometimes violent (chapters 3, 5, 6, and 7) character of modern positive law raises serious doubts about its justice and the continued possibility of justice. These doubts resonate with the metaphysical problem of nihilism and the devaluation of values that Nietzsche and Heidegger identify with our particular historical age (chapter 1). In the modern age, previously fundamental values come into question. The world threatens to become an object or resource for the social human being who would master it through knowledge. We cannot do much more than recognize this issue as the issue of our times. Recognition is a response. Such responsiveness contrasts to the tendency of modern knowledge to grasp, to conceive, to master, to posit, "to be ever itching to mingle with, *plunge into* other people and other things," the tendency, "in short [of] our celebrated modern 'objectivity.' "[1]

Third, language is very much implicated in the technical and sociological worldview that characterizes modern law. The language of modern law—the grammar of nouns that verb and subjects that predicate (chapter 2), the statements of findings and declarations of legislation (chapter 3), the assimilation of words to linguistic signs of expression (chapter 4), the rules that make decisions manageable by constraining responsibility from

---

[1] Nietzsche, *Twilight of the Idols*, "Germans," sec. 6.

the outset (chapter 5), the interpretations that are not what they pretend (chapter 6)—points to ways in which speech itself becomes a strategic resource of social empowerment and domination.

Fourth, the silence of justice. Law formerly issued from justice; now, conversely, human laws of society establish standards of judgment (chapter 1). Articulations of, and about, those human laws often fail to mention the word *justice* (chapter 2). When they do speak of it, it is as product or construction of social power, as fairness or procedure to which we do or would agree, as legitimacy we grant to authorities we obey, as conformity we show to pressures we bring to bear on one another and ourselves (chapters 1, 2, 4, 5). Justice disappears (chapter 6) into the formulations, articulations, conceptions and constructions of the talking subjects and the garrulous laws (chapters 2 and 3) of society.

Suppose we were to listen to what stays silent in this cacophony. What would we hear?

Modern law is a social and empirically knowable phenomenon, the latest manifestation of law in a tradition that has long associated law with justice. As a social and empirical phenomenon, it is the subject matter of sociology, sciences or knowledges of society, which usually identify law with social power in some form. The norms, rules, and institutions— formal and informal, official and everyday—that sociology variously takes as constituting law themselves partake in a worldview compatible with that of sociology in which the power of law involves mastering social phenomena.

Modern law and sociology both take language to be social and to be a tool or resource of potentially strategic power. Articulating themselves through language, modern law and sociology leave little room for the nonsocial, for nonpower, for noninstrumentality, be it that of law or language. At the limits of the language of law and sociology, though, in their silences, lie possibilities of which they do not speak.

The silences of modern law are many. They are not necessarily just. A refusal to speak, for instance, may be an exercise of will—a calculated strategy that aims to advance interests or to exercise or resist power in society. The unsaid may signify an absence or constitute a denial that is an effect of power or powerlessness. The unspeakable may point to an absence of words that indicates a lack of power on the part of language or of its speakers.

But invocation of the unspeakable also suggests to those who hear, not only the social domination or social power in language, but also possible injustice. Injustice calls for a hearing, and a just hearing requires that voices be heard as something other than a play of social interests. Hearing voices this way requires listening not only to their language but to what they say or, rather, attending to the event of their saying as they call to justice.

The call to justice today takes place in silence. Voices call out of and to an unsayable silence. Law issues from silence as the necessity of claims and responses and as a calling that both binds earthbound persons to a world and frees them to be and to act in that world. Law and its binding necessity manifest themselves today in the norms, rules, and institutions of modern positive and sociological law that currently tell us what to do, without necessary connection to justice.

Modern law, with its language of sociology and of power, fails to acknowledge any debt to what is unsayable. In this failure lies the particularity of the silence of modern law: it is a silence in which justice threatens to disappear. Insofar as law is exhausted by the statements of rules of officials in society or by social researchers' propositional descriptions of power, the "justice" of law becomes an empirical question of societal regularities. It becomes a matter of the ideologies and interests underlying norms and institutions. The "justice" of such social constructions is taken to be within human—social—control.

To face the threat of the disappearance of justice in modern law is to recognize the limits and possibilities of the modern law of a technical age in which everything becomes standing reserve to be utilized to advance or develop social values and goals. To face the threat of the disappearance of justice is to refrain from turning the issue of the silence of modern law into another (technical) matter of finding means to produce more desirable ends. It is to hear a voice that heeds and speaks of possibilities of law that are neither the articulations of power nor the powerful discourses of positive law. It is to hear in the air the silence of modern law as the necessary voice through which human beings sing of their earthly encounter with the world that is given them.

Voice in this encounter corresponds with law. Law arises as the event or chain of claims and responses that strive to hear and to speak in the name of justice. These calls to justice, bound as they are to an earthly world, free us for being in that world in a manner that statements of social knowledge can only ever approximate. The terminology of sociology and of the social world—the values of social ideals, the demands for social power, the capabilities of social mastery—speak today in ways that do not do law justice. Justice lies in stillness, awaiting the silent call to it that comes out of the human need to act and judge in a world that is *not* of one's own making. Out of this stillness comes a response and responsibility that corresponds (or not) with what was formerly the necessity of law, its relation to justice.

Recalling the trope of silence in the library generated no empirical knowledge of actual libraries; recalling silences of law alone establishes nothing definitive about existent law. Some silences may be just (as in *Miranda*);

some unjust (as toward Native Americans); others ambiguous (as in the absence of a right to burn the flag). Together, however, the silences of law open up questions about the speaking of law and its current grounding in social power. In an age of loquacious and powerful positive law, silences tell of what lies buried, concealed and hidden and possibly dead, within positive law.

In positive law, law's silences (or at least the silences of texts of positive law) as to law's indebtedness to justice raise questions about the continued relevance of justice and about the necessity of law. They raise questions about the way today's world is taken to be socially made and imagined, an object that our human knowledge can master and hence dominate according to our human ideas and desires. On the one hand, to show that justice lies in silence does not mean that justice is absent. On the other, showing that justice is not necessarily absent does not say what justice is nor that it will continue to be. Will silences of law as to justice become a forgetting of justice—and a forgetting of law as the tradition has known it? Or will the silences of law initiate unthought possibilities for the telling of law and the saying of justice?

We stand at a juncture in the history of relations between law and justice, a moment in which the justice of law lies as much if not more in the silences of positive law as in its speech. What will become of this moment? The answer cannot yet be known nor predicted; its determination lies in silences outside the grasp of either empirical or rhetorical analysis. As long as the justice of law lies in silence, the issue of the future of traditional concerns of jurisprudence—law and its relation to justice—remains both precarious and open.

Epilogue _____

WERE I TO WRITE this book again, it might be much shorter. It would say:

"Law on the books doesn't talk much about justice."

Then I would wait for someone to say: "It doesn't talk much, but it says much," or "Yes, it does" and to explain.

But maybe instead of waiting quietly, I—or the persons I was talking with—would first say:

"Maybe it's taken for granted."

"Maybe it's unclear what it means."

"Maybe it isn't there anymore."

And one of us would add, "In any case it's hard to talk about." Although I myself would have to resist adding this to the book, the book would just say:

"Yes, that was my point."

The conversation that then would ensue around this short book might begin, "So in what ways is justice hard to talk about?" or "But didn't you just do it?" or "If law doesn't talk much about justice, maybe it *does* justice—whatever justice turns out to be?"

Thinking back on this conversation, I wouldn't know where these questions of justice, voiced by some of us, came from. Did they come from the book's claim that law doesn't talk much about justice? Don't they run counter to it? They can't have come from nowhere—from just silence, or can they?

Appendix 1 _____

How the "Real World" at Last Became a Myth

History of an Error

1. The real world, attainable to the wise, the pious, the virtuous man—he dwells in it, *he is it.*
   (Oldest form of the idea, relatively sensible, simple, convincing. Transcription of the proposition "I, Plato, *am* the truth.")
2. The real world, unattainable for the moment, but promised to the wise, the pious, the virtuous man ("to the sinner who repents").
   (Progress of the idea: it grows more refined, more enticing, more incomprehensible—*it becomes a woman*, it becomes Christian . . .)
3. The real world, unattainable, undemonstrable, cannot be promised, but even when merely thought of a consolation, a duty, an imperative.
   (Fundamentally the same old sun, but shining through mist and skepticism; the idea grown sublime, pale, northerly, Konigsbergian.)
4. The real world—unattainable? Unattained, at any rate. And if unattained also unknown. Consequently also no consolation, no redemption, no duty: how could we have a duty towards something unknown?
   (The grey of dawn. First yawnings of reason. Cockcrow of positivism.)
5. The "real world"—an idea no longer of any use, not even a duty any longer—an idea grown useless, superfluous, *consequently* a refuted idea: let us abolish it!
   (Broad daylight; breakfast; return of cheerfulness and *bon sens*; Plato blushes for shame; all free spirits run riot.)
6. We have abolished the real world: what world is left? The apparent world perhaps? . . . But no! *with the real world we have also abolished the apparent world!*
   (Mid-day; moment of the shortest shadow; end of the longest error; zenith of mankind; INCIPIT ZARATHUSTRA)[1]

_____
[1] Nietzsche, *Twilight of the Idols*, 40–41.

Appendix 2 _____

Letter: On Abortion

The Child Has a Right to Be Born

To the Editor:

A. M. Rosenthal, in his Oct. 24 column, takes President Bush to task for his veto of Medicaid funding for abortion in cases of rape and incest, and calls his integrity into doubt for opposing Federal aid "to a young woman without money carrying her father's baby."

He addresses the pro-life position at its most vulnerable point. Who, after all, wants to ask a pregnant woman to carry to term the child whose father is actually his or her grandfather? Seen from the pregnant woman's viewpoint, that seems monstrous.

But there *is* another viewpoint, that of the child in the womb. The child has done no wrong to anyone. He or she is the most innocent of bystanders, who has been called into existence and finds him or herself washed up on the shores of the world not knowing where he came from or why he was created, and having done nothing to bring himself into existence—the same as all the rest of us.

That child is as good and as vulnerable as any one of us, for "all are created equal." He has offended no one, has caused no pain, is asking only what all of us ask: to be allowed to live. "Please don't kill me" is all the child could say if he could speak. The pro-life movement exists to be the voice of that innocent child.

Once we take the child's point of view, an interesting point comes to mind, namely that none of us know for sure who his or her father is. That is a matter of trust. Ultimately it is an act of implicit confidence in our mother. She is the only one who really knows who our father is. Even her husband does not know with absolute certitude.

This leads us to a very interesting question. Suppose I, or Mr. Rosenthal, or anyone, were to discover tomorrow, at the age, say, of 50, that the man who we thought was our father was not really our father at all; suppose indeed we were to learn that our father was, in reality, our grandfather, or that we were conceived by an act of violent rape: would we—he, I, or any one of us—wish that we were killed in the womb?

I think not. I think in the same circumstances Beethoven, Dante, Thomas Edison, Irving Berlin, Francis of Assisi or any one of us in this imperfect world would choose—if the choice were ours—to be born.

In the end, the abortion issue turns not upon the mother but upon the child. It is not a question of a woman's rights but of every child's right, of human rights, of the most fundamental right of all, the right not to be killed for no reason except through the choice of our own.

President Bush's position is not so untenable as it can be made to seem. It is quite reasonable if we believe in the equality of all human beings.

(Most Rev.) Patrick V. Ahern
Vicar of Staten Island
Oct. 25, 1989[1]

[1] *New York Times*, November 3, 1989, National Edition, A14. Reprinted by permission of the author.

Works Cited

Abel, Richard L. "What We Talk about When We Talk about Law." In *Law and Society Reader*, ed. Richard L. Abel. New York: New York University Press, 1995.

Abley, Mark. *Spoken Here: Travels Among Threatened Languages*. Boston: Houston Mifflin, 2003.

Ahern, Patrick V. "The Child Has a Right to Be Born." Letter to the Editor. *New York Times*, November 3, 1989, National Edition, A14.

Ahers, Ronald L., and Richard Hawkins, eds. *Law and Control in Society*. Englewood Cliffs, NJ: Prentice-Hall, 1975.

Ainsworth, Janet E. "In a Different Register: The Pragmatics of Powerlessness in Police Interrogation." *Yale Law Journal* 103 (1993): 259.

Alschuler, Albert. "A Peculiar Privilege in Historical Perspective: The Right to Remain Silent." *Michigan Law Review* 98 (1996): 2625.

Amar, Akhil Reed. "Foreword: The Document and the Doctrine." *Harvard Law Review* 114 (2000): 26.

American Association of Museums. "Comparison of Repatriation Legislation." Prepared by AAM Government Affairs Program, December 1989. Photocopy.

Arendt, Hannah. *The Human Condition*. 2d ed. Chicago: University of Chicago Press, 1989.

Augustine. *City of God*. Trans. Henry Bettenson. New York: Penguin, 1984.

———. *On Free Choice of the Will*. Trans. Thomas Williams. Indianapolis: Hackett, 1993.

Austin, J. L. *How to Do Things with Words*. 1962. Reprint, Cambridge: Harvard University Press, 1975.

———. "A Plea for Excuses." In *Philosophical Papers*. 3d ed. Oxford: Oxford University Press, 1979.

Austin, John. *The Province of Jurisprudence Determined*. 1832. Reprint, London: Weidenfeld and Nicholson, 1954.

Basso, Keith H. " 'To Give Up on Words': Silence in Western Apache Culture." In *Language and Social Context*, ed. Pier Paolo Giglioli. Baltimore: Penguin, 1972.

Baudrillard, Jean. *In the Shadow of the Silent Majorities; or, The End of the Social and Other Essays*. New York: Semiotext(e), 1983.

Bazemore, George. "The 'Community' " in Community Justice: Issues, Themes, and Questions for the New Neighborhood Sanctioning Models." In *Community Justice: An Emerging Field*, ed. David R. Karp. Lanham, MD: Rowman and Littlefield, 1988.

Benjamin, Walter. "Critique of Violence." In *Reflections,* ed. Peter Demetz, trans. Edmund Jephcott. New York: Schocken, 1978.

———. "The Storyteller." In *Illuminations*, ed. Hannah Arendt, trans. Harry Zohn. New York: Schocken Books, 1968.

Bennett, W. Lance, and Martha Feldman. *Reconstructing Reality in the Court-room*. New Brunswick, NJ: Rutgers University Press, 1981.

Bentham, Jeremy. *Introduction to the Principles of Morals and Legislation*. Oxford: Oxford University Press, 1948.

Benveniste, Emile. "Analytic Philosophy of Language." In *Problems in General Linguistics*, trans. Mary Elizabeth Meek. Coral Gables, FL: University of Miami Press, 1971.

Berkowitz, Peter. "On the Laws Governing Free Spirits and Philosophers of the Future: A Response to Nonet's 'What is Positive Law?' " *Yale Law Journal* 100 (1990): 701.

Berkowitz, Roger. "Friedrich Nietzsche, the Code of Manu, and the Art of Legislation." *Cardozo Law Review* 24 (2003): 1131.

Berk-Seligson, Susan. "Bilingual Court Proceedings: The Role of the Court Interpreter." In *Language and the Legal Process,* ed. Judith N. Levi and Anne Graffan Walker. New York: Plenum, 1990.

———. *The Bilingual Courtroom: Court Interpreters in the Judicial Process*. Chicago: University of Chicago Press, 1990.

Bezanson, Randall P. *Speech Stories: How Free Can Speech Be?* New York: New York University Press, 1998.

Bierne, Piers, and Richard Quinney, eds. *Marxism and Law*. New York: John Wiley and Sons, 1982.

Biskupic, Joan. "Critics of Flag-Burning Ruling Debate Next Step to Take." *Congressional Quarterly,* July 15, 1989.

———. "Flag-Burning Ruling Sparks Cries for Action on Hill." *Congressional Quarterly,* July 1, 1989.

———. "House Committee OKs Measure to Outlaw Flag Desecration." *Congressional Quarterly,* July 29, 1989.

Bix, Brian. "Conceptual Jurisprudence and Socio-Legal Studies." *Rutgers Law Journal* 32 (2000): 227.

———. "Positively Positivism: Reviewing Legal Positivism in American Jurisprudence." *Virginia Law Review* 85 (1999): 899.

Brean, Ron, and Laura Svendsgaard-Brean. "Aliens in our Midst: A Perspective on Non-Native Species." *Parklands* (newsletter, California State Parks Foundation), 1998.

Brenneis, Donald. "Language and Disputing." *Annual Review of Anthropology* 17 (1988): 221.

Brooks, Peter. *Troubling Confessions: Speaking Guilt in Law and Literature*. Chicago: University of Chicago Press, 2000.

Brown, Wendy. *States of Injury: Power and Freedom in Late Modernity*. Princeton: Princeton University Press, 1995.

Burchell, Gordon, Colin Gordon, and Peter Miller, eds. *The Foucault Effect: Studies in Governmentality*. Chicago: University of Chicago Press, 1991.

Burns, Robert P. *A Theory of the Trial*. Princeton: Princeton University Press, 1999.

Burton, Lloyd. *Worship and Wilderness: Culture, Religion, and Law in Public Lands Management*. Madison: University of Wisconsin Press, 2002.

Butler, Judith. *Excitable Speech: A Politics of the Performative.* New York: Routledge, 1997.

———. *The Psychic Life of Power.* Stanford: Stanford University Press, 1997.

Cage, John. *M: Writings '67–'72.* Middletown, CT: Wesleyan University Press, 1973.

Campbell, Lyle. *American Indian Languages: The Historical Linguistics of Native America.* New York: Oxford University Press, 1997.

Canguilhem, Georges. *The Normal and the Pathological.* 1966. Reprint, New York: Zone Books, 1989.

Carey, John L. *The Rise of the Accounting Profession to Responsibility and Authority.* New York: American Institute of Certified Public Accountants, 1970.

Cavell, Stanley. *Philosophical Passages: Wittgenstein, Emerson, Austin, Derrida.* Oxford: Blackwell, 1995.

———. *A Pitch of Philosophy: Autobiographical Exercises.* Cambridge: Harvard University Press, 1994.

Cheah, Pheng. "The Law of/as Rape: Poststructuralism and the Framing of the Legal Text." In *Legal Education and Legal Knowledge,* ed. Ian Duncanson. Bundoora, Victoria, Australia: La Trobe University Press, 1991–92.

Clastres, Pierre. *Society Against the State.* New York: Zone Books, 1987.

Clear, Todd R., and David R. Karp. "The Community Justice Movement." In *Community Justice: An Emerging Field,* ed. David R. Karp. Lanham, MD: Rowman and Littlefield, 1998.

Clemmer, Richard O. "The Hopi Traditionalist Movement." *American Indian Culture and Research Journal* 18 (1994): 125.

Clifford, James. "Identity in Mashpee." In *The Predicament of Culture: Twentieth-Century Ethnography, Literature, and Art.* Cambridge: Harvard University Press, 1988.

Coleman, Jules. "Negative and Positive Positivism." In *Markets, Morals and the Law.* Cambridge: Cambridge University Press, 1988.

———. "Rules and Social Facts." *Harvard Journal of Law and Public Policy* 14 (1991): 703.

Comaroff, Jean, and John Comaroff. "Naturing the Nation: Aliens, Apocalypse and the Postcolonial State." *International Social Science Review* 1 (2000): 7.

Conley, John, and William M. O'Barr. *Just Words: Law, Language, and Power.* Chicago: University of Chicago Press, 1998.

———. *Rules versus Relationships: The Ethnography of Legal Discourse.* Chicago: University of Chicago Press, 1990.

Constable, Marianne. "Foucault and Walzer: Sovereignty, Strategy, and the State." *Polity* 24 (1991): 269.

———. "Genealogy and Jurisprudence: Nietzsche, Nihilism, and the Social Scientification of Law." *Law and Social Inquiry* 19 (1994): 551.

———. *The Law of the Other: The Mixed Jury and Changing Conceptions of Citizenship, Law, and Knowledge.* Chicago: University of Chicago Press, 1994.

———. "Rejoinder: Thinking Nonsociologically about Sociological Law." *Law and Social Inquiry* 19 (1994): 625.

———. "The University Library at the Turn of the Century." *Chronicle of the University of California* 4 (2000): 138.

Copi, Irving M., and Carl Cohen. *Introduction to Logic.* 8th ed. New York: Macmillan, 1990.

Consortium of Social Science Associations. *Washington Update* 17 (1998): 21.

Cover, Robert. *Justice Accused: Antislavery and the Judicial Process.* New Haven: Yale University Press, 1975.

———. *Narrative, Violence, and the Law: The Essays of Robert Cover.* Ed. Martha Minow, Michael Ryan, and Austin Sarat. Ann Arbor: University of Michigan Press, 1993.

———. "Violence and the Word." In *Narrative, Violence and the Law: The Essays of Robert Cover,* ed. Martha Minow, Michael Ryan, and Austin Sarat. Ann Arbor: University of Michigan Press, 1993.

Cruikshank, Barbara. *The Will to Empower: Democratic Citizens and Other Subjects.* Ithaca, NY: Cornell University Press, 1999.

Danet, Brenda. "Language in the Legal Process." *Law and Society Review* 14 (1980): 445.

Davis, F. James. "Law as a Type of Social Control." In *Law and Control in Society,* ed. Ronald L. Ahers and Richard Hawkins. Englewood Cliffs, NJ: Prentice-Hall, 1975.

de Certeau, Michel. *The Writing of History.* Trans. Tom Conley. New York: Columbia University Press, 1988.

Derrida, Jacques. *Limited Inc.* Evanston, IL: Northwestern University Press, 1988.

Delgado, Richard, ed. *Critical Race Theory: The Cutting Edge.* Philadelphia: Temple University Press, 1995.

Dreyfus, Hubert L., and Stuart E. Dreyfus. "From Socrates to Expert Systems: The Limits of Calculative Rationality." *Philosophy and Technology* 2 (1986): 111.

Dumm, Thomas L. *A Politics of the Ordinary.* New York: New York University Press, 1999.

Dussias, Allison M. "Waging War with Words: Native Americans' Continuing Struggle Against the Suppression of Their Languages." *Ohio State Law Journal* 60 (1999): 901.

Dworkin, Ronald. *Law's Empire.* Cambridge: Harvard University Press, 1986.

Edelman, Lauren B., Steven E. Abraham, and Howard Erlanger. "Professional Construction of Law: The Inflated Threat of Wrongful Discharge." *Law and Society Review* 26 (1992): 47.

Elkins, Jeremy. "The Force of Rules." In *Rules and Reasoning: Essays in Honor of Frederick Schauer,* ed. Linda Meyer. Oxford: Hart, 1999.

Eliot, T. S. *Old Possum's Book of Practical Cats.* London: Faber and Faber, 1940.

Engel, David. "Origin Myths: Narratives of Authority, Resistance, Disability, and Law." *Law and Society Review* 27 (1993): 785.

Erickson, B. E., E. A. Lind, B. C. Johnson, and W. M. O'Barr. "Speech Style and Impression Formation in a Court Setting: The Effects of 'Powerful' and 'Powerless' Speech." *Journal of Experimental and Social Psychology* 14 (1978): 266.

Erickson, Rosemary J., and Rita J. Simon. *The Use of Social Science Data in Supreme Court Decisions.* Urbana: University of Illinois Press, 1998.

Ewick, Patricia, Robert A. Kagan, and Austin Sarat, eds. *Social Science, Social Policy, and the Law.* New York: Russell Sage Foundation, 1999.

Ewick, Patricia, and Susan Silbey. *The Common Place of Law: Stories from Everyday Life*. Chicago: University of Chicago Press, 1998.

———. "Subversive Stories and Hegemonic Tales: Toward a Sociology of Narrative." *Law and Society Review* 29 (1995): 197.

Ferrin, Scott Ellis. "Reasserting Language Rights of Native American Students in the Face of Proposition 227 and Other Language-Based Referenda." *Journal of Law and Education* 28 (1999): 1.

Finnis, John. *Natural Law and Natural Rights*. Oxford: Clarendon Press, 1981.

Fish, Stanley. "Force." In *Doing What Comes Naturally*. Durham, NC: Duke University Press, 1989.

Fiss, Owen M. *The Irony of Free Speech*. Cambridge: Harvard University Press, 1996.

Fitzpatrick, Peter. *The Mythology of Modern Law*. New York: Routledge, 1992.

Fitzpatrick, Peter, and Alan Hunt, eds. *Critical Legal Studies*. Oxford: Basil Blackwell, 1987.

"Flag Desecration Legislation." *Congressional Digest*, July–August 1989, 193.

"For the Record. Presidential News Conference [June 27]. Flag Burning, HUD Scandal Dominate Press Queries." *Congressional Quarterly*, July 1, 1989, 1650.

Foucault, Michel. *Discipline and Punish: The Birth of the Prison*. Trans. Alan Sheridan. New York: Vintage, 1977.

———. "Governmentality." *Ideology and Consciousness* 6 (1979): 5.

———. *History of Sexuality*. Vol. 1. Trans. Robert Hurley. New York: Vintage, 1978.

———. "The Order of Discourse." Trans. Ian McLeod. In *Language and Politics*, ed. Michael Shapiro. New York: New York University Press, 1984.

———. *The Order of Things: An Archaeology of the Human Sciences*. New York: Vintage, 1994.

———. *Power/Knowledge: Selected Interviews and Other Writings, 1972–1977*. Ed. Colin Gordon. New York: Pantheon, 1980.

———. "What Is an Author?" In *Language, Counter-Memory, Practice: Selected Essays and Interviews*, trans. Donald F. Bouchard and Sherry Simon. Ithaca: Cornell University Press, 1977.

Frank, Jill. *A Democracy of Distinction*. Chicago: University of Chicago Press, 2005.

Freud, Sigmund. *The Ego and the Id* (1923). In *The Standard Edition of the Complete Psychological Works of Sigmund Freud*, trans. and ed. James Strachey. London: Hogarth Press, 1966–73.

———. *The Future of an Illusion* (1927). In *The Standard Edition of the Complete Psychological Works of Sigmund Freud*, trans. and ed. James Strachey. London: Hogarth Press, 1966–73.

———. *The Question of Lay Analysis*. New York: Norton, 1950.

———. *Therapy and Technique*. New York: Collier, 1963.

Friedman, Lawrence M. "The Law and Society Movement." *Stanford Law Review* 35 (1986): 763.

Frug, Mary Joe. *Postmodern Legal Feminism*. New York: Routledge, 1992.

Goodrich, Peter. "Law and Language: An Historical and Critical Introduction." *Journal of Law and Society* 11 (1984): 173.

———. *Law in the Courts of Love: Literature and Other Minor Jurisprudences.* New York: Routledge, 1996.

———. *Oedipus Lex: Psychoanalysis, History, Law.* Berkeley and Los Angeles: University of California Press, 1995.

———. *Reading the Law: A Critical Introduction to Legal Method and Technologies.* Oxford: Blackwell, 1986.

Gould, Timothy. "The Unhappy Performative." In *Performativity and Performance,* ed. Andrew Parker and Eve Kosofsky. New York: Routledge, 1995.

Grano, Joseph. *Confessions, Truth, and the Law.* Ann Arbor: University of Michigan Press, 1993.

Habermas, Jürgen. *Between Facts and Norms: Contributions to a Discourse Theory of Law and Democracy.* Trans. William Rehg. Cambridge: MIT Press, 1996.

Hardt, Michael, and Tony Negri. *Empire.* Cambridge: Harvard University Press, 2001.

Harrington, Christine B., and Barbara Yngvesson. "Interpretive Sociolegal Research." *Law and Social Inquiry* 15 (1990): 135.

Hart, H.L.A. *The Concept of Law.* Oxford: Clarendon Press, 1961.

———. "Positivism and the Separation of Law and Morals." *Harvard Law Review* 71 (1958): 593.

Hartz, Louis. *The Liberal Tradition in America: An Interpretation of American Political Thought Since the Revolution.* New York: Harcourt, Brace World, 1955.

Heidegger, Martin. "The Age of the World Picture." In *The Question concerning Technology and Other Essays,* trans. William Lovitt. New York: Harper Torchbooks, 1977.

———. *Basic Concepts.* Trans. Gary Aylesworth. Bloomington: Indiana University Press, 1993.

———. *Poetry, Language, Thought.* Trans. Albert Hofstadter. New York: Harper and Row, 1971.

———. *Langue de tradition et langue technique.* Trans. Michel Haar. Brussels: Editions Lebeer Hossmann, 1990. Translation of *Überlieferte Sprache und Technische Sprache.*

———. "The Origin of the Work of Art." Trans. Roger Berkowitz and Philippe Nonet. 2003. Unpublished.

———. *Nietzsche.* Vol. 3. Trans. Joan Stambaugh et al. New York: Harper and Row, 1987.

———. "The Question concerning Technology." In *The Question concerning Technology and Other Essays,* trans. William Lovitt. New York: Harper Torchbooks, 1977.

Heimoff, Steve. "Angle of Repose." *East Bay Express,* July 21, 1989.

Helmholz, R. H. "Origins of the Privilege Against Self-Incrimination: The Role of the European *Ius Commune.*" *New York University Law Review* 65 (1990): 962.

Hinton, Leanne. *Flutes of Fire: Essays on California Indian Languages.* Berkeley: Heyday, 1994.

Hirschman, Albert O. *Exit, Voice, and Loyalty: Responses to Decline in Firms, Organizations, and States.* Cambridge: Harvard University Press, 1970.

Inbau, Fred E. "The Mischief of *Miranda v. Arizona.*" *Journal of Criminal Law and Criminology* 73 (1982): 797.

Inbau, Fred E., and James P. Manak. "*Miranda v. Arizona*—Is It Worth the Cost?" *California Western Law Review* 24 (1988): 185.

Kafka, Franz. *The Castle.* Trans. Mark Harman. New York: Schocken Books, 1998.

Kahan, Dan M. "Social Influence, Social Meaning, and Deterrence." *Virginia Law Review* 83 (1997): 349.

Kant, Immanuel. *Critique of Pure Reason.* Trans. Norman Kemp Smith. New York: St. Martin's Press, 1965.

———. *Groundwork of the Metaphysic of Morals.* Trans. H. J. Paton. New York: Harper and Row, 1964.

———. *Metaphysical Elements of Justice.* 2d ed. Trans. John Ladd. Indianapolis: Hackett, 1999.

Karp, David R. *Community Justice: An Emerging Field.* Lanham, MD: Rowman and Littlefield, 1998.

Keeling, Richard. "The Sources of Indian Music: An Introduction and Overview." *World of Music* 34 (1992): 3.

Keenan, Thomas. *Fables of Responsibility: Aberrations and Predicaments in Ethics and Politics.* Stanford: Stanford University Press, 1997.

Kelsen, Hans. *Pure Theory of Law.* Berkeley and Los Angeles: University of California Press, 1967.

Kessler, Mark. "Legal Discourse and Political Intolerance: The Ideology of Clear and Present Danger." *Law and Society Review* 27 (1993): 559.

Kymlicka, Will. *Multicultural Citizenship: A Liberal Theory of Minority Rights.* Oxford: Clarendon Press; New York: Oxford University Press, 1995.

Kmiec, Douglas W. "In the Aftermath of *Johnson* and *Eichman*: The Constitution Need Not be Mutilated to Preserve the Government's Speech and Property Interests in the Flag." *Brigham Young University Law Review* 19 (1990):577.

Kosslak, Renee M. "The NAGPRA: The Death Knell of Scientific Study." Comment. *American Indian Law Review* 24 (1999–2000): 129.

Krauss, Michael. "Status of Native American Language Endangerment." In *Stabilizing Indigenous Languages*, ed. Gina Canatoni. Flagstaff: Northern Arizona University, Center for Excellence in Education, Monograph Series, 1997.

Kundera, Milan. "Somewhere Behind." In *The Art of the Novel*, trans. Linda Asher. New York: Perennial Library, 1988.

Langbein, John H. "The Historical Origins of the Privilege Against Self-Incrimination at Common Law." *Michigan Law Review* 92 (1994): 1047.

Lee, Dorothy. *Freedom and Culture.* Englewood Cliffs, NJ: Prentice-Hall, Spectrum, 1959.

———. *Valuing the Self: What We Can Learn From Other Cultures.* Englewood Cliffs, NJ: Prentice-Hall, Spectrum, 1976.

Leo, Richard A. "The Impact of *Miranda* Revisited." *Journal of Criminal Law and Criminology* 86 (1996): 621.

Lessig, Lawrence. "The Regulation of Social Meaning." *University of Chicago Law Review* 62 (1995): 943.

Levi, Judith N. *Language and Law: A Bibliographic Guide to Social Science Research in the U.S.A.* Chicago: American Bar Association Committee on College and University Legal Studies, Teaching Resource Bulletin, no. 4, 1994.

———. *Linguistics, Language, and the Law: A Topical Bibliography.* Bloomington: Indiana University Linguistics Club, 1982.

———. "The Study of Language in the Judicial Process." In *Language in the Judicial Process*, ed. Judith N. Levi and Anne Graffan Walker. New York: Plenum, 1990.

Levy, Leonard W. *Constitutional Opinions: Aspects of the Bill of Rights.* New York: Oxford University Press, 1986.

Litwack, Leon. "Has the Library Lost its Soul?" *California Monthly*, February 1998, 15.

Lowell, A. Lawrence. "The Judicial Use of Torture, Parts I and II." *Harvard Law Review* 11 (1897): 290.

Lyman, Peter. "What is a Digital Library? Technology, Property, and the Public Interest." *Daedalus* 125 (1996): 1.

MacKinnon, Catharine. *Feminism Unmodified: Discourses on Life and Law.* Cambridge: Harvard University Press, 1987.

———. *Only Words.* Cambridge: Harvard University Press, 1993.

———. *Toward a Feminist Theory of the State.* Cambridge: Harvard University Press, 1989.

Macnair, Michael R. T. "The Early Development of the Privilege Against Self-Incrimination." *Oxford Journal of Legal Studies* 10 (1990): 66.

Maguire, Mary Hume. "Attack of the Common Lawyers on the Oath *Ex Officio* as Administered in the Ecclesiastical Courts in England." In *Essays in History and Political Theory in Honor of Charles Howard McIlwain.* Boston: Harvard University Press, 1936.

Matsuda, Mari J., Charles R. Lawrence III, Richard Delgado, and Kimberlé Crenshaw. *Words that Wound: Critical Race Theory, Assaultive Speech and the First Amendment.* Boulder: Westview Press, 1993.

Maynard, Douglas W. "Narratives and Narrative Structure in Plea Bargaining." In *Language in the Judicial Process*, ed. Judith N. Levi and Anne Graffan Walker. New York: Plenum, 1990.

Mellinkoff, David. *The Language of the Law.* Boston: Little, Brown, 1963.

Merry, Sally. *Getting Justice and Getting Even: Legal Consciousness among Working-Class Americans.* Chicago: University of Chicago Press, 1990.

———. "Law and Colonialism, Review Essay." *Law and Society Review* 25 (1991): 889.

———. "Wife Battering and the Ambiguities of Rights." In *Identities, Politics, and Rights*, ed. Austin Sarat and Thomas R. Kearns. Ann Arbor: University of Michigan Press, 1995.

Mertz, Elizabeth. "Language, Law, and Social Meanings: Linguistic/Anthropological Contributions to the Study of Law." *Law and Society Review* 26 (1992): 413.

———. "The Uses of History: Language, Ideology and Law in the United States and South Africa." *Law and Society Review* 22 (1988): 661.

Messick, Brinkley. "Kissing Hands and Knees: Hegemony and Hierarchy in Shari'a Discourse." *Law and Society Review* 22 (1988): 637.

Meyer, Linda Ross. "Between Reason and Power: Experiencing Legal Truth." *University of Cincinnati Law Review* 67:3 (1999): 727.

———. "Is Practical Reason Mindless?" *Georgetown Law Journal* 86 (1998): 647.

———. " 'Nothing We Say Matters': *Teague* and the New Rules." *University of Chicago Law Review* 61 (1994): 423.

Michelman, Frank. "Saving Old Glory: On Constitutional Iconography." *Stanford Law Review* 42 (1990): 1337.

Mill, John Stuart. *Considerations on Representative Government*. New York: Bobbs-Merrill, 1958.

———. *On Liberty*. London: Penguin, 1985.

———. *Utilitarianism*. New York: Meridian, 1962.

Moglen, Eben. "Taking the Fifth: Reconsidering the Origins of the Constitutional Privilege Against Self-Incrimination." *Michigan Law Review* 92 (1994): 1086.

Moore, Sally Falk. "Treating Law as Knowledge: Telling Colonial Officers What to Say to Africans about Running 'Their Own' Native Courts." *Law and Society Review* 26 (1992): 11.

Morgan, E. M. "The Privilege Against Self-Incrimination." *Minnesota Law Review* 34 (1949): 1.

Morrill, Calvin, and Peter C. Facciola. "The Power of Language in Adjudication and Mediation: Institutional Contexts as Predictors of Social Evaluation." *Law and Social Inquiry* 17 (1992): 191.

Munger, Frank. "Inquiry and Activism in Law and Society." *Law and Society Review* 35:1 (2001): 7.

Nietzsche, Friedrich. *Beyond Good and Evil*. Trans. Walter Kaufmann. New York: Vintage, 1966.

———. *On the Genealogy of Morals*. In *Basic Writings of Nietzsche*, trans. Walter Kaufmann. New York: Modern Library, 1968.

———. *Thus Spoke Zarathustra*. Trans. R. J. Hollingdale. New York: Penguin, 1969.

———. *Twilight of the Idols*. Trans. R. J. Hollingdale. London: Penguin, 1968.

———. *Will to Power*. Ed. Walter Kaufmann. Trans. Walter Kaufmann and R. J. Hollingdale. New York: Random House, 1968.

Nunberg, Geoffrey, ed. *The Future of the Book*. Berkeley and Los Angeles: University of California Press, 1996.

O'Barr, William. *Linguistic Evidence: Language, Power and Strategy in the Courtroom*. New York: Academic Press, 1982.

O'Barr, William, and John Conley. "Litigant Satisfaction versus Legal Adequacy in Small Claims Court Narratives." *Law and Society Review* 19 (1985): 661.

O'Malley, Pat. "Neo-Liberal Police: 'Partnership Policing' and the 'Empowered Community.' " Paper presented at Law and Society Summer Legal Institute, Rutgers, New Jersey, 1999.

Picard, Max. *The World of Silence*. Trans. Stanley Godman. Chicago: H. Regnery, 1952.

Plato. *The Collected Dialogues of Plato*. Ed. Edith Hamilton and Huntington Cairns. Princeton: Princeton University Press, 1963.

Power, Michael. *The Audit Society: Rituals of Verification*. Oxford: Oxford University Press, 1990.

Rawls, John. *A Theory of Justice*. Cambridge: Harvard University Press, 1971.

Raz, Joseph. *The Concept of a Legal System*. Oxford: Clarendon Press, 1970.

———. *Practical Reason and Norms*. 1975. Reprint, Princeton: Princeton University Press, 1990.

Robinson, Paul H. "The Criminal-Civil Distinction and the Utility of Desert." *Boston University Law Review* 76 (1996): 201.

Rose, Nikolas. *Powers of Freedom: Reframing Political Thought*. Cambridge: Cambridge University Press, 1999.

Rosenstock-Huessy, Eugen. *Speech and Reality*. Norwich, VT: Argo, 1970.

Rubenfeld, Jed. *Freedom and Time: A Theory of Constitutional Self-Government*. New Haven: Yale University Press, 2001.

"Sacred Sites and Federal Land Management: An Analysis of the Proposed Native American Free Exercise of Religion Act of 1993." Comment. *Natural Resources Journal* 34 (1994): 443.

Samarin, William J. "Language of Silence." *Practical Anthropology* 12 (1965): 115.

Sandel, Michael J. *Liberalism and the Limits of Justice*. Cambridge: Cambridge University Press, 1982.

Sarat, Austin. "Visuality Amidst Fragmentation: On the Emergence of Postrealist Law and Society Scholarship." In *The Blackwell Companion to Law and Society*, ed. Austin Sarat. Malden, MA: Blackwell, 2004.

———. "Robert Cover on Law and Violence." In *Narrative, Violence and the Law: The Essays of Robert Cover*, ed. Martha Minow, Michael Ryan, and Austin Sarat. Ann Arbor: University of Michigan Press, 1993.

Sarat, Austin, and William L. F. Felstiner. *Divorce Lawyers and Their Clients*. New York: Oxford University Press, 1995.

———. "Law and Social Relations: Vocabularies of Motive in Lawyer/Client Interaction." *Law and Society Review* 22 (1988): 737.

Sarat, Austin, and Susan Silbey. "The Pull of the Policy Audience." *Law and Policy* 8:1 (1986): 7.

Sarat, Austin, and Jonathan Simon. "Cultural Analysis, Cultural Studies, and the Situation of Legal Scholarship." In *Cultural Analysis, Cultural Studies, and Law*, ed. Austin Sarat and Jonathan Simon. Durham, NC: Duke University Press, 2003.

Schauer, Frederick. *Playing by the Rules: A Philosophical Examination of Rule-Based Decision-Making in Law and in Life*. Oxford: Clarendon Press, 1991.

Schauer, Frederick, and Walter Sinnott-Armstrong. *Philosophy of Law: Classic and Contemporary Readings with Commentary*. Fort Worth: Harcourt Brace College Publishers, 1996.

Schlag, Pierre. *Laying Down the Law: Mysticism, Fetishism, and the American Legal Mind*. New York: New York University Press, 1996.

Schultz, Vicki. "The Sanitized Workplace." *Yale Law Journal* 112 (2003): 2061.

Scollon, Ron. "The Machine Stops: Silence in the Metaphor of Malfunction." In *Perspectives on Silence*, ed. Deborah Tannen and Muriel Saville-Troike. Norwood, NJ: Ablex, 1985.

Scott, James C. *Domination and the Arts of Resistance: Hidden Transcripts.* New Haven: Yale University Press, 1990.

Searle, John R. "Austin on Locutionary and Illocutionary Acts." *Journal of Philosophy* 78 (1981): 720.

Sebok, Anthony. *Legal Positivism in American Jurisprudence.* Cambridge: Cambridge University Press, 1998.

Seidmann, Daniel J., and Alex Stein. "The Right to Silence Helps the Innocent: A Game-Theoretic Analysis of the Fifth Amendment Privilege." *Harvard Law Review* 114 (2000): 430.

Shapiro, Michael, ed. *Language and Politics.* New York: New York University Press, 1984.

Simon, Jonathan. "Megan's Law: Crime and Democracy in Late Modern America." *Law and Social Inquiry* 25 (2000): 1111.

———. "On Their Own: Delinquency Without Society." *Kansas Law Review* 47 (1999): 1.

Simon, William H. "Legality, Bureaucracy, and Class in the Welfare System." *Yale Law Journal* 92 (1983): 1198.

Singer, Joseph William. "The Player and the Cards: Nihilism and Legal Theory." *Yale Law Journal* 94 (1984): 1.

Snicket, Lemony. *The Bad Beginning.* New York: Scholastic, 1999.

Snyder, Gary. *The Practice of the Wild.* San Francisco: North Point Press, 1990.

Sprinkle, Robert Hunt. "Corporatism in Question: A Note on Managed Care." *Report from the Institute for Philosophy and Public Policy* 17 (1997): 13.

Stolzenberg, William. "Sacred Peaks, Common Grounds." *Nature Conservancy*, September–October 1992, 17.

Sunstein, Cass R. "Law, Economics, and Norms: On the Expressive Function of Law." *University of Pennsylvania Law Review* 144 (1996): 2021.

"Symposium: Nietzsche and Legal Theory." *Cardozo Law Review* 24:2 (2003).

Tamanaha, Brian. *Realistic Socio-Legal Theory: Pragmatism and A Social Theory of Law.* Oxford: Clarendon Press, 1997.

Taylor, R. Neill, III. "The Protection of Flag Burning as Symbolic Speech and the Congressional Attempt to Overturn the Decision." *Cincinnati Law Review* 58 (1990): 1477.

Thomas Aquinas. *The Political Ideas of St. Thomas Aquinas: Representative Selections.* Trans. Dino Bigongiari. New York: Hafner Press, 1981.

Thomas, George C., III. "Separated at Birth, but Siblings Nonetheless: *Miranda* and the Due Process Notice Cases." *Michigan Law Review* 99 (2001): 1081.

Tiersma, Peter. *Legal Language.* Chicago: University of Chicago Press, 1999.

———. "The Language of Silence." *Rutgers Law Review* 38 (1995): 1.

Tindall, Gillian. *Celestine: Voices from a French Village.* New York: Henry Holt, 1996.

Tucker, Robert. "Protecting the Guilty—True Confessions: The Long Road Back to Miranda." *National Review*, October 1985.

Tyler, Tom R. *Why People Obey the Law.* New Haven: Yale University Press, 1990.

Uchitelle, Louis. "Consumer Confidence Index Goes from an Aha to a Hmm." *New York Times,* June 8, 2002, A1.

Unger, Roberto M. *The Critical Legal Studies Movement.* Cambridge: Harvard University Press, 1983.

United Indian Nations in Oklahoma. Resolution Passed by Tribal Council, December 20, 1989.

United States Bureau of Census. *Census ABC's: Applications in Business and Community.* Washington, D.C.: Georgetown University Press, 1990.

United States Public Law 101–131. 1989. *Flag Protection Act of 1989.*

United States Public Law 101–477. 1990. *Indian Education Programs; Native American Languages Act.*

United States Public Law 101–601. 1990. *Native American Graves Protection and Repatriation Act.*

United States Public Law 102–524. 1992. *Native American Languages Act of 1992; Native Americans Educational Assistance Act.*

United States Senate. Select Committee on Indian Affairs. *Hearing on Native American Grave Repatriation Act.* S.1980. May 14, 1990.

———. Indian Affairs Committee. Senate Report 101–250 on S. 1781, March 7, 1990. Reproduced in Senate Report 101–371 on S.2167. In *Congressional Record,* vol. 136, 1841 (1990).

———. Select Committee on Indian Affairs. Senate Report 103–343, Report to Accompany S.2044, July 27, 1992. In *Congressional Record,* vol. 138, 2956 (1992).

University of California Office of the President. *Policy and Procedures on Repatriation of Human Remains and Cultural Items.* April 1, 1991.

Valverde, Mariana. *Law's Dream of a Common Knowledge.* Princeton: Princeton University Press, 2003.

Valverde, Mariana, Ron Levi, Clifford Shearing, Mary Condon, and Pat O'Malley. *Democracy in Governance: A Socio-Legal Framework. A Report for the Law Commission of Canada on Law and Governance Relationships.* Ottawa: Law Commission, 1999.

Walker, Samuel. *Hate Speech: The History of an American Controversy.* Lincoln: University of Nebraska Press, 1994.

Weber, Max. *Economy and Society.* Ed. Guenther Roth and Claus Wittich. Trans. Ephraim Fischoff et al. 2 vols. Berkeley and Los Angeles: University of California Press, 1978.

Weinraub, Bernard. "Bush Seeking Way to Circumvent Court's Decision on Flag Burning." *New York Times,* June 27, 1989, I-1.

Whately, Richard. *Elements of Logic.* 9th ed. New York: Sheldon and Co., 1873.

White, James Boyd. *Heracles' Bow: Essays on the Rhetoric and Poetics of the Law.* Madison: University of Wisconsin Press, 1985.

———. *Justice as Translation: An Essay in Cultural and Legal Criticism.* Chicago: University of Chicago Press, 1994.

White, Lucie E. "Subordination, Rhetorical Survival Skills, and Sunday Shoes: Notes on the Hearing of Mrs. G." In *At the Boundaries of Law*, ed. Martha Albertson Fineman and Nancy Sweet Thomadsen. New York: Routledge, 1991.

Wigmore, John H. "Nemo Tenetur Seipsum Prodere." *Harvard Law Review 5* (1891–92): 71.

———. "The Privilege against Self-Incrimination; Its History." *Harvard Law Review* 15 (1901–2): 610.

Williams, Patricia. *The Alchemy of Race and Rights*. Cambridge: Harvard University Press, 1991.

Willson, Meredith. *The Music Man*. New York: Frank Music Corp. and MW Music, 1986.

"With World Opening Up, Languages Are Losers." *New York Times*, May 16, 1999, 17.

Wittgenstein, Ludwig. *Tractatus logico-philosophicus*. Trans. C. K. Ogden. 2d ed. London: Routledge and Kegan Paul, 1933.

Wood, Michael. *Children of Silence: On Contemporary Fiction*. New York: Columbia Press, 1998.

Yngvesson, Barbara. "Making Law at the Doorway: The Clerk, the Court, and the Construction of Community in a New England Town." *Law and Society Review* 22 (1988): 409.

Yovel, Jonathan, and Elizabeth Mertz. "The Role of Social Science in Legal Decisions." In *The Blackwell Companion to Law and Society*, ed. Austin Sarat. Malden, MA: Blackwell, 2004.

Zuger, Abigail. "Essay: Patient Suffers from Connotations." *New York Times*, August 31, 1999.

Court Decisions

Brown v. Walker, 161 U.S. 591, 16 S.Ct. 644 (1896).
Chaplinsky v. New Hampshire, 315 U.S. 568, 62 S.Ct. 766 (1942).
Dickerson v. U.S, 530 U.S. 428, 120 S.Ct. 2326 (2000).
United States v. Eichman, 496 U.S. 310, 110 S. Ct. 2404 (1990).
Miranda v. Arizona, 384 U.S. 436, 86 S.Ct. 1602 (1966)
Texas v. Johnson, 491 U.S. 397, 109 S. Ct. 2533 (1989).

Index

Personal Responsibility and Work Opportunity Reconciliation Act, 25

Phaedo (Plato), 37

philosophy of law, 6, 15, 17–18, 18n12, 34–44. *See also* jurisprudence; legal positivism

Picard, Max, 80–81

Plato, 20, 35–37, 141, 143

pluralism, 66, 69, 81–85

poetry, 72, 75, 113, 130, 141, 148; Eliot, "The Naming of Cats," 45, 46, 72, 73

poets: John Cage, 1; T. S. Eliot, "The Naming of Cats," 45, 46, 72, 73; William Shakespeare, 74, 149, 156; Jan Skacel, 130n17, 111; Gary Snyder, 75, 90, 91

politics: of association, 23; media on partisan, 99–108; and voice, 56–71. *See also* public opinion and participation

pornography, 52

positive law

— defined, 9–10, 14, 17–18, 20, 38

— in history of jurisprudence, 38–41, 89, 112, 120–22; becomes social policy, 39–40; raises issue of nihilism, 41–44, 110, 130–31, 148, 177–78

— in age of technique: grounded in social knowledge, 74, 84–85, 88–89, 176; grounded in social pressure, 32–33, 133; as organized violence, 132–45; as system of rules, 100, 111–28, 142; as sociologically describable, 28–34, 46–55, 88; as strategically rational, 79–88, 107–10

— texts of: 6, 8, 10, 12, 13; U.S. legislation, 74–92; U.S. judicial opinions, 93–107

See also legal positivism; United States law

power: absence of, interpreted as absence of voice or justice, 8, 55, 59, 71; language of social, 6, 45–56, 93, 151; in legal and sociological texts, 9–12, 43–44, 74, 175; social, attributed to discourse and language, 8, 11, 45–56; of society, 33–34, 126–28

practices: of legal institutions, 46–55, 111–12, 132–48, 161–62; of Native Americans, 79–80, 85–86, 91–92; propositional articulation and articulability of, 31, 85, 88

pragmatism, 39

preservation: of language and culture, 74–92; of wildlife, 78n7

presumptive positivism, 12, 41, 112–13; lacks account of transformation of rules into action, 128–31, 137; legal system as, 122–28; rules of, 113–19; as systemic analog to rules, 119–22

privatization, 23

privilege against self-incrimination. *See* Fifth Amendment; right to remain silent

privacy, 161–62

pro-life position, 60–63, 182–83

property, as interest in flag, 102–4

propositions: language not simply matter of, to rhetorician, 16–17; as statements of rules, 88–89; inability of, to grasp practices, 31, 85, 88

public opinion and participation, 57; attributes of, according to media, 108; consent, 57, 59, 86; liberalism and, 56–58, 66–71, 86, 143; polls, surveys, and votes, 27, 68, 86

quality control, 24

"Question concerning Technology" (Heidegger), 11n2. *See also* technique

racial justice, 41, 51–52, 58, 65, 66, 69–71

rationality, 22–23, 39–40, 88, 98; in age of technique, 94, 109–10; of rule-based decision-making, 117, 119–20

Rawls, John, 20, 40, 57, 120n7

Raz, Joseph, 30, 114n3

reading, 3, 4–5; rhetoric as, 14–15, 17; of silences, 86

realism: as critique of Hart's legal positivism, 40, 112; of modern approaches to law, 9; in sociolegal studies of discourse. *See also* empiricism; legal realism

reason, metaphysics as error of, 34–43, 107, 141, 181. *See also* rationality

recognition: of right to speak, 15–17, 56n41; as response, 59–60, 175; of voice, 59–60, 66, 71, 147

reform of language and law, 54

religion, 12, 55, 67, 74–75, 79–85. *See also* sacredness

representation, of Native American identity, 75

Republic (Plato), 37

unpredictability, of possibilities, 12, 53, 59, 178
unsaid, 5, 69, 75, 86, 92, 176
unsayable (silence), 59, 66, 71, 72, 91
unspeakable, 69, 70–71, 72, 74–75, 85, 176–77
unspoken, 55, 69, 72
unthought, 44
unutterable, 71
users, 22–23, 26
United States law
— characteristics of: as chain of claims and responses, 14, 93–94, 101–2, 110; limits to hearing of, 91–92; loquaciousness of, 8, 88–89; rulelike character of, 74, 85; as positive law, 10, 12–13; possibilities of justice in, 149–74; as social policy, 21–28; "sociologization" of, 74
— studies of, 26–55, 132–48
— on topic of: flag-burning as expressive speech, 93–110; Native American languages and religion, 74–92; right to remain silent, 56–61, 68–71; voice, 56–61, 68–71
See also practices, of legal institutions
United States v. Eichman, 102–9; dissenting opinion (Stevens), 106–7, 109
utilitarianism, 20, 38–39, 51, 141. *See also* instrumentality
utterance: felicity and infelicity of, 156, 163–66; as performative speech act, 162–64, 163n21, 171; time and place of, 155 165–66

Valverde, Mariana, 42n63
values: of cultural pluralism and pursuit of knowledge, 81–85; in presumptive positivism, 123–25; of society, 14, 40, 141
verbs, 47–48
verdict, as speech act, 171
violence, 13, 69, 135–40, 145
voice, 56–71; calls to justice, 14, 46, 71–72, 176–77; conditions for, 59–60, 62–63, 65–66, 66–68, 71; domesticates violence, 143; equated with power or justice, 8, 46, 55, 69, 71, 72; political demand for, 58–59, 65, 86; political incoherence of, 57, 138–39, 144

voluntariness, of accused's statements, 153, 154–55
vote, 68, 86. *See also* public opinion and participation

waiver, of right to remain silent, 49, 152, 169–70
warning: *Miranda,* 149–51, 153–56, 164–70, 172–74; felicity of actual *Miranda,* 170, 174; felicity conditions of *Miranda,* 165–71, 172–74; as speech act, 150, 151, 153–56, 162–64, 165–71, 171–74
Weber, Max, 124, 134n4
welfare, 24–25
White, James Boyd, 17n10, 19n15, 135n6, 147n24; on language of concepts, 97–98; on legal interpretation and responsibility, 144–45
White, Lucie E., 51
Wigmore, John H., 158
will: free, 143–44; human, 37, 38; sociological mastery and societal, 42–43, 54–55; political, 99–108; to truth 36–44. *See also* agency; subject
Williams, Patricia, 51
Wittgenstein, 97
Wood, Michael, 75
words
— *citizen,* 21; *import,* 153; *justice,* 33, 45–46, 55, 110; *norm,* 120–21; *of,* 110, 110n37; *patient,* 21–22; *profession,* 93; *silence,* 5; *technique,* 84; *user,* 22–23; *we,* 126n12
— to rhetorician, 16–17, 19–20, 47–48
— what they are: and deeds, 47–48; and concepts, 19, 21, 78, 96–99; as interpretation, 132–45; resources, 102–3, 110, 111, 175–76; as symbols, 95–99; and things, 12, 21; violence in, 132–45
— and what they do: may become empty, 151, 159; call to justice, 12, 14, 93–94; come out of silence, 7, 80; correspond to world, 135, 145–47
writing, 58

Yngvesson, Barbara, 50

Zarathustra (Nietzsche), 41–42